ANTHROPOLOGICAL PAPERS

MUSEUM OF ANTHROPOLOGY, UNIVERSITY OF MICHIGAN

NO. 57

MIDDLE MISSISSIPPI EXPLOITATION OF ANIMAL POPULATIONS

BY

BRUCE D. SMITH

ANN ARBOR

THE UNIVERSITY OF MICHIGAN, 1975

ISBN (print): 978-1-949098-04-4
ISBN (ebook): 978-1-951519-14-8

Browse all of our books at sites.lsa.umich.edu/archaeology-books.

Order our books from the University of Michigan Press at www.press.umich.edu.

For permissions, questions, or manuscript queries, contact Museum publications by email at umma-pubs@umich.edu or visit the Museum website at lsa.umich.edu/ummaa.

FOR MY MOTHER AND FATHER

PREFACE

This publication is a somewhat revised and shortened version of a doctoral dissertation submitted to the University of Michigan in 1973.

The initial step in a study such as this is the identification and preliminary analysis of faunal samples recovered from archaeological sites. A number of individuals kindly provided access to faunal collections, while others provided assistance in the process of identification. Dr. Gerald Smith, Memphis State University, granted access to the Chucalissa site faunal sample, and provided information concerning the excavational history of the site. Dr. Paul W. Parmalee, then with the Illinois State Museum, granted access to the Banks site materials, provided space for analysis, and aided in the identification of fish remains from the Banks site. Dr. Carl Chapman of the University of Missouri, and David Evans of the Missouri Archaeological Survey granted permission to analyze the Lilbourn materials discussed here. John Cottier provided information concerning the excavational history of the site. B. Miles Gilbert generously provided work space and access to the comparative collections of the Zooarchaeological laboratory at the University of Missouri. Gregory Waselkov did the preliminary identification of the animal bones recovered from structure 25 of the Lilbourn site (Waselkov, 1972). Dr. John Walthall of the University of Alabama did the preliminary identification of the animal bones recovered from the Powers Fort site. Dr. Gerald Smith of the Division of Fishes of the Museum of Zoology, University of Michigan, generously provided working space, granted access to comparative collections, and identified many fish bone fragments recovered from the Lilbourn, Snodgrass, Powers Fort, and Gooseneck sites.

My dissertation committee, which consisted of Dr. James B. Griffin, chairman, Dr. Kent V. Flannery, Dr. Richard I. Ford, and Dr. Dale R. McCullough contributed in a variety of important ways to this study. Their encouragement, guidance, and constructive criticism has been greatly appreciated.

The manuscript was edited by Ms. Mary Coombs, of the Museum of Anthropology of the University of Michigan. Her suggestions, questions, and careful attention to accuracy have contributed in many important ways to a more accurate and more easily understood publication.

Financial assistance for the field research and the initial steps in gathering data from various sources was provided by the National Science Foundation Grant GS 3215 and by the Museum of Anthropology of the University of Michigan. These funds were administered by Dr. James B. Griffin and were for a study of the Powers Phase Mississippian society in southeast Missouri under the field direction of Dr. James E. Price. Financial assistance during much of the research and writing stages of the dissertation was provided by the Horace H. Rackham School of Graduate Studies.

I would also like to acknowledge the patience and understanding of Martha Johnson Smith, who put up with my madness during the writing of this study, and who sacrificed many evenings and weekends as a result.

CONTENTS

FIGURES

TABLES

I

INTRODUCTION

MIDDLE MISSISSIPPI

THE term "Middle Mississippi" first appeared in *Aboriginal Pottery of the Eastern United States*, written by William Henry Holmes (1903). During the seventy year span since it was first employed to denote a geographical region which had yielded pottery vessels of great similarity, the term Middle Mississippi has come to have quite specific chronological and cultural meaning in addition to the geographical significance originally given to it by Holmes.

It now refers to those agriculturally based human populations that occupied the central Mississippi valley during the late prehistoric period.

This central portion of the Mississippi valley, from the St. Louis (Cahokia) area south to Vicksburg, was the site of the earliest development of the basic adaptation which has been termed Mississippian, at approximately A.D. 700-900. From this Middle Mississippi heartland area, the Mississippian cultural tradition appears to have expanded into many regions of the eastern United States. As a result of this expansion, a number of regional traditions have been defined that share many basic Mississippian traits, yet exhibit regional variations which clearly set them apart from the central section of the Mississippi valley. The geographical location of these regional Mississippian areas is shown in Griffin's summary of the archaeology of eastern North America (1967:11). Thus the term Mississippian refers to any or all of these varied regional adaptations which share certain traits, while Middle Mississippi refers specifically to the Mississippian groups of the central section of the Mississippi valley. In addition to the geographical and cultural meaning inherent in the terms Middle Mississippi and Mississippi, the latter term is also used in a chronological sense: it refers to that period from A.D. 700 up until the contact period.

Middle Mississippi will refer in the present study to those archaeologically defined cultural units that existed in the central section of the Mississippi valley from A.D. 700 until European contact.

THE CULTURAL ADAPTATION

Having briefly defined the term Middle Mississippi, we can now turn to a general description of the ways in which the human populations adapted to the environmental setting that existed in the central section of the Mississippi valley during the Mississippi period. The basic attributes of this Middle Mississippi cultural adaptation have been succinctly described by James B. Griffin (1952b, 1967), and the following description is based in large part upon these sources.

The meander belt of the central section of the Mississippi River valley is an area of numerous cutoff oxbow lakes that are paralleled by former natural levees of the main channel. These former natural levees are rarely inundated by the floodwaters of early spring.

It is on the crest of these former natural levees, where there is fertile and easily tilled sandy and light loam soils, that many of the known Middle Mississippi settlements were situated.

The rich nature of these levee soils and the suitable climate of the central Mississippi valley combined to allow dependence upon, and development of, agricultural crops, so that large permanent villages could be established throughout much of the central Mississippi valley during the Mississippi period.

Of the numerous varieties of plants that were grown by Middle Mississippi groups, maize was undoubtedly the primary cultigen, while bean, squash, pumpkin, gourd, and sunflower were of secondary importance. These crops could be easily stored for extended periods of time, and the annual harvests produced an abundant storable food supply, enabling the Indians to develop large permanent villages. As Middle Mississippi groups increased their dependence upon agricultural crops, and gradually developed large, permanently occupied, agriculturally oriented villages, there was a corresponding development of both ownership and armed defense of arable land (Larson, 1972), and elaborate religious ceremonies concerned with crop production.

Although the flat-topped pyramidal mounds that occur at many of the larger Middle Mississippi sites likely served a variety of functions, they probably functioned primarily as high-status residence areas, and as sites of crop-oriented religious activities. These truncated, substructural mounds usually faced a central plaza area, and one mound was substantially larger when more than one mound was present. The nuclear family probably formed the basic dwelling unit, judging from the size of residential structures, which were square to rectangular in shape, and usually from twelve to twenty feet in length. Middle Mississippi villages were often surrounded by a wooden palisade and ditch, with bastions sometimes occurring.

In addition to these large fortified ceremonial centers, the Middle Mississippi pattern of settlement also characteristically included smaller subsidiary villages, hamlets, and homesteads, which were spaced over the controlled arable land areas.

It has been assumed that as the raising of agricultural crops by Middle Mississippi groups became a dominant theme in their cultural adaptation to the surrounding ecosystem, the exploitation of animal populations became relatively less important. It is very difficult at the present time, however, to make even rough estimates of the relative importance of domestic cultigens and faunal resources in the diet of Middle Mississippi groups. With a few exceptions, it has not even been possible to quantify the relative extent to which various species of animals were eaten by Middle Mississippi groups.

PRIOR STUDIES–SHORTCOMINGS

Much excavation has taken place at the larger sites, and there are, in fact, very few large Middle Mississippi villages that have not been explored by either relic hunters or professional archaeologists. These excavations have rarely, however, produced much information concerning the various species of animals that were represented at the excavated sites. Phillips, Ford, and Griffin noted that, as of 1951, archaeology had furnished practically no information about the utilization of fauna in the lower Mississippi valley (1951:31), and the situation has changed little during the ensuing two decades.

The majority of the studies of Middle Mississippi faunal assemblages are the work of a single man. Dr. Paul W. Parmalee, until recently at the Illinois State Museum, identified faunal samples recovered from the Banks site (1959*a*, 1966), the Cahokia site (1957), the Chucalissa site (1960*a*), the Aztalan site (1960*b*), the Kingston Lake site (1962*a*), the Lawhorn site (1962*b*), and the Zebree site (Parmalee & Guilday, 1973). The earlier Middle Mississippi faunal reports indicate only the various species of fish, amphibians, reptiles, birds, and mammals that contributed to the diet of these various Middle Mississippi communities. Species skeletal element counts, when they are given, sometimes allow general conclusions to be drawn concerning the relative importance of different species and species groups, but sampling problems such as non-uniform preservation and recovery are rarely discussed, which makes even basic conclusions rather difficult.

Further, although the concept of determining the minimum number of individuals of each animal species represented at archaeological sites was first suggested by Theodore White in 1953, such determinations have not been included in most Middle Mississippi faunal reports. Published Middle Mississippi faunal reports are, in fact, largely descriptive in nature (as are many such reports pertaining to the eastern United States), and in this respect they stop just where they should be beginning. They give only a limited amount of data, and little or no analysis and interpretation of that data.

As a result of this lack of adequate analysis and interpretation of faunal samples, a number of very basic questions concerning the exploitation of animal populations by Middle Mississippi groups are yet to be raised.

What was the relative importance, for instance, of various species of animals in the diet of Middle Mississippi populations?

Was exploitation of animal populations primarily a seasonal activity, and if so, during what season of the year was each species hunted?

To what degree was human predation of animal populations selective?

Was there a general Middle Mississippi pattern of exploitation of animal populations throughout the central valley, or did the specific location of sites within different environmental zones strongly influence the pattern of exploitation?

What was the impact of human predation on the biotic community? Was human predation pressure on animal populations heavy enough to place a strain on the animal populations, as many have previously suggested (Parmalee, et al., 1972:98)?

The present study will consider all these questions, and possible, though not conclusive, answers will be presented.

In considering the exploitation of animal species by Middle Mississippi communities, considerable reliance will be placed upon information obtained from wildlife studies. This information will be used to reconstruct the various animal populations that existed during the Mississippi period; relative densities, biotic potentials, seasonal movements, and food and habitat preferences will be considered in some detail.

It will be evident, I think, that such a careful and detailed consideration of the various animal populations increases the amount and type of information that can be obtained from archaeological faunal samples, and further, that by integrating modern wildlife study information with archaeological information, a number of hypotheses can be tested concerning the place of animal populations in the overall procurement system of Middle Mississippi groups.

DESCRIPTION OF SITES BEING ANALYZED

Seven Middle Mississippi sites will be considered in the present study, representing a variety of ecological zones. If lines were drawn connecting the Middle Mississippi sites being considered in the present study (Fig. 1), the resultant triangular area would measure a little over 110 miles north to south, and approximately 75 miles east to west. This triangular area is largely situated within the northern division of the alluvial valley of the lower

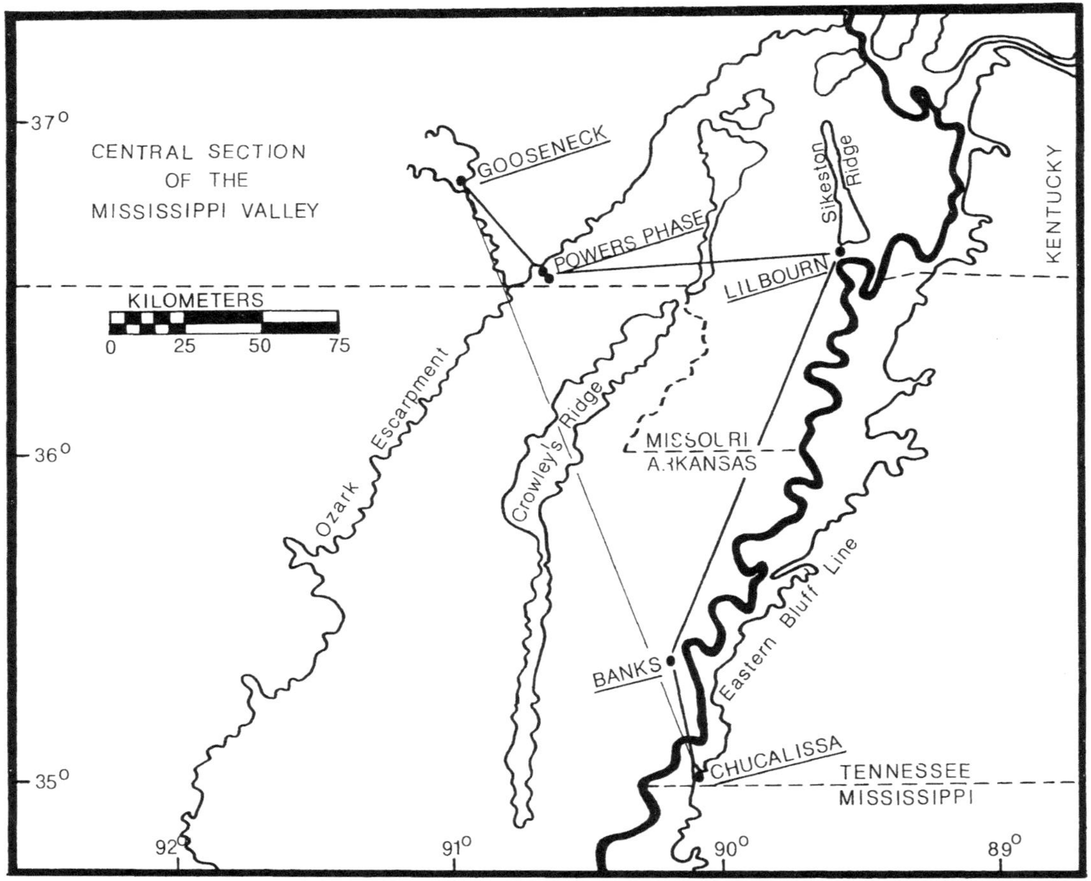

Fig. 1. The location of the seven Middle Mississippi sites being considered in the present study within the northern division of the alluvial valley of the lower Mississippi River.

Mississippi River, as defined by Fisk (1944:22), and adopted by Phillips, Ford, and Griffin (1951:11). It includes all of the distinctive aspects of topography, soil, drainage, vegetation, etc., that make the alluvial valley of the Mississippi River an area of extreme environmental diversity and complexity.

In addition to encompassing all of the ecological diversity of the alluvial valley, the sites in question also form an east-west transect of the valley, with each site being in a different ecological zone. The eastern end of the transect is at the Chucalissa site, which is a large ceremonial center occupied during the period A.D. 1000-1550, and situated on a high bluff overlooking the valley to the west (Eastern Bluffs Zone). The Banks site is a fortified site approximately ten acres in size that was occupied at about A.D. 1535, and is located in the eastern lowlands of the alluvial valley, within the meander belt of the Mississippi River (Meander Belt Zone). The Lilbourn site is a ceremonial center approximately thirty acres in size that was occupied during the period A.D. 1000-1550, and is situated on the southwestern corner of Sikeston Ridge (Meander Belt Zone). The Turner and Snodgrass sites are small fortified villages of approximately two and a half acres each that were occupied for a short period of time at about A.D. 1300. Powers Fort is a larger (fifteen acres) fortified ceremonial center of the same time period as the Turner and Snodgrass sites. The Turner, Snodgrass and Powers Fort sites are located in the western lowlands directly adjacent to the Ozark escarpment (Western Sand Ridges Zone). Continuing the transect west from the lowland sites of the Powers Phase, the western end is reached at the Gooseneck site, a small, seasonally occupied camp that probably dates somewhat later than the Powers Phase sites, and which is located about 25 miles into the Ozark uplands (Ozark Highlands Zone).

The seven Middle Mississippi sites being considered were chosen not only because they span the full ecological diversity of the Mississippi valley, but also because they show great variation in size, in date and length of occupation, and in specific cultural affiliation. This obviously heterogenous sample of sites was chosen so that it would be possible to discern any common basic pattern of exploitation that existed for Middle Mississippi groups, regardless of environmental location, site size, cultural affiliation, etc., as well as making it possible to observe variation in exploitation of animal populations between sites due to such factors. The most obvious factor that would produce variation in the pattern of exploitation of animal populations from site to site is the environmental setting of each site. The four major environmental zones in which the sites being considered are located will be briefly described below. More detailed descriptions of the specific environmental setting of the sites can be found in the site appendixes.

The Chucalissa site is located in the eastern bluffs zone. The eastern border of the northern division of the lower alluvial valley of the Mississippi River is defined by a high loess mantled bluff line that rises to an elevation of

125 to 250 feet above the floodplain. This eastern bluff zone is characterized by an abrupt, steep-sided bluffline, cut by small, narrow, and steep-sided stream valleys, with the upland area consisting of numerous low ridges interspersed with stream valley ravines.

The complex topography of the western margin of the eastern bluffs loess hills zone is paralleled by a rather complex species composition in the forest vegetation. Although the loess hills area is included within the Mississippi Embayment section of Braun's western mesophytic forest region (1950:125), she describes the forest vegetation of the area as being largely mixed mesophytic in character. In typical mixed mesophytic climax associations, dominance is shared by a number of species, particularly beech, tulip tree, several species of basswood, sugar maple, chestnut, red oak, white oak, and hemlock (Ibid.:35, 40-41, 160). The composition and relative abundance of these dominant species varies greatly from place to place. Within the eastern bluff loess hills zone, one could expect oaks to predominate on the narrow ridge tops, with mixed mesophytic forest occurring on ridge-ravine slopes. A few floodplain species would be present on the lower slopes and ravine bottom areas within the uplands.

The Banks and Lilbourn sites are located within the meander belt zone of the Mississippi, the second of four major environmental zones being sampled. The Mississippi River is the dominant feature of the meander belt zone, and almost every facet of the environment in this zone, from the shape and composition of the earth to the distribution of vegetation can be traced to the effects of its moving, muddy waters. The constant lateral shifting of the course of the Mississippi River occurs within a zone which is called a meander belt. The present meander belt of the Mississippi River is at least 3000 years old, and the constant formation of new channels and associated natural levees has eventually formed a continuous ridge of superimposed and coalesced former levees, interspersed with channel remnants in varying stages of vegetational succession. This meander belt ridge is approximately fifteen feet higher than the adjacent backswamp areas, and is about fifteen miles wide.

Braun has defined four general subdivisions of bottomland forest (1950:291), and although they obviously do not reflect all the possible variation in plant community composition and successional stages, they will be adequate for our purposes. 1) Braun's stream margin communities occur on newly formed land on the streamward side of natural levees, as well as on suitable sites on the landward side, with cottonwood and black willow being early dominants. 2) The swamp forest subtype occurs in backswamp and low lying areas of permanently standing water. Dominant species are bald cypress and water tupelo. 3) The hardwood bottom subtype, which is flooded for a considerable period during the spring and early summer, occupies lower ridge areas, with sweetgum, red maple, elm, and numerous species of oaks occurring. 4) The ridge bottom community consists of advanced species such as shagbark hickory, white oak, and cherrybark oak, in addition to most of the species that are represented in the hardwood bottom type.

A wide variety of plant communities and successional stages can be found in close association with each other within the meander belt zone, resulting in maximization of interface or edge area between plant communities. This high occurrence of edge area has great significance, for it results in high carrying capacity for a great variety of animal species.

The lowland sites of the Powers Phase are situated within the western sand ridges zone at the extreme western edge of the Mississippi valley. The topography of the western sand ridges zone is characterized by small parallel ridges which are natural levee remnants of the braided stream drainage pattern that existed when the Mississippi River flowed west of Crowley's Ridge. When the course of the Mississippi river shifted to the east of Crowley's Ridge, the characteristic braided stream channel topography remained as a distinctive feature of the landscape. The low areas between these sand ridges were swampy prior to modern drainage efforts, with small streams flowing southwest into the Little Black River.

The composition, distribution, and successional stages of the forest vegetation in the western sand ridges zone is similar to that of the meander belt zone. More detailed reconstructions of the vegetation in the Powers Phase area can be found in appendix D.

The Gooseneck site is located within the eastern Ozark highland zone. The Ozark highlands area is characterized by small, well-drained ridge systems and irregular hilly land areas composed of stony, fairly acidic residual soils, interspersed quite regularly with small stream-formed valleys or hollows. Occasional deeply entrenched rivers such as the Current River have produced narrow, steep-sided floodplain valleys with distinctive vegetational succession. The eastern Ozark highlands generally has some phase of oak–hickory or oak–pine forest prevailing (Braun, 1950: 164), with geomorphological conditions determining in many instances the types of vegetation succession that will take place at a specific locality. The distribution of vegetation within the eastern Ozarks will be discussed in some detail in the context of seasonal movements of the white-tailed deer (pages 000-000), and the environmental setting of the Gooseneck site will be discussed in appendix E.

Having briefly described the four major environmental zones within which the Middle Mississippi sites being considered are located we can now turn to a consideration of the animal species that were most intensively exploited during the Mississippi period.

II

EXPLOITATION OF ANIMAL POPULATIONS

PRIMARY PREY SPECIES

AGRICULTURAL crops are generally considered to have been of primary importance in the diet of Middle Mississippi populations. It is difficult, however, to quantitatively determine the relative importance of agricultural crops and wild species of plants and animals in terms of total food value in the diet of Middle Mississippi populations. While agricultural crops were an increasingly important source of carbohydrates, and contributed significantly to the caloric demands of Middle Mississippi populations, wild animal populations remained an important source of protein, though less so than previously.

Even though a large variety of animal species were harvested during the Mississippi period (as indicated by the more than one hundred species of vertebrates represented at the Middle Mississippi sites being presently considered), only a few dozen species contributed very much to the protein requirements of the human populations in question.

In order to obtain some indication of which species and species groups contributed significantly to the diet of the Middle Mississippi populations, the projected meat yield values of each animal species for each site (see Appendixes A through E) were added together, and the species were then ranked according to their total projected meat yield values. All fish were considered together in this ranking procedure, as were all waterfowl; the fox and gray squirrel; the swamp and cottontail rabbit; and the alligator snapping turtle and snapping turtle. The top thirteen species and species groups are ranked in Table 1 by total projected meat yield values. The projected meat yield values for these thirteen species and species groups are given by site in Table 2. (Each of the three structures excavated at the Lilbourn site is listed separately in Table 2, as are the village midden area and temple mound at the Chucalissa site). The first column in Table 2 lists the total projected meat yield values at each site, while the last column lists the combined meat yield values at each site for the species listed. By comparing these two columns one can see that the species listed represent a very high percentage of the total projected meat yield at each of the seven sites. This is even more clearly illustrated in Table 3, which gives the percentage equivalents of the meat yield values in Table 2. The last column in Table 3, giving the percentage of the total projected meat yield values that the listed species account for at each site, ranges from a low of ninety-two percent (Lilbourn site, structure 9), to a high of ninety-nine percent (Turner site). Because the high proportion of white-tailed deer obscures the relative importance of the other species listed in Table 3, the deer meat yield for each site was subtracted from the total meat yield value, and the percentage values for each species was recomputed in terms of the total non-deer meat yields at each site

TABLE 1

THE THIRTEEN ANIMAL SPECIES/SPECIES GROUPS PRIMARILY EXPLOITED BY THE MIDDLE MISSISSIPPI GROUPS BEING STUDIED, RANKED ACCORDING TO THEIR TOTAL PROJECTED MEAT YIELD VALUES.

SCIENTIFIC NAME	COMMON NAME
1. *Odocoileus virginianus*	White-tailed deer
2. *Procyon lotor*	Raccoon
3. *Class pisces*	Fish
4. *Anas, Aythya, Branta*, etc.	Migratory waterfowl
5. *Meleagris gallopavo*	Wild turkey
6. *Castor canadensis*	Beaver
7. *Didelphis marsupialis*	Opossum
8. *Sylvilagus aquaticus* *Sylvilagus floridanus*	Swamp rabbit Cottontail rabbit
9. *Macroclemys temminicki* *Chelydra serpentina*	Alligator snapping turtle Snapping turtle
10. *Canis familiaris*	Aboriginal dog
11. *Sciurus niger* *Sciurus carolinensis*	Fox squirrel Gray squirrel
12. *Ursus americanus*	Black bear
13. *Cervus canadensis*	Wapiti (elk)

TABLE 2

PROJECTED MEAT YIELD VALUES FOR THIRTEEN SPECIES/SPECIES GROUPS AT EACH OF SEVEN MIDDLE MISSISSIPPI SITES. (in pounds)

SITES	TOTAL PROJECTED MEAT YIELD REPRESENTED AT SITES	WHITE-TAILED DEER	RACCOON	CLASS PISCES	MIGRATORY WATERFOWL	WILD TURKEY	BEAVER	OPOSSUM	RABBITS	SNAPPING TURTLES	DOMESTIC DOG	SQUIRRELS	BLACK BEAR	WAPITI	PROJECTED MEAT YIELD REPRESENTED BY THESE 13 SPECIES/ SPECIES GROUPS
Chucalissa Village	12224	10192	296	—	48	179	80	86	74	23	64	78	420	350	11,890
Chucalissa Temple Mound	365.3	245	9	20	16	17	20	—	5	8	8	13	—	—	361
Banks Village	9093	7250	368	170	270	145	60	133	78	60	144	13	210	—	8901
Lilbourn Structure 9	2667	1323	48	893	170	26	20	17	29	15	8	20	—	—	2569
Lilbourn Structure 12	863.8	544	32	65	70	17	20	9	15	8	8	8	—	—	796
Lilbourn Structure 25	1510	930	64	148	124	26	40	9	34	45	—	17	—	—	1437
Turner Site	3559	2948	184	—	14	26	60	26	9	23	24	6	210	—	3530
Snodgrass Site	13429	12031	624	2	9	43	60	45	25	75	24	7	—	350	13,295
Powers Fort Site	674.9	515	24	2	3	36	20	17	9	8	8	5	—	—	647
Gooseneck Site	1199	1092	8	8	2	36	20	9	2	8	—	3	—	—	1188

TABLE 3

PERCENTAGE OF TOTAL PROJECTED MEAT YIELD WHICH EACH SPECIES/SPECIES GROUP REPRESENTS AT EACH OF SEVEN MIDDLE MIDDLE MISSISSIPPI SITES.

SITES	WHITE-TAILED DEER	RACCOON	CLASS PISCES	MIGRATORY WATERFOWL	WILD TURKEY	BEAVER	OPOSSUM	RABBITS	SNAPPING TURTLE	DOMESTIC DOG	SQUIRRELS	BLACK BEAR	WAPITI	TOTAL
Chucalissa Village	83.4	2.4	—	.4	1.5	.7	.7	.6	.2	.5	.6	3.4	2.9	97.3
Chucalissa Temple Mound	67.1	2.5	5.5	4.4	4.7	5.5	—	1.4	2.2	2.2	3.6	—	—	98.8
Banks Village	79.7	4.0	1.9	3.0	1.6	.7	1.5	.9	.7	1.6	.1	2.3	—	98.0
Lilbourn Structure 9	49.6	1.8	33.5	6.4	1.0	.7	.6	1.1	.6	.3	.7	—	—	96.3
Lilbourn Structure 12	63.0	3.7	7.5	8.1	2.0	2.3	1.0	1.7	.9	.9	.9	—	—	92.2
Lilbourn Structure 25	61.6	4.2	9.8	8.2	1.7	2.6	.6	2.3	3.0	—	1.1	—	—	95.2
Turner Site	82.8	5.2	—	.4	.7	1.7	.7	.3	.6	.7	.2	5.9	—	99.2
Snodgrass Site	89.6	4.6	.01	.06	.3	.4	.3	.2	.6	.2	.05	—	2.6	99.0
Powers Fort Site	76.3	3.6	.3	.4	5.3	3.0	2.5	1.3	1.2	1.2	.7	—	—	95.9
Gooseneck Site	91.1	.7	.7	.2	3.0	1.7	.7	.2	.6	—	.2	—	—	99.1

(Table 4). It can be seen that the other species listed account for very high percentages of the non-deer meat yield from each site (78.8-96.4 percent).

Because this group of thirteen animal species/species groups consistently accounts for a very high percentage of projected total meat yield values at each site (although they do not always rank above all other species at every site), this study will be restricted largely to these primary prey species.

SELECTIVE RECONSTRUCTION OF BIOTIC COMMUNITIES

Because of the number of detailed wildlife studies that have been done over the last two decades, it is possible to partially reconstruct the niches of those animal species and species groups that were of primary importance to the Middle Mississippi human populations being studied. Only those aspects of the niches of the species in question that are directly relevant to their interrelationships with the human component of the ecosystem will be considered here.

In reconstructing the niches of those animal species and species groups that were of primary importance to the Middle Mississippi groups being studied, we will also be selectively reconstructing a portion of the faunal section of the biotic community that existed: that portion that had the strongest and most important interrelationships with the human component.

In selectively reconstructing the niches of a number of species and species groups, many interrelated aspects of their role within the ecosystem will be considered, including the following:

Seasonal events–

1) seasonal movement,
2) seasonal variation in food preference, foraging patterns, and daily movements,
3) seasons of mating and birth,
4) seasonal variation in density,

Population dynamics–

1) biotic potential,
2) mortality factors and recruitment rates,
3) density,
4) annual reproduction, available harvest.

The validity of these selective niche reconstructions is dependent upon the strict adherence by the author to a number of important principles in selecting data:

1) The modern data was taken mainly from original case studies rather than from secondary sources such as Shelford (1963) or Taylor (1956).

2) The wildlife studies were done on natural populations that were relatively undisturbed by modern man.

TABLE 4

PERCENTAGE OF TOTAL PROJECTED NON-DEER MEAT YIELD WHICH EACH SPECIES/SPECIES GROUP REPRESENTS AT EACH OF SEVEN MIDDLE MISSISSIPPI SITES.

SITES	TOTAL PROJECTED MEAT YIELD OTHER THAN VENISON AT SITES (IN POUNDS)	RACCOON	CLASS PISCES	MIGRATORY WATERFOWL	WILD TURKEY	BEAVER	OPOSSUM	RABBITS	SNAPPING TURTLE	DOMESTIC DOG	SQUIRRELS	BLACK BEAR	WAPITI	TOTAL
Chucallisa Village	2032	14.6	—	2.4	8.8	4.0	4.2	3.6	1.1	3.1	3.8	20.6	17.2	83.6
Chucalissa Temple Mound	120.3	7.5	16.6	13.3	14.1	16.6	—	4.2	6.7	6.7	10.8	—	—	96.4
Banks Village	1843	19.9	9.2	14.6	7.8	3.2	7.2	4.2	3.2	7.8	.7	11.3	—	89.2
Lilbourn Structure 9	1344	3.6	66.4	12.8	1.9	1.5	1.3	2.2	1.1	.6	1.5	—	—	92.8
Lilbourn Structure 12	319.8	10.0	20.3	21.9	5.3	6.3	2.8	4.7	2.5	2.5	2.5	—	—	78.8
Lilbourn Structure 25	580	11.1	25.5	21.4	4.4	6.9	1.5	5.9	7.8	—	2.8	—	—	87.4
Turner Site	611	30.1	—	2.3	4.3	9.8	4.3	1.5	3.8	3.9	1.0	34.4	—	95.2
Snodgrass Site	1398	44.6	.1	.6	3.0	4.3	3.2	1.8	5.4	1.7	.5	—	25.0	90.4
Powers Fort Site	159.9	15.0	1.3	1.9	22.5	12.5	10.6	5.6	5.0	5.0	3.1	—	—	82.5
Gooseneck Site	107	7.5	7.5	1.9	33.6	18.7	8.4	1.9	7.5	—	2.8	—	—	89.7

3) The wildlife studies were done in locales that were close to the Middle Mississippi sites being considered, and were in areas that were similar in variety and distribution of micro-ecological zones to the site locations.

4) All the pertinent data from primary sources was cross-checked with numerous other references to confirm its general accuracy.

These four basic principles were adhered to as closely as possible. The large number of excellent wildlife studies that have been done in locales that were both geographically and environmentally similar to the site locations was encouraging. It is hoped, however, that the reconstructions contained herein, and the subsequent combining of the reconstructions with ethnohistorical and archaeological data will not be accepted by the reader as being completely valid, but will rather be criticized according to one's level of knowledge and interest in the subject. It is only through constructive criticism that the procedures followed in this kind of study can be further improved and refined.

It may seem that this study includes much unnecessary data. This may be true in some cases, but it is a result of an attempt to avoid careless and incorrect applications of modern wildlife data to archaeological situations.

It must also be stressed that the selective reconstructions of prehistoric animal populations contained herein are based upon the specific geographical and environmental setting of the Middle Mississippi sites being considered, and may not be applicable to other areas.

It is hoped that by describing and interpreting the seasonal movements, population dynamics, food preferences, etc., of certain species of animals, it will be possible to "put life and flesh onto the bones, to think in terms of animals, of flocks and herds, and not of their mortal remains." (Chaplin, 1965:205)

Once the niches of these animal populations have been selectively reconstructed, three interrelated topics dealing with the relationships that existed between these animal populations and the human populations will be considered:

A. *Determining the most probable season of exploitation of various animal species, and the procurement techniques that may have been employed.*

Data from three separate sources will be combined in this discussion. The value of integrating archaeological data with ethnological descriptions has been recognized for some time, but information pertaining to prey species has rarely been considered in any detail by anthropologists (Flannery, 1966, is a notable exception).

Our approach will be to first describe the yearly cycle of each species, and then attempt to determine if there is any period of time that the species could be more advantageously exploited. In some cases there are, indeed, obvious seasons of the year when a particular species is more accessible to human predation. Once a logical hypothesis has been formed concerning the most advantageous time or times of the year to exploit a certain species, and procurement techniques that could have been employed (based upon the species' yearly cycle), we can then compare it with any pertinent ethnohistorical accounts that may exist. Unfortunately, the quality and quantity of ethnohistorical accounts of aboriginal hunting of animals in the southeastern United States are quite limited. Any archaeological data that may bear upon seasonality and techniques of exploitation will then be introduced, and the three classes of data will be combined to estimate a time of year of exploitation, and the probable techniques of procurement. The level of confidence of these final projections will vary with the quality and amount of data available for each species. In some cases the final projection will be little more than a logical construct based upon wildlife data and limited archaeological information, while in other cases the available data will allow more firm conclusions to be reached.

B. *Determining the extent to which Middle Mississippi groups selectively exploited the faunal portion of the biotic community.*

The projected meat yield values for each species represented at an archaeological site usually gives a fairly accurate representation of the importance of different animals in the diet of prehistoric human populations. It is not possible, however, to accurately determine from such meat yield values alone if some animal species were being exploited more intensively than others. The white-tailed deer, for example, represents a significant percentage of the total meat yield at many archaeological sites in the eastern United States. Is this high representation a function of selective human predation, concentrating on white-tailed deer populations to the relative exclusion of other species? Or is it, on the other hand, simply a function of the high biomass levels and high biotic potential of the white-tailed deer? To measure the extent to which exploitation of animal populations by Middle Mississippi groups was selective, some idea of the composition of the faunal portion of the prehistoric biotic community is obviously needed as a reference base. By comparing the representation of various species of animals at archaeological sites with the projected potential annual yield and the biomass levels of those species, we should be able to determine if various species were in fact selectively exploited.

The potential annual yield of each species is not simply a function of biomass levels (population density times average weight of the species) as Munson et al. have indicated (1971:415,425), but is, in fact, a slightly more complicated matter. Potential annual yield values for each species were obtained in the following way: once the density of the breeding population of a specific species was estimated (number of individuals/square mile), the number of young of the year could be estimated from the reproductive rate of the population. The number of young of the year per unit of area represents the potential annual yield of that species. This is not to say that human predation will account for the total cropping that will reduce the prey population back to the stable breeding population level, but rather that the potential annual yield values accurately represent the amount of meat that can be culled from the population of a certain species through a variety of mortality factors without causing a reduction in the breeding population.

There are a number of problems, however, in determining potential annual yield values for certain species groups. Such yield values are easily determined for many species of land animals, and can be applied with a high degree of confidence. It is quite difficult, however, to produce potential yield values for species groups such as fish and migratory waterfowl.

In considering the relative extent to which the Middle Mississippi groups being studied practiced selective exploitation of various animal species, the following hypotheses will be tested:

H_0 Middle Mississippi populations exploited all animal populations in direct proportion to the potential annual yield of each species.

H_2 Middle Mississippi populations selectively exploited animal populations according to the concept of maximization—they attempted to gain a maximum meat yield with a minimum of effort.

H_3 A common subsistence base consisting of a few broad niche species can be identified at all of the Middle Mississippi sites being considered. Significant exploitation of many other species varied according to the location of each of the sites within one of four major environmental zones of the Mississippi Valley.

C. *Determining the role of man as a predator within the ecosystem.*

The interrelationships that existed between the Middle Mississippi populations and the various animal populations of the biotic community will be analyzed and classified according to Haskell's coaction theory, as modified by Clarke (1954).

WHITE-TAILED DEER (*Odocoileus virginianus*)

Subspecies Represented

The white-tailed deer (*Odocoileus virginianus*) has a geographical range which includes most of the temperate forest and grassland areas of North America, and extends south through Middle America. Of the three subspecies of *Odocoileus virginianus* which originally occurred in the Mississippi valley area, one was largely restricted to areas east of the Mississippi and north of the Ohio River (*O.v. borealis*), while another (*O.v. virginianus*) commonly occurred only east of the Mississippi and south of the Ohio River. The subspecies of white-tailed deer represented at six of the seven sites being considered is therefore most likely *O.v. macoura*, which occurred along the west side of the Mississippi river from mid-Wisconsin south to mid-Louisiana (Hall and Kelson, 1959). *O.v. virginianus* is the subspecies most likely represented at the Chucalissa site, situated on the eastern bluffs of the Mississippi valley.

It is not possible, however, to be certain about the subspecific identification of deer represented at these sites. The estimated original ranges of these three subspecies (which were drawn rather arbitrarily in many cases) have since been obscured by extensive transplantation programs, and it is impossible to make subspecific identification through analysis of archaeological samples, since only subtle physical characteristics differentiate the subspecies.

Seasonal Habits

The seasonal habits of deer vary very little in a given region from year to year. The rutting period, the fawning period, the seasonal groupings, and the periods during which antlers are grown and shed are reasonably consistent from year to year, as are seasonal food preferences and seasonal movements. The peak of the fawning period in the southeast Missouri-northeast Arkansas area is approximately the first of June (Dunkenson, 1958), with most births occurring in late May and the first two weeks of June. During this spring fawning period the female is usually alone, but her young from the previous spring may rejoin her soon after the fawning period is over. These small family groups remain together through summer in white-tailed deer populations, while mature bucks usually form small all-male groups. Antler growth in males usually begins around the middle of May. Full antler development is usually attained by the end of July, but rubbing does not begin until the beginning of September, when the antlers have fully hardened. Velvet rubbing lasts through the month of September. This habit of polishing antlers is accentuated by the rut, and develops into a characteristically belligerent activity, with bucks making fitful assaults on shrubbery as well on other males. During the rutting season (late September through November), the antlers are in near perfect condition. The bucks use them in frequent combat until the mating season is over. They are usually dropped between the middle of January and the first of February. About one-third of the females born each spring will be sexually mature in time for that fall's rutting season, with the rest of the young of the year (both males and females) not breeding until the following fall. Mature bucks will join females for a few days at a time during the rut, moving from female to female. After their antlers have been shed, bucks will join the small bands of females and young for the winter months, leaving, however, prior to the spring fawning period.

Winters in the southeast Missouri-northeast Arkansas area are relatively open, with few heavy snowfalls. Since snow does not restrict travel or feeding, white-tailed deer do not yard, or collect in small areas, during the winter, as is common in areas farther north.

Feeding Habits and Seasonal Movements

The white-tailed deer is a browsing ruminant. Its diet consists of tender shoots, twigs, and leaves, a wide assortment of herbaceous foodstuffs, acorns of a number of oak species, and certain fruits. When undisturbed, they generally feed in the early morning and late afternoon. Deer are selective in their feeding habits, and the types of plants that make up a deer's diet shift significantly and predictably from season to season. This concept of differential palatability applies not only between species of plants, but to the same species at different stages in its development (a species may be highly favored in March, yet go untouched in July). Since an important part of the diet of *Odocoileus virginianus* consists of the twigs, shoots, and leaves of low growing shrubs and bushes, their population densities are low in climax forest situations where a closed canopy has been established. Highest population densities occur where there are many small areas of varying types, producing maximum edge areas between habitat zones.

A number of detailed studies have defined and described the distribution and distinctive vegetation associations of each of the four main forest types that occur in the southeastern Ozarks, as well as the food habits and seasonal movements of the white-tailed deer population in this area (Segelquist and Green, 1968; Segelquist et al., 1969). These studies make it possible to reconstruct with some degree of confidence the seasonal occurrence of white-tailed deer in the different forest types of the upland hardwood zones which border the Mississippi valley.

The four main forest types that occur in the southeastern Ozarks are as follows:

1) Upland hardwoods–north and east exposure of ridge tops and slopes,
2) Upland pine hardwoods–south and west exposure of ridge tops and slopes,
3) Cedar glades–rocky outcrop areas on western and southern slopes,
4) Stream bottom hardwoods–narrow stream bottoms and lower slopes.

Acorns are the single most important food source for deer in this area. As the month of August comes to a close, the deer quite abruptly shift their attention to the acorns that are beginning to litter the ground beneath the various species of oaks. These will make up almost their total diet for the next few months, and will continue to be important throughout the winter until the first green grasses of early March signal the start of a new feeding cycle. If the acorn crop is good, it will form the bulk of the diet for fall and winter. If the oak mast yield is poor, on the other hand, deer will be forced to shift to other plant species as the acorns disappear. This most important fall and winter food item occurs primarily in the upland hardwood areas.

The four different forest types produce quite comparable annual vegetation yields (oven dried weight), with each type producing different food plants during different seasons. Deer, therefore, move seasonally to take advantage of the changing availability of browse material. During the spring and summer, the sparsely timbered cedar glades produce large amounts of herbage and grasses and a good amount of browse; these glades also provide good browse yield during the winter. The densely timbered stream bottom hardwood forest type has less herbage and browse than the glades during the spring and summer, but sedges and ferns, forms commonly associated with moist sites, are common.

The upland hardwood area is the most heavily timbered, and produces sparcer browse yields than any other type, but, of course, offers abundant acorn yields.

Knowing the location and seasonality of vegetation utilized by deer, we can describe their seasonal feeding movements with a good degree of accuracy. During the fall, when oak mast is abundant, deer eat little else, and concentrate their feeding in the heavily wooded areas, especially the upland hardwoods. The extent to which deer feed within this forest type during the winter months is a function of the continuing availability of acorns: when the oak mast yield is abundant enough, deer will feed in the upland hardwoods throughout the winter; when oak mast yields are low, deer are forced to shift to forage, and forest type preference changes, with deer browsing throughout the forest types. During the spring the deer concentrate their feeding in the stream-bottom hardwood areas, eating the early emerging grasses and sedges. As the growing season progresses, deer expand their range to include the cedar glades and lower slopes. They feed in these areas throughout the summer. It would seem evident, then, that deer definitely concentrate on a consistent basis during the period September-October-November in the upland hardwoods, and during March-April in the stream-bottom hardwoods, with the fall concentration being the more reliable of the two (Fig. 2).

Home Range

The white-tailed deer probably has the smallest home range of any member of the deer family in America. A number of studies have been done during the last twenty years, and Severinghaus and Cheatum (1956:154) summarize these studies as follows: "It therefore appears that the seasonal range of an individual deer does not greatly exceed a mile." Progulske and Baskett (1958) determined that the average minimum home range of deer in

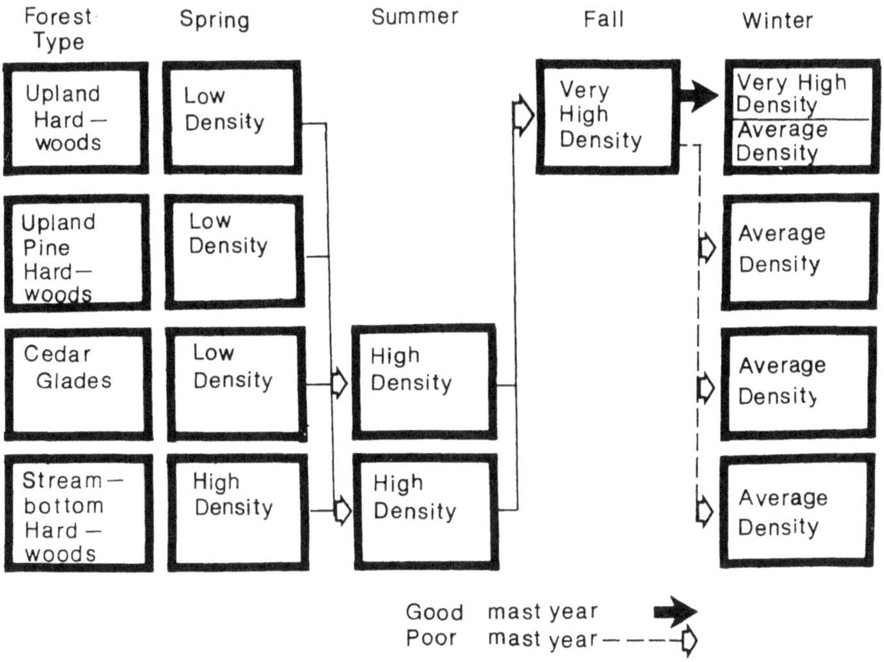

Fig. 2. Seasonal density of the white-tailed deer within each of 4 forest types in the eastern Ozarks.

an area of central Missouri was 695 acres, or a little more than one square mile. This home range is not a defended territory, but rather the area used by a single individual. Obviously a great amount of overlap of individual home ranges exists. There is some seasonal variation in the size of home ranges, which are largest during the fall rutting season.

Population Dynamics

Within any animal population there exists what Andrewartha and Birch (1954) have termed "an innate capacity for increase." This theoretical maximum growth rate, which occurs only when a species reproduces under ideal conditions and in the absence of mortality, is also referred to as the biotic potential of a species. Biotic potential is determined by inherent genetic factors, and is just as characteristic of a species as physical size, or any other measurable trait. The biotic potential of a population is usually only approached for short periods of time in wild populations. If the number of animals is quite low in relation to the available food, as when they are introduced into new and favorable habitats, the birth rate will be high, and the rate of increase may approach the biotic potential of the species. Studies done in Michigan (O'Roke and Hamerstrom, 1948) and in Missouri (Brohn and Robb, 1955) have estimated the biotic potential of the white-tailed deer at about sixty percent per year (see also Robertson, 1969). If this maximum rate of increase continued for any period of time, it would produce a larger deer population than the plant food base of an area could support. This critical level above which the available food resources cannot support the growing population is loosely termed the carrying capacity of the specific area. This "carrying capacity" concept has been employed in a wide variety of ecological and wildlife studies. Unfortunately there is a corresponding variety of interpretations of the term, depending upon both the investigator and the animal species involved. Since there are many different interpretations of "carrying capacity," wildlife ecologists have developed a number of concepts concerning the relative density of animal populations, and have strictly defined several different density levels, three of which apply to deer populations.

1. *Security density:* White-tailed deer usually inhabit brushy or wooded edge areas during most of the year. Hunting pressure elicits highly effective avoidance behavior which includes prolonged hiding and a shift to nighttime feeding. For these and other reasons the white-tailed deer is considered a "resistant species" by wildlife ecologists. This means that, given suitable habitat conditions, it is almost impossible to remove high percentages of white-tailed deer populations by shooting (Dasmann, 1964:198). Once a white-tailed deer population has been reduced to a certain density level by modern hunting, it is theoretically impossible to further harvest the population. This density level at which the population is almost invulnerable to further predation is termed the security density level. Given the excellent cover conditions that must have existed in the Mississippi valley during the Mississippi period, there is little doubt that this security density concept can be applied to white-tailed deer populations subject to predation by Middle Mississippi hunters. No matter how great the predation pressure by Middle Mississippi hunters, they could not harvest enough deer each year to endanger the ultimate survival of the local deer population. This was probably true, in fact, for all of southeastern North America prior to the extensive deer driving which occurred during the contact period (Larson, 1969:248). This security density concept does not necessarily apply, however, to those northern areas where deer yard during the winter months, and are thus more vulnerable to human predation (Hickerson, 1965).

2. *Subsistence density:* Dasmann defines subsistence density as "the upper limit that a population can reach in a given environment" (1964:183). A population at such a high level "obtains enough food for bare survival, but not enough to maintain good health, optimum growth, optimum body size, vigor, or fecundity" (loc. cit.). Subsistence density has been aptly described as a disaster level. Deer populations at such high levels are very vulnerable to

such factors as disease and predation, and when a deer population at a subsistence density level is faced with a sudden reduction of the carrying capacity of an area, widespread starvation and a subsequent rapid decline in population (a crash cycle) will result. Paradoxically enough, an insufficient deer harvest by Middle Mississippi hunters was a greater threat to the continued existence of their primary animal food source than extreme predation pressure would have been.

3. *Optimum density:* There is an optimum density between the security and subsistence density levels. It corresponds to the meaning ascribed to "carrying capacity" in range management studies. At this density, maximum health, growth, and productivity will be realized. Mortality due to shortages of food, water, and shelter does not occur.

The value of these density concepts in understanding the relationship that existed between the prehistoric deer population and Middle Mississippi hunters can be more easily demonstrated by first considering studies done of the George Reserve deer population. The Edwin S. George Reserve in southeastern Michigan is an enclosed 1200 acre study area. The deer population of the reserve has been harvested, censused, and studied during the last six years under the direction of Dale R. McCullough of the School of Natural Resources, University of Michigan. This discussion of the George Reserve deer population is a simplified version of the information presented by Dr. McCullough in a wildlife ecology course during the spring of 1971. Figure 3 illustrates the different density values determined for the George Reserve deer herd. Subsistence density was found to occur at a population level of about 170 for the 1,200 acre enclosure (84 deer per square mile). Security density was estimated at a population level of approximately 40 to 60 for the reserve (20 deer per square mile). Because of the excellent available cover on the reserve, it was very difficult to reduce the deer population below this level.

To explain how the optimum density of the deer population of the George Reserve was determined, it is necessary to introduce the concept of recruitment. Because it is so difficult to measure the number of births in most animal populations, wildlife ecologists instead measure the number of young which reach breeding age. Recruitment, then, can be defined as the number of animals added to the breeding population each year. The recruitment rate of the George Reserve, as illustrated in Figure 3, approaches the biotic potential, or maximum possible rate of increase up to a level of about 60 individuals. This high recruitment rate indicates both that the birth rate approaches the biotic potential of the population, and that a very high percentage of the fawns survive to be included in the breeding population. If the deer population is at a higher level than 60, the recruitment rate is correspondingly lower. As the density of the deer herd increases, fewer births occur, and fawn mortality increases. This reduction in the recruitment rate is largely a result of a reduced food supply. At subsistence density, recruitment theoretically equals zero—none of the young of the year survive to reach breeding age. At this point the food supply has stabilized the deer population. It is possible to determine the optimum density of the George Reserve deer herd from Figure 3 in the following manner: multiply the number of deer in the breeding population by the recruitment rate value. The result of this step is shown in Figure 4, which illustrates the number of fawns which survive to join the breeding population in relation to the size of the breeding population. It can be seen that given a population level of 90 deer, which has a recruitment rate of 0.5, a total of 45 fawns will be born and survive to join the breeding population each year. It is at this population level that the productivity of the population is maximized. That is, a population of 90 deer produces more young that survive to join the breeding population than any other population level. If one wishes to maintain the deer population at this optimum density of 90 animals, the yearly harvest must equal the annual recruitment: 45 deer must be killed each year to stabilize the population at 90 deer. If less than 45 deer are killed each year, the population will increase until a balance between predation pressure and recruitment is attained, at which point the population will stabilize. If more than 45 deer are killed each year, the population will be reduced until it reaches the security density level, at which point it will become impossible to sustain the previous high level of predation, and the population will stabilize.

Prehistoric Situation

Given these basic population parameters of the George Reserve deer herd, let us now consider what inferences can be drawn concerning the relationship which existed between the prehistoric deer population and the Middle Mississippi hunters. Obviously it would have been advantageous for Middle Mississippi groups if the deer population was stabilized at close to optimum density. This would allow a maximum consistent harvest from the deer population and would maintain the deer population at a healthy level. If, on the other hand, the deer population was allowed to increase toward subsistence density, the general health of the deer herd would be reduced, and the possibility of a rapid decline in the deer population (a "crash") would be greatly increased.

It has been clearly established that deer populations have no inherent capacity to control their level of population, and in the absence of inhibitory factors will quickly reach a subsistence density. What, then, was the density of prehistoric deer populations during the Mississippi period in our study area? Were they at a subsistence density? And if not, what inhibitory factors were functioning to stabilize the deer population below subsistence density? One of the primary inhibitory factors which maintained the deer population below

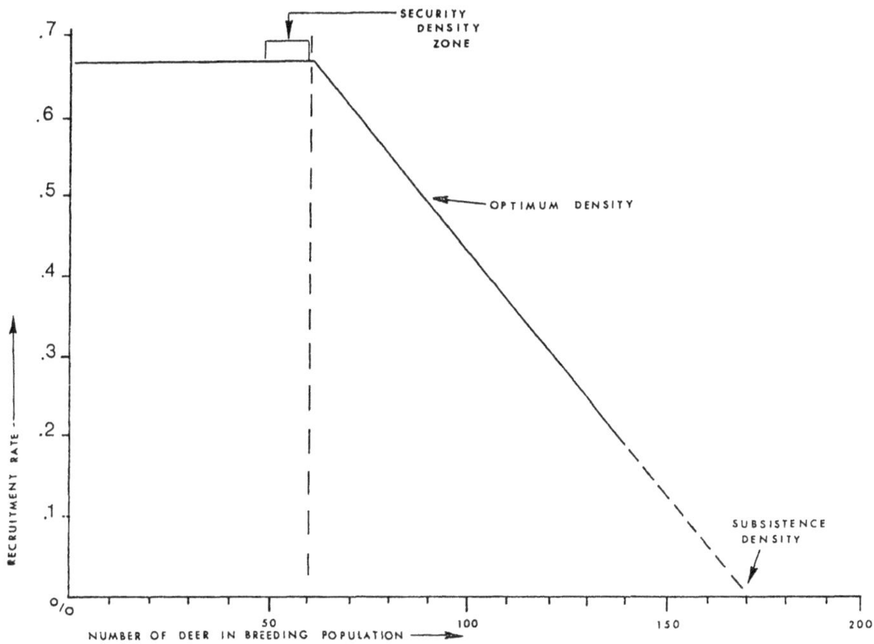

Fig. 3. Decline of recruitment rate as George Reserve deer population increases.

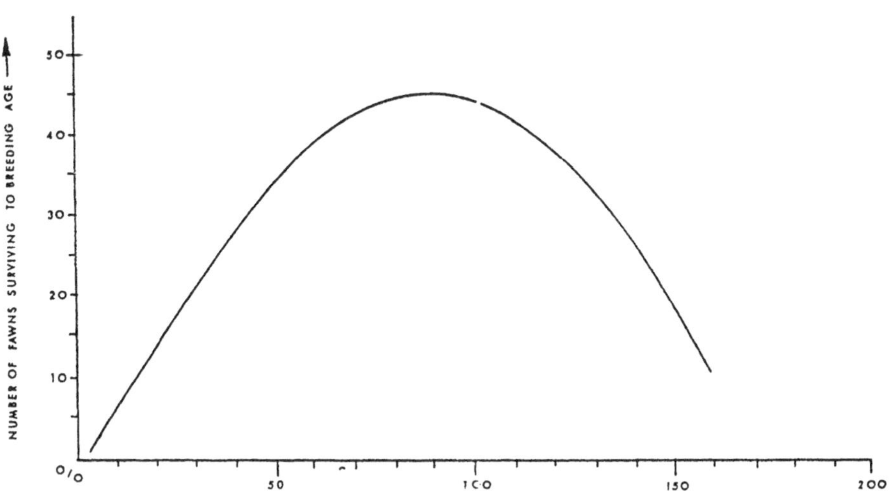

Fig. 4. Relative productivity of the George Reserve deer herd.

subsistence density during the Mississippi period in our study area was continual predation, which was beneficial to both predator and prey. This can be illustrated with a model containing three components: vegetation food source, prey population, and predator populations. If left unchecked, the prey population would over-utilize the plant supply, causing serious disruption of the plant life, which would, in turn, result in a crash in its own population due to starvation. By keeping the prey population from reaching a subsistence density level, the predator populations would not only provide for their own survival and insure a future source of food, but would also protect the prey population from crashing due to starvation and the plant food supply from severe overbrowsing (see Fig. 6).

Whether predation by specialized carnivores such as wolves, pumas, and man is the primary inhibitory factor operating on herding populations in undisturbed situations has been a point of debate for some years. While the argument has not been settled, a recent statement by D. H. Pimlott is of interest:

> In considering the population dynamics of some big game species, deer and moose in particular, the question arises, as to why intrinsic mechanisms of population control have not evolved to prevent them from increasing beyond the sustaining level of their food supply. It seems reasonable to postulate that it may be because they have had very efficient predators, and the forces of selection have kept them busy evolving ways and means not of limiting their own numbers but of keeping abreast of mortality factors. (1967:275)

L. David Mech makes the following comment on Pimlott's statement:

> If Pimlott's theory is correct, as I believe it is, wolf predation could very well have been the main limiting factor on most, if not all, big game before man so greatly disturbed the habitat. (1970:272).

It seems certain that wolves (*Canis lupus*) were present in the Mississippi valley area during the prehistoric period. Early historical accounts as well as fairly recent kill records attest to their abundance later in time, and the red wolf (*Canis rufus*) is still encountered in the Missouri Ozarks today. If both wolves and Middle Mississippi hunters were present in the Mississippi valley, and the white-tailed deer was a major source of food for each, what relationship existed between the two predator populations? Were they competing for the same food source? This question has been dealt with in reference to the Powers Phase area in Smith (1974*a*), and the conclusions reached concerning the western edge of the Mississippi valley would seem to be just as applicable to the larger area now being considered.

The relationship between these two predator populations can be better understood after we consider the age composition of the deer kill from six of the seven sites under study (the Powers Fort sample was too small to be included). The age composition of the deer kills are listed in Table 5, and graphically illustrated in Figure 5. Deer mandibles recovered from the sites were aged according to the eruption pattern of permanent dentition and relative amount of tooth wear (Severinghaus, 1949). Aging by the molar cementum method (Ransom, 1966) was attempted on a limited sample of the most well-preserved mandibles, but proved unsuccessful because of the almost complete fragmentation of the dental cementum zone. These age composition curves (Fig. 5) are similar in form for all but the Banks site, which will be discussed in some detail later. In the rest, there is low representation of the zero age class (ten percent or less of the harvest), while the first, second, and third age classes represent the bulk of the sample. The older age classes are represented in lower percentages, though all but the two smallest samples include a few relatively old individuals (7½ years or more). This general pattern is similar to that obtained by Elder (1965) from three prehistoric sites in Missouri. These age composition curves of prehistoric deer harvests are extremely different from the age composition curves obtained from modern sport-hunting deer harvests: "(1) Nearly one-third of the modern white man's bag is made up of fawns. (2) Very few deer live as long as 8½ years. (3) The proportion of all older deer, 6½ years or more, in the bag is again greatly reduced, to approximately 2%." (Elder, 1965:368). Middle Mississippi hunters were obviously harvesting a quite different portion of the deer population in the Mississippi valley area than is being taken there today.

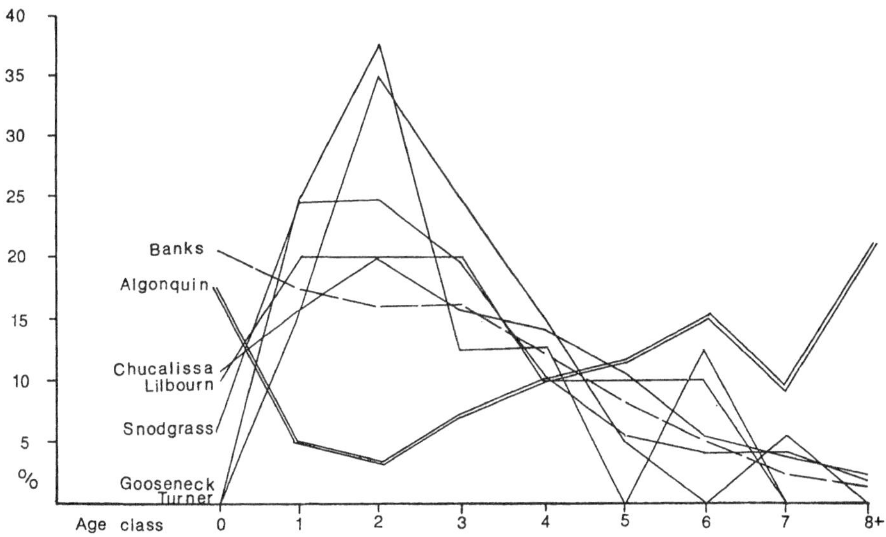

Fig. 5. Age composition of the deer kill from 6 Middle Mississippi sites, compared with the age composition of the deer kill due to wolf predation at Algonquin Park, Ontario.

TABLE 5

AGE COMPOSITION OF THE DEER KILL AT SIX MIDDLE MISSISSIPPI SITES BASED ON MANDIBLES AGED BY THE SEVERINGHAUS METHOD (1949) COMPARED WITH THE AGE COMPOSITION OF THE DEER KILL DUE TO WOLF PREDATION AT ALGONQUIN PARK ONTARIO. (FROM WOLF PREDATION DATA, PIMLOTT ET AL., 1969)

AGE CLASS	CHUCALISSA SITE	BANKS VILLAGE SITE	LILBOURN SITE	TURNER SITE	SNODGRASS SITE	GOOSENECK SITE	WOLF PREDATION, FROM PIMLOTT ET AL., 1969
0	10.9% (6)	20.9% (17)	10.0% (1)	----	6.9% (9)	----	17% (56)
1	16.4% (9)	17.3% (14)	20.0% (2)	15.0% (3)	24.6% (32)	25.0% (2)	5% (19)
2	20.0% (11)	16.1% (13)	20.0% (2)	35.0% (7)	25.4% (33)	37.5% (3)	3% (10)
3	16.4% (9)	16.1% (13)	20.0% (2)	25.0% (5)	19.2% (25)	12.5% (1)	7% (24)
4	14.5% (8)	12.3% (10)	10.0% (1)	15.0% (3)	9.2% (12)	12.5% (1)	10% (32)
5	10.9% (6)	8.7% (7)	10.0% (1)	5.0% (1)	5.4% (7)	----	12% (39)
6	5.5% (3)	5.0% (4)	10.0% (1)	----	3.8% (5)	12.5% (1)	15% (50)
7	3.6% (2)	2.5% (2)	----	5.0% (1)	3.8% (5)	----	9% (29)
8+	2.0% (1)	1.3% (1)	----	----	1.5% (2)	----	22% (72)
Total (n)	100% (55)	100% (81)	100% (10)	100% (20)	100% (130)	100% (8)	100% (331)

One of the most interesting characteristics of the Middle Mississippi hunter's harvest is the low percentage of fawns (zero age class) represented in the kill. This is most unusual since young of the year are a large, very vulnerable segment of the deer population, and would seem to be very susceptible to exploitation by predators. In attempting to determine the most probable explanation for the low percentage of young of the year in the prehistoric deer kills, Elder considered the impact of nonhuman predators such as wolves, but rejected this in favor of the hypothesis that prehistoric cultures were practicing "a voluntary and effective conservation measure—sparing the fawns to grow into better hides and more meat." (Elder, 1965:369). A closer look at the selective nature of wolf predation on deer populations, however, strongly suggests that it was indeed the impact of wolves, rather than any conscious conservation measure by human predators, that was producing the low percentage of young of the year in the Middle Mississippi deer kills. It is well-known that wolf populations characteristically exploit the zero age class, along with the older, more vulnerable individuals, in a prey population. It was not, however, until 1969 (Pimlott et al.), that an accurate, detailed analysis of the pattern of wolf predation on an undisturbed deer population became available.

Pimlott's data on wolf predation patterns were obtained from a study of the wolf population in Algonquin Park, Ontario. Since no sport-hunting was allowed, the primary mortality factors that operated to control the growth of the deer population of the park were wolf predation, research sampling, and accidents. The age composition curve for wolf predation obtained by Pimlott will be considered representative of the predation pattern of wolf populations in general, including the pattern during the Middle Mississippi period.

The age distribution curve of wolf predation obtained by Pimlott is included in Table 5 and Figure 5, along with the age distribution curves of the deer harvests from the six archaeological sites. A comparison of these two age distribution curves shows the relationship that existed between these two predator populations. The very high negative correlation between the two strongly suggests that there was very little direct competition between the two predator populations. Predation by wolves and Middle Mississippi hunters concentrated on quite separate portions of the deer population. Man's role as predator in the system can most accurately be viewed as complementary to that of the wolf.

The relationship between predators, prey, and the vegetation food source of the prey species can be illustrated by the use of a systematic model. The system can be considered (1) functional—since it maintains its structure; (2) dynamic—since its elements can change over time; (3) coherent—since a change in one element of the system causes change in all other elements; (4) in equilibrium—since it maintains itself with a certain range of values. This rather simple system contains three interacting elements:

(1) Predation:

a. Wolf predation—concentrates upon specific age groupings in the deer population (fawns and 4½ years plus).

b. Human predation (Middle Mississippi hunters)—concentrates upon specific age groupings (1½-4½ years).

(2) Prey population: White-tailed deer populations have a very high biotic potential, and as a result deer populations will reach a subsistence density within a short period of time, unless inhibitory factors (predation) continually function to offset their high potential rate of increase.

(3) Vegetation Base: The vegetation base defines the sustaining level of the area, with the frequent low oak mast yield years being the specific limiting factor that determines the carrying capacity of the area. The number of deer that can be supported without damage to the vegetation base during a poor oak mast year equals the carrying capacity, for deer, of the southeastern Ozarks.

The interaction of these variables is shown in Figure 6.

With healthy, functioning predator populations present, the deer population is maintained below subsistence density levels, and perhaps approaches optimum density levels. This in turn assures that the vegetation base which supports the prey population will not be degraded. With a stable vegetation base, the deer population remains healthy and numerous enough to support predator populations. This system is functioning adequately when the deer population is maintained below a subsistence density level and above the predator support level. This, then, is the range variable in the system, with the goal state of the variable being (predator support level < deer population < subsistence density level). This system is balanced, meaning that with any large change at any point in the system, a non-functioning state will ensue. Any radical change in the status of any one of the three main components could bring on such a collapse. Once this system has collapsed, a crash cycle will begin. When the crash cycle has run its course, and the prey population has recovered, the original system will begin to function once again (unless, of course, some factor of the system has been permanently altered, in which case the system will never be re-established).

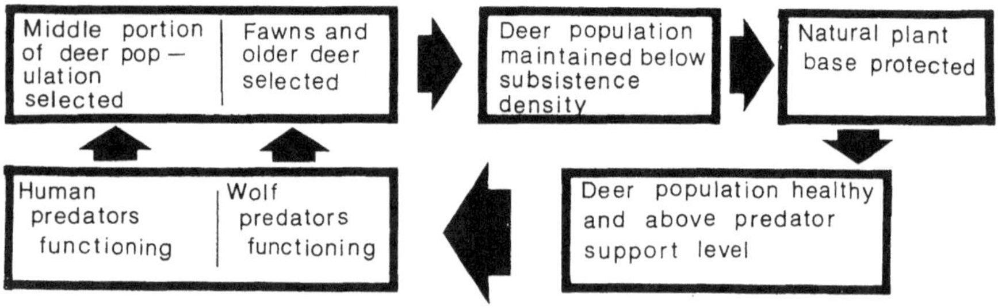

Fig. 6. Predator–prey–plant food source equilibrium system.

It is also important to note that by clearing fairly large areas for fields on the lowland ridges, Middle Mississippi communities may very well have provided a safety valve for the natural system described above. Access to these fields would allow the local deer population to survive small, infrequent breaks in the natural system without slipping into a crash cycle. The increased edge areas around the fields, as well as the crops themselves (mainly corn) would provide an excellent alternate food source during an oak mast failure, or other decrease in the natural vegetation base. This alternate food source would not be used by the deer population to any great extent while the natural system was functioning, but would be turned to when the system temporarily broke down, judging from relative usage of agricultural crops by modern deer populations in poor and good mast years in the southeastern Ozarks. This artificial improvement of the environment would, in effect, raise the carrying capacity of the area, and would reduce the impact of any temporary disruption in the system.

The age composition of the deer kill from the Banks site differs from the sites just discussed in that the zero age class represents a much higher percentage of the deer kill. This increase in the representation of young of the year in the deer kill indicates a change in at least one of many factors. If the level of predation by *Canis lupus* were reduced, more fawns would survive until the fall, and would represent a greater percentage of the Banks site harvest. A similar increase in the representation of young of the year would occur if predation of white-tailed deer by Banks site hunters was extended seasonally into the summer months, placing them in direct competition with the wolf population for the fawn crop. A third possibility is the influence of a greatly increased harvest by Banks site hunters. If human predation of the deer population was significantly increased, the rate of turnover of the deer population would rise as a result. Therefore, young of the year would make up a higher percentage of the deer herd and the deer harvest. Modern sports hunting produces high turnover rates in deer populations, and modern age composition curves, as previously mentioned, have high representation of young of the year, and a low representation of the older age classes. Of these three possibilities, the third can probably be ruled out, since the age composition of the Banks site deer kill shows no drop in the representation of older age classes. The second possibility, a greater effort by Banks site hunters to exploit the deer population during the summer months, is not supported by the evidence for seasonality of the Banks deer harvest (Fig. 7). Even though more young of the year are represented in the Banks site deer harvest, the seasonal nature of their exploitation does not appear to explain this. Although Banks hunters may have hunted deer throughout the winter months, this would not result in a higher representation of young of the year. It is, therefore, suggested that the increase in representation of young of the year in the Banks deer harvest was a function of a decreasing influence of nonhuman predation (wolves and pumas). This was quite probably a result of the expanded range of human activities in the Bradley Ridge area, which contained the large Wappanoca and Bradley sites, and at least two known Walls-Pecan Point hamlets in addition to the Banks site (Perino, 1966:140).

Sex Ratio of the Deer Kill

Two skeletal indicators of sex were used to estimate the sex ratio of deer kills: the presence or absence of antlers on skull fragments, and morphological characteristics of the pelvis (Taber, 1956). Variations in morphological characteristics of the first cervical vertebra have been used to determine the sex of a number of species of deer in the Old World, but the applicability of this method to the genus *Odocoileus* has not yet been established. Table 6 shows the sex ratio of the deer harvests suggested by each of these two methods. There is an obvious discrepancy between the two

TABLE 6

SEX RATIO OF THE DEER KILL FROM SEVEN MIDDLE MISSISSIPPI SITES, BASED ON TWO OSTEOLOGICAL SEXING CRITERIA.

SITE	SEXING CRITERIA	MALE	FEMALE
Chucalissa	antlers	3	0
	pelvis	14	17
Banks	antlers	41	14
	pelvis	10	12
Lilbourn	antlers	1	0
	pelvis	7	5
Snodgrass	antlers	5	1
	pelvis	2	4
Turner	antlers	4	0
	pelvis	3	2
Powers Fort	antlers	0	0
	pelvis	1	3
Gooseneck	antlers	2	0
	pelvis	1	0
TOTAL	antlers	56	15
	pelvis	38	43

sets of results. Judging from pelvis morphology the sex ratio of the deer kill was fairly evenly balanced. (The small sample size of pelvic indicators of sex is due to the extensive destruction inflicted on the pelvis during butchering.) On the other hand, the presence or absence of antlers on skull fragments suggests a definite selection of male over female individuals by Middle Mississippi hunters. This seeming selection for male animals is most likely not a result of hunter preference, but rather a bias introduced by two factors. Female skull fragments, because of their more delicate nature, are less likely to survive in recognizable form the battering they would be subjected to during extraction of the brains. Also, male skulls and skull fragments with attached antlers would be more likely to be brought back to the villages, where the antlers were used in a variety of ways. The pelvic sample, therefore, is believed to more accurately represent the sex ratio of the deer kill, and it strongly suggests a sexually balanced exploitation of the deer population.

Estimation of Deer Meat Yield

The size of white-tailed deer depends largely upon their age and sex. Males are larger than females in all age classes. The first seven months after birth is a period of rapid growth, followed by a second period of significant growth the following summer. During the third and fourth summers smaller increments in weight occur, with males showing greater increases (Severinghaus and Cheatum, 1956). Deer have reached their full physical stature and weight by the fifth year. After this peak at five years of age, weight usually tends either to level off or to decrease gradually with age, although a continuing increase in weight was observed in the study by Brohn and Robb (see Table 7). The quality and quantity of forage per capita available to the deer population will obviously influence the size of deer in each sex and age category. Seasonal variations in weight also occur, with dramatic increases during the fall acorn season, followed by gradual weight loss through the winter. Considering the number of factors which influence the amount of meat which prehistoric Indian hunters would obtain from an individual deer, it becomes difficult to accurately estimate how many pounds of deer meat are represented at a prehistoric site. White (1953) has estimated the average live weight of a white-tailed deer at 200 pounds. Since usable meat is about fifty percent of live weight, White suggests that the average deer should yield 100 pounds of meat. This figure of 100 pounds has been widely accepted and applied to many archaeological sites. If, for example, a prehistoric site has a minimum of twenty-five deer represented, this would indicate a yield of at least 2,500 pounds of deer meat according to White's criteria.

A much more accurate total deer meat yield value for an archaeological site can be obtained by using a slightly more complicated procedure. In attempting to estimate the deer meat yield values for each of the sites, we first obtained a large modern sample of deer weight values by sex and age of a deer population in close proximity to the area being considered. This was necessary since the size of white-tailed deer varies markedly with latitude. A seven year study of the age composition and weights of the Missouri deer population (Brohn and Robb, 1955) contained the needed information. Table 7 lists the average fully dressed weights in each age category for males, females and both sexes combined. The wide variation in meat yield for the different age and sex categories can be easily seen in this table. Knowing the age composition of the deer kill for each site (Table 5) and these average weights, the relative contribution of each age class in pounds of meat can be calculated for each of the sites. The way in which the deer meat yield for the Banks site was determined is illustrated in Table 8. A sample of eighty-one deer mandibles complete enough to be aged were recovered from the Banks site. Of these, ten (12.34 percent) fell into the fourth year age class. Assuming

TABLE 7

FULLY DRESSED WEIGHTS[1] OF MISSOURI WHITE-TAILED DEER, BY SEX AND AGE CLASSES (IN POUNDS; COMPUTED FROM BROHN AND ROBB, 1955[2]).

AGE CLASS	SEX MALE	 FEMALE	AVERAGE	SAMPLE SIZE
0	41.6	38.1	39.9	201
1	69.9	61.7	65.8	116
2	88.2	63.8	76.0	96
3	103.8	64.0	83.9	47
4	114.3	66.8	90.5	46
5	109.5	71.4	90.5	26
6	107.2	71.4	89.3	15
7	129.4	66.8	98.1	15
8+	134.5	77.6	106.0	3

1. Fully dressed weight refers to the amount of edible meat obtained from an individual deer. Of the numerous estimates available, the value .57 given by Schwartz and Schwartz (1959), was employed as the fully dressed/live weight ratio in this analysis.

2. Age classes 0 through 3 were computed from data for the southeastern Ozarks, while age classes 4 through 8 were computed from state-wide data, because of the small sample size for these age groups in the southeastern Ozarks.

that the age composition of the sample of recovered mandibles accurately reflects the actual age composition of the prehistoric Banks site deer kill, 12.34 percent of the one hundred deer (minimum) represented at the site would be four years old, producing 1116.77 pounds of usable meat. The average combined weight value was used since archaeological evidence indicates a sexually balanced harvest. In a similar manner the meat yields of the other age classes were estimated and combined to produce a deer meat yield for the Banks site. These meat yield figures are not estimates of the total amount of deer meat obtained during the occupation of the sites, but are used to indicate the importance of deer in the diet relative to the other species that were exploited.

There are a number of possible sources of bias in applying the modern deer weight values to prehistoric sites. The deer population from which the modern data was drawn is located in the upland hardwood areas of the state of Missouri. Since these upland hardwood areas provide less desirable deer habitat than the bottomland hardwoods of the Mississippi valley, it would be expected that the deer of the Mississippi valley would be larger, all other factors being equal. If such were the case, these modern weight values would

TABLE 8

ESTIMATED DEER MEAT YIELD BY AGE CLASSES FOR THE MINIMUM NUMBER OF DEER (100) REPRESENTED AT THE BANKS SITE.

AGE CLASS	NUMBER OF MANDIBLES	PERCENT OF KILL	NUMBER OF ANIMALS IN EACH AGE CLASS	ESTIMATED WEIGHT (IN POUNDS)	ESTIMATED MEAT YIELD BY AGE CLASS (IN POUNDS)
0	17	20.98	20.98 x	39.9 =	837.10
1	14	17.28	17.28 x	65.8 =	1137.02
2	13	16.04	16.04 x	76.0 =	1219.04
3	13	16.04	16.04 x	83.9 =	1345.75
4	10	12.34	12.34 x	90.5 =	1116.77
5	7	8.64	8.64 x	90.5 =	781.92
6	4	4.93	4.93 x	89.3 =	440.24
7	2	2.47	2.47 x	98.1 =	242.30
8	1	1.23	1.23 x	106.0 =	130.38
Total	81	100%	100		7250.52

be slightly low for the Banks and Lilbourn sites. Since the Chucalissa site and the Powers Phase sites are situated along the edge of the Mississippi valley, this source of bias would not apply to them. The fact that the modern study by Brohn and Robb sampled deer killed during the late fall, when the greatest yearly weight is attained by white-tailed deer, might affect the applicability of the data to prehistoric deer kills if prehistoric hunters did not restrict their hunting to this late fall period of maximum weight. Such sources of bias balance each other out, we hope. Accurate estimates of the relative importance of deer in the diet of prehistoric groups depend upon: (1) the applicability of modern data concerning weight values by age, (2) accurate estimates of the age composition of prehistoric deer harvests, and (3) accurate estimates of the total number of deer represented at prehistoric sites.

Seasonality of Deer Hunting

I proposed in an earlier article (Smith, 1974*a*) that the exploitation of white-tailed deer in the Powers Phase area was largely a seasonal activity, occurring during the fall and early winter. The evidence for seasonality from the other sites, while quite limited for the Lilbourn site, at least corresponds fairly closely with the Powers Phase data. The conclusions reached for the Powers Phase area, are, therefore, considered generally applicable to the larger geographical and temporal range considered in the present study. Although it is difficult to show conclusively the extent to which deer hunting was a seasonal, rather than a year-round subsistence activity for Middle Mississippi hunters, a strong argument can be made that deer were most intensively exploited during the late fall and early winter in the uplands areas (Chucalissa and Powers Phase areas), while the hunting season extended somewhat later in the first bottom areas (Lilbourn and Banks sites).

The feeding habits and seasonal movements of deer in the upland areas bordering the Mississippi valley follow a consistent, predictable pattern. Deer tend to concentrate their feeding in specific areas during the early spring (March and April) and during the fall (September-October-November). The fall concentration in the upland hardwood areas is a result of the abundant acorn yields, and is the more reliable of the two periods of concentration. A similar fall feeding concentration of deer in hardwood first bottom ridge areas would be expected in the region closer to the Mississippi River. This seasonal occurrence of high availability of a prime food source (acorns) within upland hardwood and bottomland hardwood areas produces a higher density of deer for several months, and with this higher density of deer within known zones, the probability of a hunter-prey encounter is substantially increased. This increase in the probability of a hunter encountering deer is a matter of both higher prey density, and the fact that hunters, knowing of this seasonal concentration, would tend to take advantage of it. In terms of the feeding habits and seasonal movements of the prey, the fall and early winter would be the most advantageous time to hunt. It is also during this late fall and early winter period that deer attain their maximum yearly weight (Severinghaus and Cheatum, 1956:83).

Another factor which must be taken into consideration in the first bottoms areas around the Banks and Lilbourn sites is the late winter and early spring floods, which would maintain high deer density levels on the hardwood first bottom ridges throughout this time. Thus Banks and Lilbourn hunters would be able to concentrate their hunting on Bradley and Sikeston ridges respectively throughout the winter months.

Perhaps the greatest problem for a hunter armed only with a bow and arrow is getting near enough for a shot at the prey without being detected. But from the time a buck's antlers drop their velvet (the first week in September) until the end of the rutting season (the last week in November) a behavioral change occurs which greatly increases the hunter's chances. During this period the "personality" of the male deer changes radically from timidity to both curiosity and belligerence, as he avidly seeks out other deer of both sexes. This rut-induced change in behavior seems to have been exploited in early historical times. Swanton (1946) cites nine ethnographic accounts of individual stalking of white-tailed deer by Indians in the southeast United States. Of these nine references, eight made specific, detailed reference to the use of deer skins or heads both to conceal the hunter and to attract the deer. This sometimes involved violent rustling of bushes and trees with stuffed deer heads held in the hunter's hand. Such a method closely parallels the way in which deer attack trees and bushes immediately prior to and during the rutting season. This hunting strategy is one of slow stalking, concealment, and attraction of the deer prior to shooting. During most of the year this tactic would probably not attract the prey, but would, on the contrary, frighten it away. But such is not the case from September to December. In one passage concerning this strategy, F. G. Speck (in Swanton, 1946:317) referring to Yuchi informants, said,

> My informants also remember this style of hunting. They said that, as it was usually undertaken in October or November when the bucks seek the does or seek each other to fight, either the head of a buck or the head of a doe could be used. Wonderful skill was claimed for some hunters.

Obviously, if Banks and Lilbourn hunters exploited deer throughout the winter months, a technique other than this one of concealment and attraction must have been employed during the post-rut winter months.

Judging from seasonal movements, feeding habits, maximum seasonal weights, rut-induced behavioral changes, and the seasonal flood stages of the Mississippi River, the period from September through December was the most advantageous time of year to hunt deer in the upland areas, while the winter flood stage of the Mississippi River would have extended this optimal period throughout the winter months in the first bottoms areas. We can also confidently state that it was a widespread practice during the early historical period to take advantage of these possibilities for exploitation.

Archaeological evidence for the seasonality of deer hunting can be obtained by analysis of the growth and shedding of deer antlers and the eruption and wear patterns of mandibular dentition.

Deer antlers begin growing in May, becoming fully hardened during the month of September. They are dropped between the middle of January and the first week in February. During the summer velvet period the antler tips exhibit bulbs or terminal growth centers. It is theoretically possible to determine the time of death of a deer using the following criteria:

a) Antlers present + still in velvet stage = May to September.
b) Antlers present + fully hardened = September to February.
c) Antlers absent = January to May.

Unfortunately for the archaeologist, it is rarely possible to determine antler condition in archaeological situations. Since antler shafts and tines were used for a variety of tools, they were almost always separated from the skull just above the base. Unless the whole antler is recovered, including the tips, it is very difficult to determine when the deer was killed. Antler tips showing the terminal growth bulb characteristic of summer are rarely found in archaeological sites, perhaps because of their rather spongy quality. None were observed in the present study. It is unfortunate, but unavoidable, that the only seasonal determination that archaeologists can make from the antlers of white-tailed deer is the following:

a) Antlers present = killed during the period May-February.
b) Antlers shed = killed during the period January-May.

It is possible to determine the season of death of white-tailed deer within finer limits by analysis of deer mandibles from archaeological sites. The eruption of permanent dentition, and the replacement of deciduous pre-molars in *Odocoileus virginianus* during the first 20 months of life proceeds at a relatively standard rate. This allows mandibles of individuals less than 20 months old to be accurately aged within a two to three month range (Severinghaus, 1949).

The fawn dropping period begins in late May in the southeastern Missouri area, about a week earlier than in the more northern parts of the state. Fawning peaks on the first of June, give or take a few days, and drops off slowly, ending about June fifteenth. By using June first as the date of birth of each deer, an estimate of the date of death can be computed for each. Each deer mandible recovered from the sites in question that was complete enough to be aged and that represented an individual less than 20 months of age, was aged within a two to three month range. Histograms of the computed age of death for these juvenile deer are presented for each site in Figure 7. Since only a single mandible was recovered from the Lilbourn site that was less than 20 months of age, and was complete enough to be aged, the conclusions that may be drawn concerning the seasonality of deer hunting at the Lilbourn site are limited. The histograms of seasonality for the other sites, however, are quite similar, with the peaks corresponding closely to the availability of acorns in the hardwood areas, and to the rutting period. It is not possible, however, to determine from the archaeological evidence if deer hunting peaked during the "acorn-rutting" period, and then continued at a lesser intensity through the winter months, or if it was at a constant level through the late fall and winter. The ratio of antlered to antlerless skulls (Figure 7) indicates that deer hunting in the late winter months, after antlers had been dropped, was more common at the Banks site than it was at the sites closer to the edge of the Mississippi valley (the Powers Phase and Chucalissa sites). The high late winter deer population densities on Sikeston and Bradley ridges, caused by inundation of low areas during the high water period probably allowed the extension of the hunting season through the winter months. The low mortality levels through the rest of the year suggest that late fall-winter was the period of most intensive exploitation.

Density Estimates

According to available data, the carrying capacity for white-tailed deer in the eastern United States ranges from a high of 64 per square mile in Mississippi (Goodrum, 1949) to a low of 8 per square mile in Florida (Newman, 1948). The carrying capacity of the Ashland Wildlife Refuge in Boone County, Missouri was estimated at 20 per square mile (Progulske and Baskett, 1958). This same figure of 20 per square mile is cited by Hosley (1956:225) as an average figure for nine eastern and southern states in which studies had been done. A number of problems must be considered before attempting to apply these modern carrying capacity values to the Mississippi valley area during the prehistoric period. The most obvious problem, of course, is interpreting how "carrying capacity" was defined in each of the studies cited. Are they estimates of subsistence density values, or optimum density values, or simply population estimates? It is also possible that they are too conservative for our purposes, since they all refer to areas outside major river valleys. Moore's study (1967) of the Savannah River area in South Carolina showed a carrying capacity of 50 deer per square mile for the bottomland areas, a figure which probably closely approximates the optimum density level for deer in the Mississippi River valley during the prehistoric period. Because of the relatively small home range of the white-tailed deer, and its shifting seasonal food preferences, the carrying capacity of an area depends in large part upon its variety of vegetation zones. Those areas with a

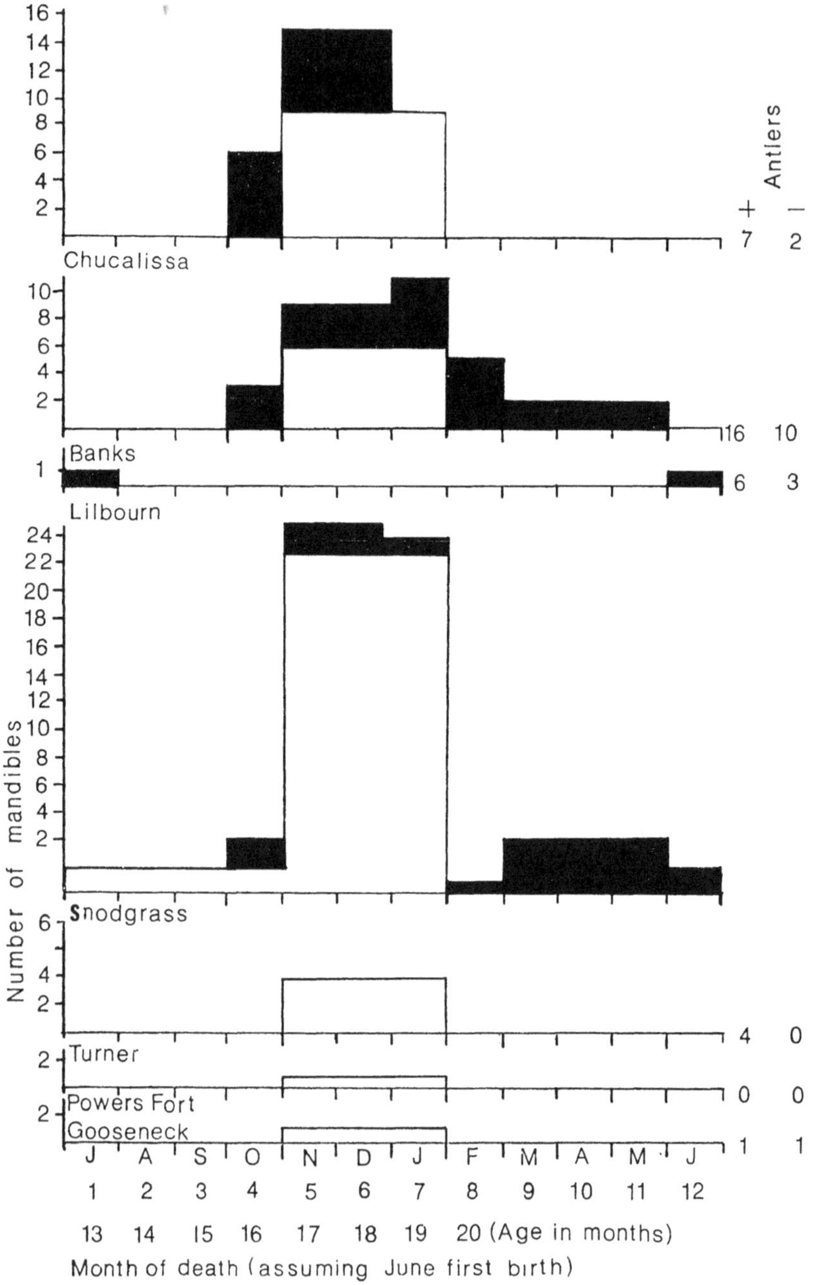

Fig. 7. Archaeological evidence from 7 Middle Mississippi sites indicating seasonality of the exploitation of white-tailed deer populations.

large variety of habitat zones, and a correspondingly large linear distance of interface or edge area per unit of area will obviously support larger deer populations. This "edge effect" holds true for many species with low mobility that require a variety of vegetation types. The number of different species of animals, and the total biomass will subsequently be greater in such edge areas than in areas of uniform vegetation. It has been well established that, of the four major forest types in the southeastern United States, bottomland hardwood provides the best deer habitat (Stransky, 1969). This is because of both the fertile soils of the bottomlands and the great amount of edge area that exists along oxbow lakes, swampy areas, river bank succession zones, and topographic vegetation zones. The study of the George Reserve deer herd discussed earlier is the only accurate analysis ever done of the subsistence and optimum density levels of a white-tailed deer population. The estimated optimum density for the George Reserve deer herd is 44 deer per square mile. This is quite close to the population level of 50 deer per square mile reported by Moore (1967) for a major river bottomland area in South Carolina, and to the 40 per square mile projected optimum density for an undisturbed eastern deciduous forest situation (Shelford, 1963:26). Since the Shelford estimate and the George Reserve estimate are for habitat situations slightly less fertile than the first bottoms area of the Mississippi River, an optimum density level of 50 deer per square mile will be projected for the first bottoms area adjacent to the Banks and Lilbourn sites. This can be considered a conservative estimate. Since the upland habitat areas adjacent to the Chucalissa and lowland Powers Phase sites are much closer in type to the George Reserve and Shelford habitat areas, a rather conservative optimum density level of 30 deer per square mile will be projected for these areas.

It was proposed earlier that human and nonhuman predation combined to stabilize the deer population below subsistence density, perhaps as low as optimum density level. Let us assume for the moment that the deer populations were maintained at close to optimum density by the inhibitory effect of predation. The projected optimum density values of 30 to 50 deer per square mile would represent deer biomass values (live weight) of approximately 3,000 to 4,500 and 5,000 to 7,500 pounds per square mile respectively. If the deer populations were stabilized at a level above optimum density, these biomass values would, of course, be higher. Since the recruitment rate of stable deer populations at optimum density is 0.5, the potential harvest of deer is fifteen and twenty-five per square mile per year. This means that to maintain the deer population at optimum density, 25 deer per square mile would have had to have been killed each year in the first bottoms areas, and 15 deer per square mile per year in the upland areas. The deer populations could sustain such a harvest on a continual basis in a healthy state. The continued harvest would be an important factor, in fact, in assuring the continued healthy existence of the deer population.

In estimating the potential annual meat yield and fall-winter biomass values for deer populations during the Mississippi period, an average edible meat yield value of 72.5 pounds is combined with a mean spring breeding population estimate of 40 deer per square mile (a fall-winter population estimate of 50 deer per square mile) and a recruitment rate of 0.5. The potential annual meat yield for the species is therefore projected as 1450 pounds of edible meat per square mile (40 x 0.5 x 72.5). The fall-winter biomass level is projected as 3,625 pounds of edible meat per square mile (50 x 72.5). These values will later be compared with similar values for other species of animals that were exploited by Middle Mississippi groups.

Raccoon (*Procyon lotor*)

The raccoon (*Procyon lotor*) has a very wide geographical range, which encompasses most of north and middle America south of the Canadian border. Its remains have been recovered in some quantity from many archaeological sites in the eastern United States, indicating its continued importance as a food source from the early Archaic to the proto-historic period.

Recognized as a very generalized, wide niche species, the raccoon can adapt to, and exist in, a wide variety of habitat situations. This ability is most clearly indicated by the wide spectrum of plants and animals that make up its diet.

Of the numerous studies of raccoon food habits conducted in various parts of the eastern United States, the one done closest to our area of study is that of Calhoun Point by Yeager and Rennels (1943). Calhoun Point is a four square mile area situated at the confluence of the Mississippi and Illinois Rivers, just north of St. Louis. It is typical of the larger flood plains north of the Ohio River, and is similar to the Mississippi bottomlands in our area of interest. A variety of habitat subtypes are found at Calhoun Point, with the most important being the margins of large rivers, sloughs, small lakes and marshes, flooded woodland, forested ridges, brushland, cut-over land, fallow land, and levees. Such bottomland habitat "... is undoubtedly the preferred habitat of raccoons and over much of the vast Mississippi basin is the best range available for numerous forms of wildlife." (Yeager and Rennels, 1943:45).

Analysis of raccoon scats (droppings) from Calhoun Point indicated that seasonal availability dictated in large part the quantity and kinds of food taken. The main winter foods were carrion, winter-killed fish, corn, and mice. Mulberries, dewberries, crayfish, and insects made up the spring and early summer diet, while corn, wild grapes, and blackberries were eaten in the last half of the summer. The most important raccoon food resources in the fall were fruits and nuts (persimmons, pecans, acorns, etc.) (Ibid:59). A similar study done in eastern Texas (Baker, Newman, and Wilke, 1945:48) indicated that acorns and crayfish made up over fifty percent of the yearly diet, with raccoons concentrating in timbered river bottoms during the winter and spring to take advantage of these two food sources. In the summer and autumn months raccoons dispersed through the uplands as well, in search of seasonal foods such as persimmons, grapes, and insects.

These two area studies of raccoon food habits and seasonal movements, along with numerous other studies, clearly indicate that rather than having a fixed range of food species, the raccoon is highly adaptable, consuming whatever a specific area has to offer in most abundance.

Raccoons are nocturnal feeders. During the daylight hours they usually remain secluded in dens, occasionally sunning themselves on tree limbs close to the den. Dens are often located in tree cavities, but if such sites are lacking, fallen logs, crevices, and ground holes are used. Raccoons in southern regions like the southeast Missouri area remain active throughout the winter, denning up for only a few days at a time. In Stuewer's study of a Michigan raccoon population (1943:220), he noted that even though upland hardwood areas provided an important food supply (oak mast), most raccoon dens were found in trees in the lowland areas, with the average distance from the nearest creek, bayou, or river being 400 feet. Over half of the dens observed were between twenty and forty feet above the ground.

Although raccoons cover large distances and use a variety of habitat situations in their foraging for food, their home range is relatively small and well-defined. The average range of adult male raccoons has been estimated at 503 acres (a circle one mile in diameter). A lower value of 268 acres (a circle seven tenths of a mile in diameter) was estimated for adult females and juveniles (Stuewer, 1943:226).

Most raccoons breed during February in southeast Missouri, with males being promiscuous in their mating. Some litters are born in June, July, or August, as a result of late matings, but most arrive in April or early May. The average litter contains three to four young (Schwartz and Schwartz, 1959:276).

Analysis of present day raccoon populations indicates a balanced sex ratio in stable populations (Bennitt and Nagel, 1937; Stuewer, 1943; Mech, et al., 1968).

Stuewer has estimated the breeding potential (biotic potential) of raccoons at 1.5 young per adult. This means that in the absence of mortality, winter populations would have a ratio of three young of the year for every two adults, i.e., sixty percent of the population would be young of the year. Because of the great reduction in the predator populations which originally preyed upon raccoons (fishers, wolves, bobcats), juvenile mortality during the spring and summer is low (Sanderson, 1951:400). As a result of this low natural mortality, a high percentage of the young of the year survive to be taken during the winter hunting and trapping seasons. Young of the year usually represent half of the winter kill (Ibid.: 401). This figure of fifty percent, compared with the theoretical maximum of sixty percent, indicates the low juvenile mortality prior to the hunting season. These estimates of biotic potential and hunting harvest also indicate that to maintain a stable raccoon population in the absence of natural predation, it is necessary to harvest fully sixty percent of the population each fall (Stuewer, 1943:218).

Estimates of the density of raccoon populations vary widely, depending upon the habitat studied and the census techniques employed, as well as the time of year the census is taken. Twitchell and Dill estimated the raccoon population in 102 acres of excellent raccoon habitat in the Swan Lake National Wildlife Refuge (Chariton County, Missouri) at 166 individuals, and estimated a density of one raccoon per two acres for a larger 2,000 acre section of good habitat in the refuge (1949). These are the highest density values ever recorded for this species. A number of sources give much lower density estimates. Sonenshine and Winslow have estimated a fall raccoon population of 1 raccoon per 14.3 acres (44.8 per square mile) in an average raccoon habitat situation in Virginia (1972), while Butterfield (1944) estimated a winter population of 1 raccoon per 11.7 acres (54 per square mile) in Ohio. Similarly, Yeager and Rennels (1943) estimated the fall raccoon population at Calhoun Point as 53 raccoons per square mile.

Using these modern studies of raccoon populations as a frame of reference, we can now project with some degree of confidence the raccoon population which existed in the Mississippi valley area during the Mississippi period.

In estimating the potential annual meat yield and fall-winter biomass values for raccoon populations during the Mississippi period, an average edible meat yield per individual value of eight pounds will be combined with a mean spring breeding population estimate of 30 raccoons per square mile, a fall-winter population estimate of 40 raccoons per square mile, and a biotic potential of 1.5. The potential annual meat yield for the species is therefore 360 pounds of edible meat per square mile (30 x 1.5 x 8). The fall–winter biomass level is projected as 320 pounds of edible meat per square mile (40 x 8).

The bottomland areas directly adjacent to the Banks, Lilbourn, and Chucalissa sites would have provided generally excellent habitat for raccoons, for the great amount of margin areas around oxbow lakes, marshes, and seasonally flooded low areas provide abundant insect and crayfish populations. Raccoons would concentrate their foraging during the spring and summer months along the margins of these permanent and seasonally flooded watercourses, where crayfish, insects, and a variety of berries would make up the bulk of their diet. The abundant mast crops of the bottomland hardwood areas (acorns, persimmons, pecans) would provide an easily accessible and important food source during the fall and winter months.

In the Powers Phase area, the pattern of small ridge systems surrounded by low areas of marsh and swamp, as well as the numerous streams, would also provide good habitat for raccoons. Here, too, raccoons most likely concentrated their foraging during the summer months along the edges of streams and swamp areas, moving up onto the ridges during the fall and winter to eat mast crops. Raccoon populations in the Ozark highlands probably occurred only along stream valleys that did not run dry during the summer months.

Assuming that denning trees were abundant in the Mississippi valley area, and judging from preference patterns of present day raccoons, most of the raccoon dens would have been located from twenty to forty feet above the ground in large trees, usually within 400 feet of the nearest water source.

Before beginning a discussion of the possible techniques used by Middle Mississippi hunters to capture racoons, the following preliminary assumption will be offered–raccoons were not hunted by Middle Mississippi hunters during the hours of darkness. Hunting at night would have almost certainly required the use of dogs, and although the Middle Mississippi groups being considered had "domestic" dogs, ethnohistorical evidence suggests that dogs were rarely used for hunting during the late prehistoric period.

Granted this preliminary assumption, Middle Mississippi hunters logically would have had to depend upon one or both of the following techniques to capture raccoons:

a) The setting of snares or traps along the margins of marshes, oxbow lakes, streams, etc.

b) The searching out of raccoon denning trees.

These are the techniques used today, in addition to night hunting, in capturing raccoons.

Raccoons cover relatively long distances each night as they forage for crayfish, insects, etc., along the marsh, stream, and lake margins. Modern trappers take advantage of this forage pattern by setting traps along shoreline routes. Trapping methods include both baited sets in shallow water and blind sets on and next to logs (Yeager and Rennels, 1943:50; Stuewer, 1943:207).

Judging from modern attempts (Stuewer, 1943:208; Twitchell and Dill, 1949), locating of denning trees was done by concentrating on large trees within 400 feet of water, and looking for possible den cavities twenty to forty feet up. The locating of denning trees was occasionally facilitated by surprising raccoons while they were sunning on the ground or on branches close to their den. Once the denning tree was located, it could be climbed, or a small tree could be leaned against the denning tree to allow access to the den cavity. It is unlikely that raccoons were captured by destroying the denning trees, since once denning trees were located, they could be expected to yield results for years to come.

Twitchell and Dill (1949) searched out denning sites of raccoons in the manner just described on a 102 acre area of the Swan Lake National Wildlife Refuge (Chariton County, Missouri) during January of 1948:

> Den trees climbed were those that showed the most activity, such as scats at the base of the tree, well-scratched bark, or a smooth appearance around the den entrance. In shallower dens the raccoons were removed by grasping them by a hind foot and the tail and pulling them out. With deeper dens, it was often possible to use a forked stick, which was twisted into the animal's hair and skin until it could be drawn within reach. (1949:131)

During a four and a half day period, Twitchell and Dill, along with a crew of ten men, collected one hundred raccoons from this 102 acre area. Unfortunately, there is neither archaeological nor ethnohistorical evidence concerning hunting techniques used in capturing raccoons. The techniques discussed above must therefore be considered as unconfirmed hypotheses rather than fact.

Recent studies of dental indicators of age and sex in raccoons have made it possible to determine the sex ratio and age distribution of the raccoon kills from each of the seven sites being considered.

Sexual dimorphism in canine size is a reliable indicator of sex in the raccoon (Grau et al., 1970:368). The difference in lower canine root thickness is the specific measurement employed–all male canines were found to be thicker than 4.0 mm, while ninety-three percent of the female canines were thinner than 4.0 mm. Root thickness measurements taken on all raccoon lower canines recovered from each site were recorded as shown in Table 9 (Banks site sample). All canines with a root thickness greater than 4.0 mm were classed as males, those with a thickness less than 4.0 mm as females. Those canines in each sample with a borderline root thickness of 4.0 mm were omitted from the counts. Most of the canine roots measured were in excellent condition, with minimal shrinkage due to drying and weathering. When dentition was complete enough to allow aging of the mandible, the lower canine root thickness measurements were placed in the appropriate age column. Those canines for which no age determination was possible were plotted in the unknown age column. The sex ratio of the raccoon kill for each site, according to age category, is shown in Table 10. The sex ratio of the total raccoon kills from each of the sites is roughly balanced, suggesting procurement techniques which did not select by sex. This suggests that neither sex-linked behavioral variation (such as the larger home range of male raccoons, and the summer family groupings of females and their young), nor culturally biased hunter selection influenced the raccoon harvest. When total sex ratios (all sites combined) within each age class are considered however, there appears to be an imbalance favoring females in the 0-14 month age class, and an opposite selection for males in the next three age classes. This pattern is not, however, consistent for all age classes within a single site, or within a single age class for all sites.

TABLE 9

ROOT THICKNESS MEASUREMENTS OF LOWER RACCOON CANINES RECOVERED FROM THE BANKS SITE.

TOOTH WEAR AGE CLASS		I	II	III	IV	V	?	
Canine Diameter (in mm)	4.8		1					
	4.7							
	4.6		1	2	2			
	4.5	1					2	
	4.4	2		1	2		4	
	4.3	1	2	4				
	4.2			2	1			
	4.1		1		1			
	4.0		1	1		1	2	
	3.9	2	1	3	1			
	3.8		1			1	1	
	3.7		1	1				
	3.6	1					1	
	3.5		1	1	1		3	
	3.4		1	2			1	
	3.3	1	1	1				
	3.2	1						
	3.1							
	3.0							
Sex	Male	4	5	9	6	0	6	30
	Female	5	6	8	2	1	6	28

TABLE 10

SEX RATIO OF THE RACCOON KILL AT SEVEN MIDDLE MISSISSIPPI SITES, BASED UPON THE THICKNESS OF THE ROOT OF LOWER CANINES.

AGE IN MONTHS	TOOTH WEAR CLASS	SEX	CHUCALISSA SITE	BANKS SITE	LILBOURN SITE	SNODGRASS SITE	TURNER SITE	POWERS FORT SITE	GOOSENECK SITE	TOTAL
0-14	I	Male	0	4	0	0	0	0	0	4
		Female	2	5	2	3	0	0	0	12
15-38	II	Male	4	5	3	2	2	0	0	16
		Female	0	6	1	1	2	0	0	10
39-57	III	Male	2	9	3	7	0	0	0	21
		Female	1	8	0	2	1	1	0	13
58-86	IV	Male	1	6	0	0	1	0	0	8
		Female	0	2	1	1	0	0	0	4
> 86	V	Male	0	0	0	1	0	0	0	1
		Female	0	1	0	0	0	0	0	1
Unknown	?	Male	4	6	2	3	1	0	0	16
		Female	5	6	2	3	0	0	1	17
Total		Male	11	30	8	13	4	0	0	66
		Female	8	28	6	10	3	1	1	57

Working with known age raccoons, Grau et al. have established five age classes based upon the relative amount of tooth wear on mandibular teeth (1970:368-69). Their established age classes do not represent year classes, but rather cover varying lengths of time. They were able to assign mandibles to correct age classes with a success rating of 82.7 percent (1970:369).

By employing these wear criteria, it was possible to assign a total of 182 raccoon mandibles recovered from the sites being studied into one of the five age classes. The percentage values and actual counts for each wear class for each site are shown in Table 11 and graphically illustrated in Figure 8. These age distribution curves are similar in a number of ways: (1) young of the year (age class I, 0-14 months) are only 11 to 20 percent of the sample from any one site; (2) age classes II and III (1 to 5 years) are from 50 to 73 percent of the samples; (3) except at the Chucalissa site, animals older than five years (classes IV and V) are 9 to 20 percent of the kill.

Although no detailed age distribution studies of modern raccoon kills have been published, a number of studies indicate that young of the year usually make up approximately fifty percent of the present-day sport-hunting kill. This high juvenile representation in modern kills is attributed to low juvenile mortality resulting from the lack of natural mortality factors--predators such as wolves, fishers, and bobcats. The much lower representation of young of the year in the Middle Mississippi samples is probably a result of higher juvenile mortality in the raccoon population because of nonhuman predation. The relative extent to which different age classes of raccoon populations are killed by nonhuman predators is not known. It is, therefore, impossible to determine to what extent Middle Mississippi hunters, wolves, bobcats, and other nonhuman predator species were in direct competition in their exploitation of raccoon populations.

Deliberate sparing of young of the year raccoons by Middle Mississippi hunters is not a likely factor in low juvenile representation in raccoon kills: it would be quite difficult for Middle Mississippi hunters to identify juvenile raccoons older than seven months from older raccoons without resorting to close anatomical inspection; sparing raccoons younger than seven months, on the other hand, would in many cases also logically have meant sparing the mother of the family group, since they could not survive without the protection of their parent. Such a sexually selective practice would have resulted in an unbalanced sex ratio in the raccoon kill; such an imbalance does not exist.

The relatively high representation of the older age classes (animals five years or older) in the raccoon kills, especially at the Chucalissa site, suggests that the turnover rate of the raccoon populations was rather slow during the Mississippi period. It would seem that predation pressure was light enough to allow a long life expectancy for most raccoons once the period of high juvenile mortality was passed. This light predation pressure is also indicated by

TABLE 11

PERCENTAGE BY AGE OF THE RACCOON KILL FROM SIX MIDDLE MISSISSIPPI SITES, BASED ON AGING CRITERIA OF GRAU ET AL. (1970) (n IN PARENTHESES)

AGE IN MONTHS	TOOTH WEAR CLASS	CHUCALISSA SITE	BANKS SITE	LILBOURN SITE	SNODGRASS SITE	TURNER SITE	POWERS FORT SITE	TOTAL	
0-14	I	11.8 (4)	17.8 (12)	20.0 (3)	13.2 (7)	18.2 (2)	(0)	15.3	(28)
15-38	II	26.6 (9)	33.9 (23)	40.0 (6)	43.4 (23)	54.5 (6)	(0)	36.8	(67)
39-57	III	23.6 (8)	29.2 (20)	26.6 (4)	30.2 (16)	18.2 (2)	(1)	28.0	(51)
58-86	IV	20.4 (7)	13.2 (9)	13.3 (2)	9.4 (5)	9.1 (1)	(0)	13.2	(24)
> 86	V	17.6 (6)	5.9 (4)	0.0 (0)	3.8 (2)	0.0 (0)	(0)	6.6	(12)
Total		(34)	(68)	(15)	(53)	(11)	(1)	99.9%	(182)

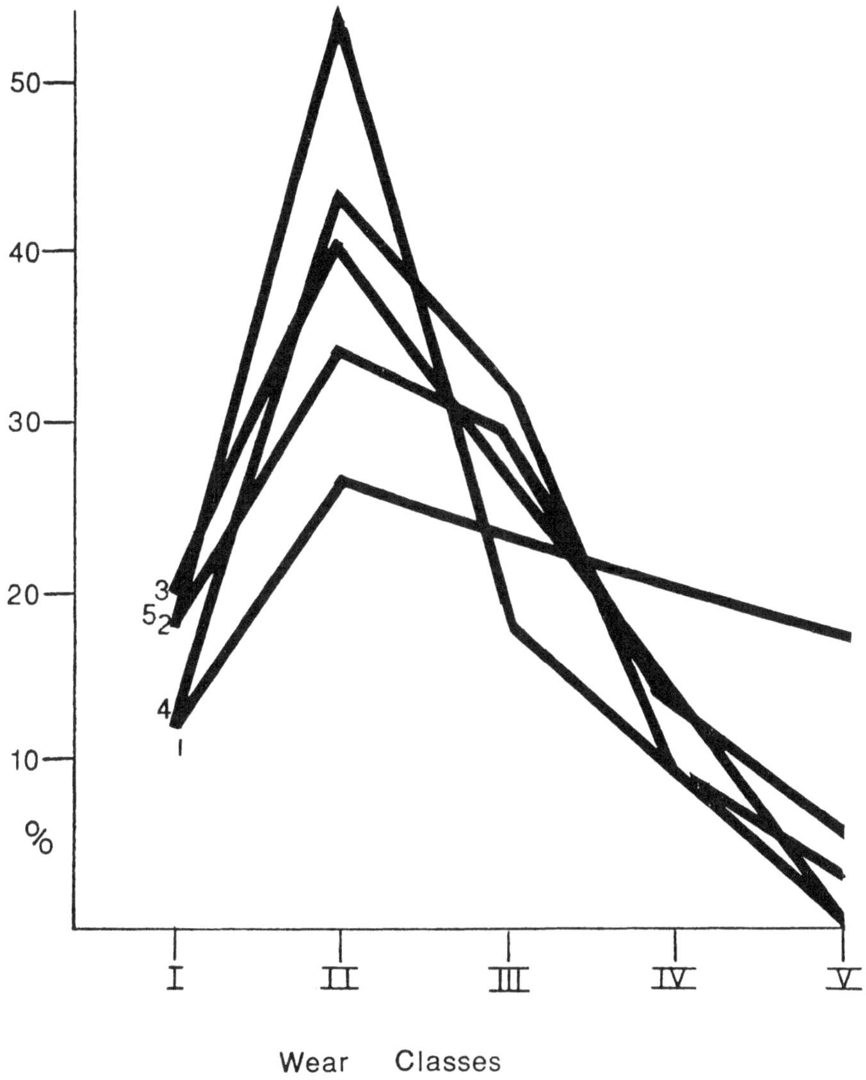

Fig. 8. Age composition of the Raccoon kill from 5 Middle Mississippi sites: 1-Chucalissa, 2-Banks, 3-Lilbourn, 4-Snodgrass, 5-Turner.

the small number of raccoons represented at the Snodgrass and Turner sites, both of which have been almost fully excavated. A minimum of seventy-eight raccoons are represented at the Snodgrass site, while the Turner site has a minimum of twenty-three.

Because of the excellent raccoon habitat which probably existed during the Mississippi period, a density of 30 breeding adults per square mile has been projected. Such a density of breeding adults would produce a potential harvest of 45 raccoons per square mile per year. If we assume for the moment that the Snodgrass and Turner sites were occupied at the same time, and that a hunting territory of ten square miles was utilized, the combined total raccoon harvest of 101 individuals represents less than 23 percent of the potential annual harvest from the hunting territory. Even if we assume that the Snodgrass and Turner sites were occupied for only five years, the minimum number of raccoons represents less than five percent of the potential raccoon harvest from the projected hunting territory of ten square miles for a five year period.

Both the presence of older individuals in the human kills, and the relatively low number of raccoons represented at the two extensively excavated Powers Phase sites support the light predation hypothesis. We hope to test this hypothesis further as life expectancy curves for modern raccoon populations are developed, and as more Middle Mississippi sites are fully excavated.

A single mandible recovered from the Turner site is the only direct archaeological evidence indicating seasonality of exploitation of raccoon populations. Judging from its tooth eruption pattern, this animal was from three to five months old (Montgomery, 1964), and was most likely killed during the period July-September. This single mandible is obviously not sufficient evidence from which to infer seasonality of exploitation.

The projected seasonal habits and movements of raccoons in the southeast Missouri area do not indicate any one time of the year when it would be easier to capture raccoons.

A late fall-winter period of exploitation would be most advantageous for maximizing weight and pelt quality. The weight of raccoons varies greatly from season to season, with weights peaking in November, then dropping sharply through the winter. Raccoons weigh the least in the early spring (Stuewer, 1943:215; Schwartz and Schwartz, 1959:273). Adult raccoon pelts are usually prime by November, with juvenile pelts becoming prime during the month of December (Stuewer, 1943:250).

If raccoons were hunted primarily during the late fall and winter, this would explain in part the low representation of young of the year in the human harvest, since nonhuman predators would have culled out many of the young during the spring, summer, and fall, before the human season of exploitation.

CLASS *PISCES*

Although some skeletal elements of fish were recovered from each of the sites being considered, the number of fish bones recovered varied greatly from site to site. While over five thousand identifiable fish bone fragments were recovered from the Lilbourn site, for example, the Snodgrass site yielded only four.

The most obvious explanation for this variation between sites is that fish were more intensively exploited at certain sites. This would certainly seem to be the case, but variation in the degree of preservation of delicate fish skeletal elements, as well as variation in archaeological recovery techniques from site to site are also important factors influencing the relative amount of recovered fish bone.

The techniques employed in the excavation of each site are discussed in some detail in the site appendixes, as is the extent to which bone was preserved at each site. It is important to note here, however, that since the skeletal elements of fish are often delicate or quite small, recovery techniques and preservation are important sources of bias in the faunal sample.

The Chucalissa site offers an excellent example of the variation which can result from different excavation techniques. While the fish bones recovered from earlier excavations at the Chucalissa site were relatively few in number and all from large fish, water screening of several features in the temple mound has recently yielded large quantities of small skeletal elements of fish (mostly undiagnostic elements). Thus it is difficult to determine the actual importance of fish in the Chucalissa diet, because of the bias introduced by partial recovery. The fish bone recovered from the Banks site is also biased because of partial recovery, although a fairly large sample was obtained (Appendix B).

Although only portions of the Snodgrass site were water screened, all the dirt removed from structures and refuse pits was screened through quarter-inch mesh. The small sample of fish bone recovered from the Snodgrass site is largely a function of poor preservation rather than of partial recovery.

Because the Lilbourn site is the only one where both recovery methods and preservation were adequate, minimizing bias, it is the only site that will be discussed in detail.

The extent to which different species of fish are represented in the faunal samples recovered from each site is also subject to bias. The scales and vertebrae of most species of fresh water fish are morphologically quite similar, and are, therefore, undiagnostic. Although further study of fish vertebrae may allow generic or specific identifications, it is impossible at our present level of knowledge to determine in most cases which species, genus, or even family a fish vertebra represents. There are, however, two notable exceptions to this rule. The bowfin (*Amia calva*) is the only surviving species of a once-prominent order, and its scales and vertebrae are diagnostic to the species level. The gar family (*Lepisosteidae*), which includes a number of fresh water species, also has very distinct characteristics. Thus, the scales and vertebrae of the gars are also diagnostic, but only to the generic level.

The fresh water drum (*Aplodinotus grunniens*) is the single fresh water member of a typically salt water family of fishes. The hard button-like teeth of its pharyngeal jaws, which function to crush the shells of mollusks, are usually well-preserved in archaeological sites, and are easily recognizable. Because the scales and vertebrae of the bowfin and the gars are diagnostic to the species or genus level while those of other species are not, and because the pharyngeal teeth of the drum are usually numerous and easily recognizable, faunal reports for archaeological sites quite often list these fish as being represented by higher skeletal element counts than other species. These high skeletal element counts, however, usually contrast markedly with the corresponding values for the minimum number of individuals represented, with the latter values giving a much more accurate indication of the relative importance of these species.

Skeletal elements of the paddlefish (*Polydon spatula*) and the sturgeons (*Family Acipenseridae*) are rarely recovered from archaeological sites, because of the cartilaginous nature of their skeleton. The absence of these species in the faunal samples may represent a significant bias, since they are known to reach quite large sizes, and could have represented an important source of protein for Middle Mississippi groups.

The Lilbourn Site

Over 15,000 fish bones and fragments were recovered from structures 9, 12, and 25 at the Lilbourn site. Of these, it was possible to identify almost 6,000 to the species, generic, or family level. At least 403 individuals, representing sixteen species were included. This fairly high ratio of identified to unidentified fish bone (5788 to 9373) is partly because of recovery techniques: flotation and water screening were unfortunately used only occasionally, with a resultant loss of many small unidentifiable fragments from the sample. The bone counts at the species, generic, and family level for each of the three structures are shown in Table 12. The faunal materials from structure 25 were identified by G. A. Waselkov (1972), and identification was usually only carried to the family or generic level. The analysis techniques described below were only applied to the fish bone samples from structures 9 and 12.

Unlike most other animal species, fish do not cease growing once they reach maturity. Andreas Paloumpis, working with modern specimens recovered from the Illinois River area, has developed linear regression charts for many species of fish, making it possible to estimate total length from the relative dimensions of certain diagnostic skeletal elements. Nancy Wilson (see Parmalee, Paloumpis, and Wilson, 1972) was kind enough to make these linear regression charts available to me. Length estimates were made from those skeletal elements which were diagnostic to the species level and were complete

TABLE 12

RELATIVE IMPORTANCE OF SPECIES OF FISH REPRESENTED AT STRUCTURES 9,12,25 OF THE LILBOURN SITE.

SPECIES OF FISH REPRESENTED	STRUCTURE 9 NUMBER OF SKEL. ELEMENTS	STRUCTURE 9 MINIMUM NUMBER OF IND.	STRUCTURE 9 ESTIMATED POUNDS OF MEAT	STRUCTURE 12 NUMBER OF SKEL. ELEMENTS	STRUCTURE 12 MINIMUM NUMBER OF IND.	STRUCTURE 12 ESTIMATED POUNDS OF MEAT	STRUCTURE 25 NUMBER OF SKEL. ELEMENTS	STRUCTURE 25 MINIMUM NUMBER OF IND.	STRUCTURE 25 ESTIMATED POUNDS OF MEAT
Bowfin	1084	23	15.0	74	4	3.0	170	8	6.0
Alligator gar				1	1	1.0			
Shortnose gar	25	5	2.5	2	1	1.0			
Longnose gar	10	2	5.0						
Gar	189	6	6.6	14	2	2.0	2014	38	34.0
Bigmouth buffalo	25	8	69.0						
Black buffalo	9	5	45.0						
Black/smallmouth buffalo	11	6	53.0						
Smallmouth buffalo	19	9	95.0						
Buffalo	257	17	160.0	10	2	19.0			
Northern redhorse	3	3	1.0	1	1	0.7			
Redhorse	12	9	3.0	14	3	2.1			
Suckers	68	12	88.8	6	3	22.2	237	6	44.5
Channel catfish	143	31	42.5						
Blue catfish	42	9	14.0						
Yellow bullhead	8	5	2.0						
Black bullhead	58	12	3.7	1	1	0.3			
Brown bullhead	10	5	1.0						
Catfish/Bullhead	653	85	116.5	26	4	4.8	92	13	18.0
Flathead catfish	14	7	31.5	4	1	0.5	4	1	0.5
Largemouth bass	4	2	1.0						
Bass	29	4	2.0						
Freshwater drum	129	29	135.0	5	3	8.0	314	17	45.0
TOTALS	2802	294	893.1	158	26	64.6	2831	83	148.0

TABLE 13

ESTIMATED TOTAL LENGTH OF FISH RECOVERED FROM STRUCTURES 9 AND 12 AT THE LILBOURN SITE (IN INCHES).

		LENGTH																								
		0	2		4	6	8		10	12		14		16	18		20		22	24	26		28	30		32
	9					2		1		7			4		5				1							
Bowfin	12												1						2							
	9																									
Alligator gar	12														1											
	9									1						1			1							
Shortnose gar	12									1																
	9																			1						1
Longnose gar	12																									
	9						1											1			2				1	
Bigmouth buffalo	12																									
	9															1					1					
Black buffalo	12																									
	9													1						2				3		
Smallmouth buffalo	12																									
	9							1		1																
Northern redhorse	12									1																
	9		1		2	5			7			8							4		2					
Channel catfish	12								1			1							1							
	9					2		1		1				1		2			1	1						
Blue catfish	12																									
	9					1			2			1														
Yellow bullhead	12																									
	9			2	1	3			1	1		2														
Black bullhead	12								1																	
	9					2			1	2																
Brown bullhead	12																									
	9											2								2		1		1		
Flathead catfish	12									1																
	9								1	1																
Largemouth bass	12																									
	9					3	2		4		1									7			1	5		2
Freshwater drum	12								1					1						1						

enough to allow the required measurements. Table 13 shows the estimated total length values for different species of fish for structures 9 and 12. The smaller species of fish, and the smaller individuals within species were selected against in the recovery techniques, and the resultant bias shows clearly in the low representation of small individuals in this table. It should also be noted that the number of individuals of each species for which length was estimated is in most cases less than the minimum number of individuals represented for each species. This is a result of the high percentage of skeletal elements that were too fragmentary to allow estimation of total length, yet were diagnostic to the species level. Because of the fragmentary nature of many of the skeletal elements, it was not possible to increase the minimum number of individuals represented through estimation of length. The minimum number of individuals represented for each species was determined, therefore, by minimum osteological element counts. Fragmentation did not seem to be as significant a problem at the Apple Creek site. Paloumpis and Wilson were able to substantially increase the minimum number of individuals represented through estimation of length (Ibid.: 11).

The relative importance of each species of fish in the Lilbourn diet, expressed in terms of estimated pounds of meat, was determined in the following way, which is quite similar to the method employed by Paloumpis and Wilson (Ibid.: 16-17). It was possible to estimate the weight of each fish for which an estimated total length had been obtained, using length-to-weight ratio tables. An average individual weight value for the measured sample for each species was then determined, and this average weight was multiplied by the minimum number of individuals represented to obtain estimated poundage values for each species.

For fish identified only to generic and family levels, all the individual weight values for the appropriate species were averaged, with the average weight value multiplied by the minimum number of individuals in that genera or family, to obtain poundage estimates. These average weight values obtained from structures 9 and 12 were also used to obtain poundage estimates for structure 25. It is obvious from the foregoing discussion that there are numerous sources of bias in these poundage estimates, and these figures are minimums.

It was hoped that age composition data for the various species of catfish could be obtained by sectioning of pectoral spines (Appleget and Smith, 1951; Sneed, 1951; Marzolf, 1955), but sectioning attempts did not yield specimens satisfactory for microscopic examination.

Judging from the species represented at the Lilbourn site, only two basic water habitat zones were used: the main channel of the Mississippi River, and the backwater lake areas of the adjacent floodplain. Although the backwater oxbow lakes, ponds, and seasonally flooded areas can be considered a separate water habitat zone from the main channel, the two habitats are not mutually exclusive. The quite level floodplain of the alluvial valley of the Mississippi River was subject to frequent flooding during the late winter and spring high water stages. This seasonal flooding of large areas during high water periods was an important factor in determining the quality of the backwater lake habitat zone. Sediments deposited during the flooding would obviously have a fertilizing effect on the oxbow lake areas, increasing the abundance and quality of the aquatic vegetation. This seasonal flooding of backwater areas also influenced fish populations in important ways. Since the high water periods often corresponded with the spawning season of many species of fish, great numbers of a variety of types moved from the main channel into the shallow water areas to spawn during the spring floods. This spring spawning period would have been an optimum period for the harvesting of fish populations, with large numbers of fish occurring in extensive shallow water areas. A few modern descriptions of harvesting fish populations during the spring spawning period will be discussed later. By the time the flood waters had receded below the level of the natural levee, many of the adult fish would have returned to the main channel. The backwater ponds and lakes, cut off from the main channel as the flood waters receded, contained a harvestable surplus of the various fish populations, since much of the breeding populations returned to the relative safety of the river.

The backwater areas, now largely isolated from the main river channel, would contain large areas of flooded land (see Parmalee, Paloumpis, and Wilson, 1972:18-20). The majority of these flooded areas were strictly seasonal impoundments (Lambou, 1959:7). As the summer progressed, the depth of the water in these flooded areas would decrease, with the numerous shallow pools slowly shrinking in size, and many eventually drying up completely. The rate at which these temporary pools dried up, and the percentage of pools which dried up completely during the summer-fall low water stage would, of course, vary from year to year, depending largely upon summer rainfall levels. As the volume of water in lowland pools decreased, fish trapped in isolated pools would either fall prey to a variety of predators, or would die of suffocation when the pools dried up completely (Paloumpis, 1957:62). More and more fish would move into the permanent oxbow lake areas during the summer and fall as other contingent shallow water areas decreased in size and number. These permanent oxbow lakes could support the subsequent large fish populations, judging from modern studies of Louisiana backwater lakes (Lambou, 1959:15).

Throughout the summer and fall, the numerous shallow, isolated pools would have provided an excellent opportunity for Middle Mississippi groups using seines or other simple devices to collect large quantities of fish with a minimum of effort. Carlander describes the abundant harvests realized by modern attempts to capture and relocate fish stranded in such isolated pools (1954:28). The relatively shallow, permanent oxbow lakes, with their high fish biomass levels, would also yield large quantities of fish with a minimum of effort. The importance of such backwater pools and lakes for Woodland groups in the Illinois valley has been discussed in some detail by Paloumpis and Wilson (in Parmalee et al., 1972:23-24). Some idea of the extent to which the Middle Mississippi inhabitants of the Lilbourn site exploited the easily accessible fish populations of the backwater lakes and ponds, rather than the main channel populations, can be obtained by considering the habitat preference of the different species of fish included in the Lilbourn harvest.

The following habitat preference descriptions are based upon a variety of sources, particularly Forbes and Richardson (1920), and Pflieger (1971).

The bowfin (*Amia calva*) accounted for only 2.1 percent of the Lilbourn harvest, by poundage. A predatory species which prefers sluggish waters and weedy places, it is most often found in backwaters and oxbows rather than the main channel. Because the bowfin (like the gars) has a cellular air bladder, it can survive for long periods in the mud bottoms of ponds that have almost completely dried up. Bowfins are spring spawners, moving into shallow weedy areas with the flood waters.

The gars (*Lepisosteus*), which made up almost 5 percent of the Lilbourn fish harvest, are also predatory species which prefer quiet stagnant water. They are most often found in backwater pools and lakes, with young individuals found in thick beds of shallow water vegetation, while adults are found in large deep pools.

Almost 40 percent of the fish harvest consisted of the three species of buffalo fish (*Ictiobus*), the smallmouth buffalo fish being the most abundant of the three. These bottom feeding suckers' primary habitat is the quiet waters of lowland lakes and the backwater pools of large streams. Although buffalo fish do occur in some numbers in larger streams, they are most abundant in backwater lakes (Forbes and Richardson, 1920:62). Buffalo fish have been reported in very high densities during spring spawning runs into shallow water areas, where it was a common practice during the early nineteen hundreds to spear them by the thousands as they rolled in the shallow water (Bartlett, 1917).

The northern redhorse (*Moxostoma macrolepidotum*) is a bottom feeding sucker which occurs most frequently in moderately large rivers, although it does inhabit streams of all sizes. Five species of redhorse occur in Missouri today, largely in the Ozark and Prairie streams. Of them, *Moxostoma macrolepidotum* has the most flexible habitat requirements. The very low representation of this species in the Lilbourn sample is not surprising, considering its present distribution.

Those skeletal elements which could only be identified as belonging to the sucker family (*Catostomidae*) represent another 15 percent of the Lilbourn harvest. Buffalo fish quite likely comprised almost all of this.

Of the bullheads, which made up less than one percent of the Lilbourn harvest, the yellow and black species prefer the quiet, heavily vegetated backwaters and overflow pools of low gradient creeks and small rivers, while the brown bullhead occurs more commonly in the muddy waters of ponds and oxbow lakes.

Twenty-one percent of the Lilbourn harvest consisted of bullheads and catfish, with the three larger species of catfish making up almost all of this figure. The channel catfish is today the most abundant of the three larger species, and has the greatest habitat flexibility. Like the blue and flathead species, it is most abundant in the deeper waters of larger streams and rivers. These species do, however, move into bayous and backwater areas in large numbers during the spring spawning runs.

The freshwater drum (*Aplodinotus grunniens*) made up 17 percent of the Lilbourn fish kill. It feeds almost entirely on thin-shelled species of mollusks, and prefers the soft muddy bottoms of large rivers and lakes.

The water habitat preferences of the species of fish represented at the Lilbourn site, which have been briefly described above, are listed in Table 14, which is drawn from Forbes and Richardson (1920:cxiv-cxix), and Parmalee, Paloumpis, and Wilson (1972:20). It is apparent from this short consideration of the habitat preferences of the different species of fish represented at the Lilbourn site that the oxbow lakes and backwater ponds were far more intensively exploited than the main channel of the Mississippi River. The catfish are the only species that occur in greater numbers in the main channel, suggesting that Middle Mississippi groups also used the main channel, but to a lesser degree than the backwater lakes and ponds.

Interestingly enough, the percentage values noted above for the different types of fish represented in the Lilbourn sample correspond fairly closely with the percentage values for different fish types represented in the commercial catch on the Mississippi River in 1895, prior to the proliferation of the introduced European carp (Carlander, 1954:Figure 16). Buffalo fish composed from 40 to 54 percent of the Lilbourn sample, and approximately 45 percent of the 1895 catch, while catfish, 21 percent of the Lilbourn sample, were approximately 24 percent of the 1895 catch. Freshwater drum, which made up approximately 11 percent of the 1895 sample, accounted for 17 percent of the Lilbourn sample. On the basis of this comparison with the 1895 catch, it might be suggested that the Lilbourn fish harvest represents a non-selective sample of the fish population rather than a selective harvest of only certain species. Taking into consideration the various feeding habits and habitat preferences of the different species, the most likely method of harvesting the fish populations was intensive seining or collecting in small backwater pools and oxbow lakes.

In addition to spearing and seining fish during the spring spawning season and throughout the low water stage of summer and fall, the occupants of the Lilbourn site may have used a variety of other fishing techniques, little of which can be inferred from the preserved material culture (though simple bone fish hooks are not uncommon in Middle Mississippi sites). It is questionable whether any species other than catfish, bullheads, and bass could be caught using a hook and line. The freshwater drum, buffalo fish and suckers are bottom feeders, and, therefore, difficult to catch on a hook and line, and the bowfin and gars would be difficult to land successfully because of their sharp teeth. Wire lines are usually used today when these sharp-toothed species are sought with a hook and line technique. Rostlund (1952) has an excellent summary of the fishing techniques used by Indian groups of the eastern United States.

We hoped that some archaeological data concerning the seasonality of exploitation of fish populations could be obtained through microscopic

TABLE 14

HABITAT AND WATER MOVEMENT PREFERENCES OF THE FISH SPECIES REPRESENTED AT THE LILBOURN SITE. (HABITATS RANKED NUMERICALLY–1=MOST PREFERRED, X INDICATES WATER MOVEMENT PREFERENCE; AFTER FORBES AND RICHARDSON, 1920:CXIV-CXIX)

SPECIES	LARGE RIVERS	SMALL RIVERS	CREEKS	LAKES & PONDS	CURRENT PRESENT	QUIET, SLUGGISH WATERS
Bowfin	2	3	3	1		X
Longnose gar	1	2	3	1		X
Shortnose gar	1	2	3	1		X
Bigmouth buffalofish	2	-	3	1		
Smallmouth buffalofish	2	2	3	1	X	
Blue catfish	1				X	
Black bullhead	4	3	1	2		X
Yellow bullhead	3	3	1	2		
Brown bullhead	2	3	3	1		X
Channel catfish	3	1	2	4	X	
Flathead catfish	1	2	3	3		
Largemouth bass	4	2	3	1		
Freshwater drum	1	2	3	1		

analysis of the annual rings occurring on vertebral centri or scales. It became apparent, however, that not enough information exists at this time on the actual mechanics of deposition of annual rings in different species of fish to allow reliable conclusions to be drawn from any data analysis.

The Banks Site

The total number of fish elements recovered from the Banks site is not known, since unidentifiable fragments were discarded. A total of 449 identifiable elements were examined and found to represent at least nine species of fish. The skeletal element counts, minimum number of individuals, and poundage estimates are shown in Table 15. The poundage estimates should not be considered much more than rough estimates, since average weight

TABLE 15

RELATIVE IMPORTANCE OF SPECIES OF FISH REPRESENTED AT THE BANKS SITE.

SPECIES	NO. OF SKELETAL ELEMENTS	MINIMUM NO. OF INDIVIDUALS REPRESENTED	PROJECTED MEAT YIELD (IN POUNDS)
Bowfin	18	5	5.0
Alligator gar	16	4	4.0
Shortnose gar	1	1	2.0
Longnose gar	22	4	4.0
Gar	129	16	16.0
Bigmouth buffalo fish	3	1	8.0
Black buffalo fish	--	-	---
Black/Smallmouth buffalo fish	3	1	8.0
Smallmouth buffalo fish	--	-	---
Buffalo fish	31	3	24.0
Eastern redhorse	--	-	---
Redhorse	--	-	---
Suckers	12	6	48.0
Channel catfish	--	-	---
Blue catfish	--	-	---
Yellow bullhead	--	-	---
Black bullhead	--	-	---
Brown bullhead	126	17	20.0
Flathead catfish	--	-	---
Smallmouth bass	--	-	---
Spotted bass	--	-	---
Largemouth bass	--	-	---
Bass	4	2	1.0
Freshwater drum	50	4	20.0
TOTAL	415	64	160.0

values obtained for the Lilbourn site were applied to the Banks site data to arrive at meat values.

Because of the very biased nature of the fish bone sample from the Banks site, only a few comments will be made. The importance of fish in the Banks site diet was certainly much greater than is indicated by the present sample. The relative occurrence of the various species in the Banks site sample seems roughly comparable to the Lilbourn site sample, with the gars being represented in greater numbers and the buffalo fish to a lesser extent. The exploitation pattern of fish populations at the Banks site was probably very similar to that proposed for the Lilbourn site, since the sites occur in similar locations. The close proximity of a large lake (Lake Wapanocca) and its associated bayou certainly provided excellent opportunities for exploitation of fish populations by the inhabitants of the Banks site.

The Chucalissa Site

Because of the extremely small sample of fish bone from the Chucalissa site, the single point that can be made beyond a listing of the species recovered (Table 16) is that the species represented suggest exploitation of lowland pools and oxbow lakes rather than upland streams. The relative extent to which upland streams contributed to the Chucalissa diet cannot be ascertained until larger samples are recovered through more sophisticated excavation techniques.

TABLE 16

RELATIVE IMPORTANCE OF SPECIES OF FISH AT THE CHUCALISSA SITE (TEMPLE MOUND)

SPECIES	NUMBER OF SKELETAL ELEMENTS	MINIMUM NUMBER OF INDIVIDUALS REPRESENTED	PROJECTED MEAT YIELD (IN POUNDS)
Bowfin	6	1	1.0
Shortnose gar	1	1	2.0
Gar	8	3	3.0
Redhorse	1	1	3.0
Channel catfish	5	3	4.5
Catfish/bullhead	10	2	3.0
Freshwater drum	3	1	4.0
TOTAL	34	12	20.5

Sites of the Powers Phase

Very few fish bones were recovered from the lowlands sites of the Powers Phase because of poor preservation.

The water habitat zones available for exploitation in the Powers Phase areas were more varied than in the Mississippi lowlands area, yet not as productive in terms of the number and easy accessibility of fish. In addition to the Little Black River, which flows along the edge of the Ozark escarpment, and its associated oxbow lakes, the Powers Phase area would have included a number of small creeks and swampy areas. The spring high water stage of the Little Black River, which floods extensive areas of the lowlands even today, would produce temporary shallow pools similar to those in the Mississippi River area. It is impossible to determine the extent to which these different water habitat zones were utilized by Powers Phase groups, because of the inadequate archaeological fish bone sample. It is interesting to note the occurrence of bass (*Micropterus* sp.) at Powers Fort, since this genus was exploited only in very small quantites at lowlands sites closer to the Mississippi River.

The Gooseneck Site is situated on the second terrace of the Current River (see Appendix E). Preservation and recovery techniques at the Gooseneck site were excellent, yet few skeletal elements of fish were recovered. This very low occurrence of fish bones indicates little exploitation of the fish resources of the Current River, with larger species of land animals predominating. Most of the species represented are bottom feeding types, which were probably taken during spring spawning runs.

MIGRATORY WATERFOWL

A flyway can be defined as a geographical region which has its own population of different species of ducks, geese, and swans. Within the boundaries of a flyway are wintering and breeding grounds connected by a system of migration routes.

First defined by Frederick C. Lincoln in 1935, the Mississippi flyway has been likened to an enormous funnel, with the almost continent-wide northern mouth of the flyway stretching across the tundra of the arctic archipelago from Baffin Island in the east to northeastern Alaska in the west. The spout of this funnel is delineated by the floodplain of the lower Mississippi valley. This region south of the mouth of the Ohio River, which extends from Cape Girardeau, Missouri, to the Gulf of Mexico, ends in the coastal prairies and marshes of Louisiana.

Together these two areas (the lower Mississippi valley and the coastal marshes of Louisiana) were, and are, the principal wintering ground for

Mississippi flyway waterfowl. The fourteen states which are in the path of the Mississippi flyway have been divided into north, central, and southern sections by the Mississippi Flyway Council to facilitate the gathering of migration and wintering information on a regional basis. Northern states include Minnesota, Wisconsin, and Michigan; central states include Iowa, Missouri, Illinois, Ohio, Indiana, and Kentucky; and southern states of the flyway include Tennessee, Arkansas, Alabama, Mississippi, and Louisiana. Our area of study is located at the southern boundary of the central section of the flyway.

More than half of the forty-eight species of swans, geese, and ducks that frequent continental North America use the flyway today. Only a dozen species are bagged with any regularity today, however, and ten species make up 95 percent of the modern day duck bag. Each of the two dozen species of waterfowl that use the Mississippi flyway today can be classified according to what part of its yearly migratory route the central section represents. Waterfowl move north to breeding grounds in the spring and south again to wintering grounds in the fall. Thus we might theoretically expect three patterns of central section flyway utilization:

1. Those species that breed but do not winter in the central section of the flyway,
2. Those species that winter but do not breed in the central section of the flyway,
3. Those species that neither breed nor winter in the central section of the flyway.

These three mutually exclusive categories must be altered somewhat to accommodate those species of birds that have small percentages remaining within the central flyway area during the winter, although the great majority of the migrating flocks move on to their primary wintering ranges to the south. The following four categories group the species of waterfowl according to their seasonal occurrence in the central section of the Mississippi flyway.

The technical information concerning seasonal movements and densities of waterfowl was obtained from Mississippi Flyway Council reports (1958*a*, 1958*b*). Information concerning food preferences was obtained from Martin, et al. (1951).

1. Those species that breed but do not winter in the central section of the flyway:

The wood duck (*Aix sponsa*) is truly a bird of the Mississippi flyway. A few have been recorded migrating into Canada, but most nest in the United States, and the breeding range includes all fourteen states of the flyway. Wood ducks move south from the northern section of the flyway by November first, and from the central section by November fifteenth. Most winter within the southern states of the flyway, with the mid-January population wintering in Arkansas, Alabama, Mississippi, and Louisiana. Wood ducks nest in trees, rest and hide in swampy areas, depend heavily on acorns, and occur almost everywhere within the flyway. The Mississippi River and its tributaries provide excellent breeding grounds for wood ducks, with the numerous timber-bordered sloughs and ponds being ideal nesting, feeding, and rearing areas. The actual density of breeding birds is low along most small streams and sloughs (0.3 to 0.5 broods per mile), but the extent of this habitat allows for many broods.

The hooded merganser (*Lophodytes cucullatus*) is found across the continent in wooded timberlands surrounding ponds and streams. It is often found in association with the wood duck in the watery woodlands in which both build their nests. It feeds mainly on small fish, frogs, tadpoles, crawfish, etc. Its large breeding range includes the central Mississippi valley, and as it is said to winter not only in the southern states but as far north as open water is available, small wintering populations may have occurred within the study area. The wood duck, too, may have remained in the study area through the winter in limited numbers. These two species are the only ducks which occur in significant numbers in the central section of the flyway during the summer months.

2. Those species that winter in the central section of the flyway in significant numbers, but do not breed there:

The Mississippi flyway is also sometimes termed "The Mallard Flyway" because this highly successful species uses the flyway in such great numbers. The mallard is the most numerous duck in the flyway, and at peak numbers makes up more than seventy percent of the duck population. The fall mallard migration, which originates in breeding ranges in Canada and the Dakotas, is characterized by a mass movement into all flyway states within a few days time. This "Grand Passage" usually occurs during the first week of November. The population of mallards in the central states section rises from around 100,000 on October first to 2.6 million on November fifteenth, increases to 3.2 million by December first, and levels off thereafter at about 2.5 million through the middle of January. Central flyway states winter more than half of the flyway mallard population. Preferred habitats are inland ponds, shallow lakes, sloughs, and rivers. Mallards occasionally leave the water and forage on upland areas for food, with land foods of preference being acorns and such farm crops as corn, barley, and wheat.

The black duck (*Anas rubripes*) breeds commonly in Michigan, northern Ohio, and west into Minnesota and western Ontario. The majority winter north of the Ohio River, and this near-relative of the mallard has a fairly restricted range. Eighty-five percent of the population winters north of Tennessee. Small numbers move south into the central section by September fifteenth, and the central section population increases slowly to a peak of 150,000 by December fifteenth, thereafter dropping slightly to 125,000 in mid-January. Although the wintering range of the black duck is well to the northeast of our study area, its original winter range may have included the bottomlands of southeast Missouri.

The Canada goose (*Branta canadensis*) winters in significant numbers in the central section of the flyway. Two separate populations are involved. The Mississippi valley population originates in western Quebec, migrates south through Ontario, the lake states, western Ohio, Indiana, Illinois, and eastern Iowa to its major wintering area in southern Illinois. The eastern prairie population breeds in Ontario and Manitoba, migrates through the eastern Dakotas, western Minnesota and Iowa, and winters in greatest numbers in north central Missouri. Peak populations reach central flyway states by mid-November, and the wintering population remains stable thereafter. Eighty percent of the Canada geese wintering in the Mississippi flyway were found in the central section, with Illinois being the most important wintering area.

The American and red breasted mergansers (*Mergus* sp.) are diving ducks, feed primarily on fish, and occur in very small numbers in the flyway. They are generally late migrants, with the major population increase in the central section occurring in mid-December, although some arrive by the first of November. The population of these species is believed to be underestimated because of their tendency to scatter over remote areas and extensive bodies of water and disperse among the more abundant species of ducks.

These six species are the primary winter residents in the study area.

3. Those species that do not breed in the central section of the flyway, and winter there only in small numbers:

The lesser scaup is the most abundant of the diving ducks within the flyway, and is second only to mallards among ducks generally. By September fifteenth a few migrants have arrived in the northern section from breeding ranges in Canada. The major influx starts after the first of October and builds up to a peak by November first. Following the peak build-up each year in the first part of November, a major portion of the scaup population migrates south out of the central section of flyway. Thus, of the 170,000 birds noted in the central section during the November peak, only 10,000 still remain by January first, while the rest move southward to winter in the southern states. Most of the birds remaining in the central section of the flyway are found in southern Illinois. Although the winter population which occurs in the central section of the flyway is quite small, and is located north of our study area, the original wintering range may have extended farther south.

Most pintails (*Anas acuta*) breed in grasslands to the west and north of the flyway, but some small numbers breed in Minnesota. Their southward migration extends over a considerable period of time. Peak numbers occur in the central section during late August, although some flocks have already reached the Louisiana Gulf coastal marshes by this time. Pintails use the western half of the flyway during migration, and winter almost entirely in the southern states, with Louisiana being the most important wintering area. Of the peak population of 130,000 recorded on October fifteenth, only 10,000 remained in the central section by December fifteenth. One of the wintering areas in the southern section, however, is in northeast Arkansas directly adjacent to our study area.

The ring-necked duck (*Aythya collaris*) is the second most abundant among the divers. It breeds in the lake states and northward. By October fifteenth large populations are present in the northern section of the flyway, and some occur as far south as Tennessee. The peak population density in the central section (85,000) is reached by November first, after which the population dwindles rapidly except for small concentrations in Illinois and Tennessee. Its wintering area in Tennessee is quite close to the study area.

The canvasback duck (*Aythya valisineria*) is ranked third in abundance among the divers. The peak population of 25,000 is reached in the central states by November first, and drops gradually to a level of 5,000 by January fifteenth. This population most likely represents dropouts from a secondary migration route via the Mississippi valley to Mobile Bay in Louisiana and Alabama. The central section wintering range is restricted to Illinois, but may have originally extended southward into the study area.

Gadwalls (*Anas strepera*) breed almost entirely outside the flyway. They tend to accompany the mallard on their mass migrations, and use the western half of the flyway. Their peak population in the central section is only 10,000 on November first and drops to very low levels by December first. A pocket of wintering individuals occurs on Reelfoot Lake in Tennessee, however, directly adjacent to the study area.

These four species have small wintering populations within the central section of the flyway.

4. Those species that neither breed nor winter in the central section of the flyway:

Snow and blue geese (*Chen caerulescens/hyperborea*) leave concentration areas (the largest being southern James Bay) by mid-October and arrive at the coastal marshes of Louisiana between October twenty-second and December first. After a peak of 67,000 on November first, the population in the central section drops to only 5,000 by January first. The spring flight from the Gulf Coast is in slow easy stages up the Mississippi and Missouri Rivers, and then by a direct flight from the Dakotas to James Bay, arriving about June first.

Most baldpates (*Mareca americana*) are produced on breeding grounds in Canada, with some breeding in Minnesota. Adult drakes are the vanguard of the fall migration in September, but peak numbers are not reached in the central section until late October (44,000). This population decreases rapidly to 5,000 by December fifteenth. A pocket of wintering individuals occurs on Reelfoot Lake in Tennessee directly adjacent to the study area.

The shoveler (*Spatula clypeata*) is another species which uses the western half of the flyway. It is an early migrant, reaching a peak of 3,000 on October fifteenth in the central section, and dropping to zero by December first.

Redheads (*Aythya americana*) are prairie marsh breeders, with nesting occurring largely outside the flyway. One of the redhead's two major flight lanes goes through the Mississippi valley to Laguna Madre on the Gulf Coast. They are early migrants, with peak population levels of 7,500 in the central section by October fifteenth. This peak value decreases to 2,500 by December fifteenth, and zero by January first. There is, however, a small wintering population on Reelfoot Lake, Tennessee, directly adjacent to the study area.

The green-winged teal (*Anas carolinensis*) breeds almost entirely outside the flyway, in an extensive range from the prairies to the arctic. The western half of the flyway carries the heaviest traffic, and the birds are seldom found in major concentrations during migration. The fall migration spans a long period from late in August until the final freezeover. The main flights occur late in October or early in November, with the central section peak population of 30,000 occurring in early November. This drops to 5,000 by December fifteenth, and to zero by January first. The green-winged teal is one of the major birds taken by modern hunters.

The blue-winged teal (*Anas discors*) is second to the wood duck in number breeding within the flyway, using a wide variety of wetland habitat from Iowa northward. Known as a fair weather duck, the blue-winged teal is the earliest migrant, leaving summer homes long before either cold weather or a food shortage occurs. Substantial numbers have reached the Gulf Coast by mid-August. The peak population of 75,000 occurs in the central section by early October. Most are flyway transients, but some occasionally winter in Louisiana. Spring censuses in Louisiana indicate the northward movement of this species in the Gulf area occurs primarily in April and May.

The ruddy duck (*Oxyura jamaicensis*) enters the flyway in mid-October, with a major portion of the population in Minnesota and Wisconsin. The peak of 5,000 birds in the central section occurs in early November, and drops to zero by December first as the birds move south to Louisiana.

The common coot (*Fulica americana*) occurs in small numbers in the central section of the flyway by September first, with the first large influx of birds from Canada occurring by October first. The peak population of 90,000 occurs in mid-October in the central section of the flyway. This decreases to 10,000 by December first and to zero by December fifteenth. Though large numbers of coots winter in other flyways, only a few remain in the Mississippi flyway, principally in Alabama and in southern Arkansas and Tennessee.

The seasonal movements of migratory waterfowl within the Mississippi flyway have been accurately defined within the last twenty years. There are a number of interesting problems, however, in determining the extent to which these modern day migration patterns correspond to the seasonal movements of waterfowl seven hundred years ago.

The arrival dates of waterfowl from breeding ranges in the north during the fall, and the departure dates from wintering grounds in the spring remain stable over a long period of time. Detailed research into the physiological mechanisms which elicit migrational movements has shown such arrival and departure dates to be consistent. The impetus for homeward migration to breeding grounds in the spring is sexual, though the exact timing is affected by the weather. Fall migration movements are also governed by physiological changes, and altered somewhat by changes in the weather. Each species of waterfowl has its own schedule and rate of migration, and variables in the environment affect each species differently. But the migrational patterns of each species (i.e., arrival of first birds, peaks of movement, total period of migration, etc.) change very little from year to year, and the variations that exist are a function of fluctuations in weather conditions. Any significant changes in the established, consistent patterns of yearly migration would, therefore, have to be the result of major changes in the onset of physiological changes, which in turn could be produced only by major climatic changes. It is highly unlikely that such changes occurred within the last 750 years.

Thus the exploitation of migratory waterfowl by these prehistoric human populations was strictly of a seasonal nature, with the maximum seasonal range of exploitation for each species shown in Figure 9. These maximal seasonal ranges of exploitation are based on the assumption that all of the species winter within the central section of the flyway. Among the birds placed in classes three and four, however, only a small percentage remain within the central section of the flyway through the winter, while most have moved on to primary wintering grounds farther south. Whether these species ever wintered in significant numbers within the study area, or have always been primarily fall and spring migratory visitors would be difficult to determine. The alteration of the prime wintering habitat of the Missouri bottomland area during the last hundred years has been considerable. The alluvial valley of the Mississippi River, extending from the Gulf to Cape Girardeau, Missouri, is estimated to have originally encompassed some 22,720,000 acres. Only about one-seventh of this original area remains natural, and timber cutting has removed most of the mast-bearing hardwoods from this remaining area. Missouri's wetland habitat has been reduced by almost ninety percent in the period from 1850 to 1950. Such a drastic reduction in potential wintering areas has probably driven many species which were unable to adapt to the altered environment in the central Mississippi valley to wintering areas farther south. The rapid development of isolated wintering populations of many species after the impoundment of the Tennessee River and the creation of Reelfoot Lake in western Tennessee provided suitable habitat suggests that their original wintering range formerly extended much farther north. The development of these wintering populations north of their present day primary wintering grounds probably represents the partial re-establishment of wintering populations within the central section of the flyway. Thus the degree to which the species placed in classes three and four may have been

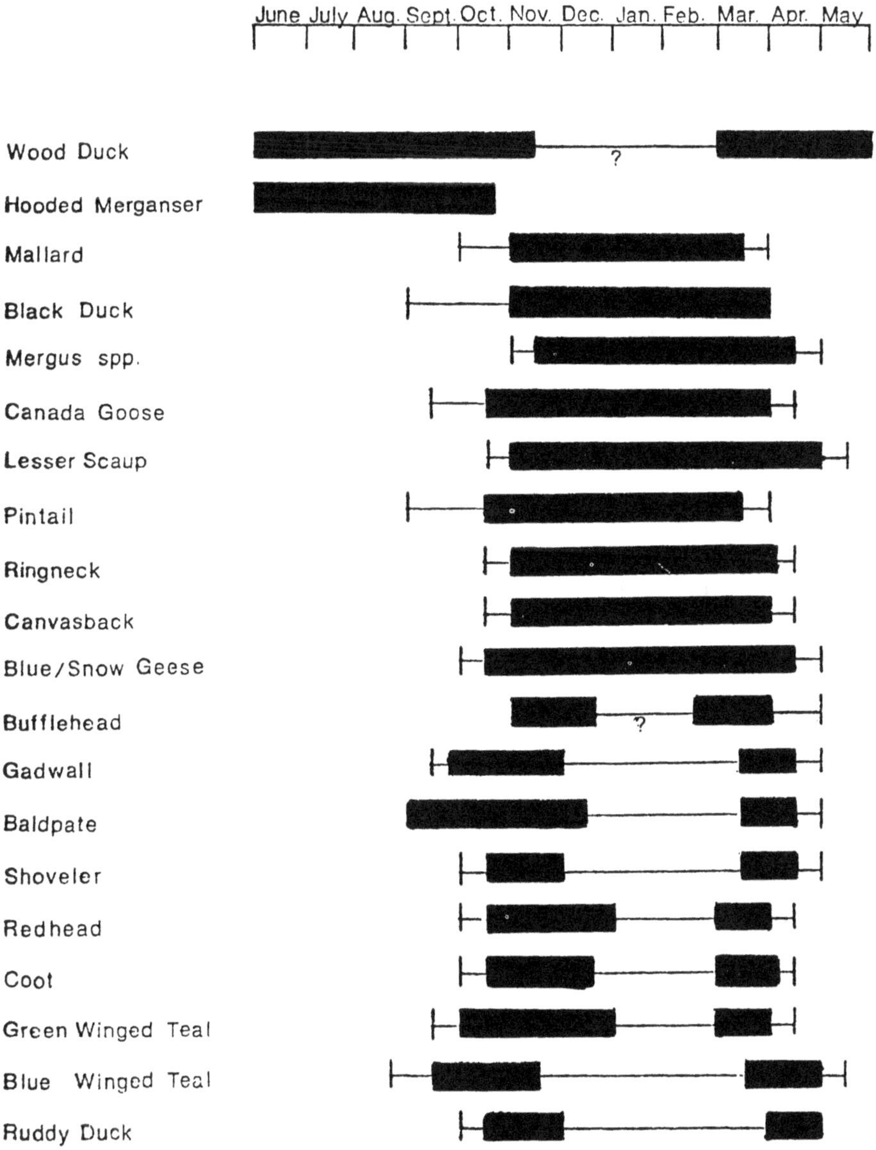

Fig. 9. The migrational profiles of 22 species of ducks and geese for the central section of the Mississippi flyway. Lines indicate maximum seasonal range of availability, bars indicate periods of population peaks within the central section of the flyway.

winter residents of the study area during the prehistoric period cannot be determined with any degree of accuracy. But whether or not wintering populations of these species existed in the study area in A.D. 1100-1500, the number of birds would have been much higher during periods of fall and spring migration, because of the influx of birds on their way to or from wintering areas farther south.

Five of the species of waterfowl which have been recorded as using the Mississippi flyway today, use only the western half, and are primarily found farther west in the central flyway. These are the shoveler, gadwall, pintail, green-winged teal, and white-fronted goose. The eastern fringe of the ranges of these species touches the western-most part of the Mississippi flyway.

Another interesting problem involves the relative abundance of different species of waterfowl within the flyway today. The great success of some species, and the drastic reductions in the numbers of others, is largely a matter of food habits and the ability of some species to adapt to changing food sources as man alters the habitat. Ducks can be divided into two groups according to their feeding habits. Surface feeding ducks obtain food by "tipping" and by "dabbling" along in the shallow waters at the edges of oxbow lakes, ponds, and smaller bodies of water. They generally eat more vegetable matter, and are, with few exceptions, considered more palatable today than the second group of ducks, the divers. The following species are surface feeders: mallard, gadwall, pintail, green-winged teal, blue-winged teal, shoveler, black duck, wood duck, Canada goose, white-fronted goose, lesser snow goose, and blue goose.

Most of these twelve species of surface feeders can also be described as "stubblers" since they also use available land plant resources that occur rather far from water. Thus the mallard, whose traditional principal feeding grounds are the shallow waters of sloughs, ponds, lakes and rivers has been able to shift to upland feeding on wheat, barley, corn, and buckwheat, which it gleans from stubble fields. Mallards also resort to abundant acorn crops for sustenance. Most species of geese similarly obtain much of their food by grazing on land, in the fields of stubble and sprouting grain, although they are classed as shallow water surface feeders. Black ducks resort to grain fields in the fall, and consume wheat, barley, and buckwheat, as well as acorns and beechnuts. The green-winged teal and wood duck both wander far from water in search of berries, acorns, seeds, grapes, etc. The gadwall, too, wanders far from water, visiting nearby fields, as well as seeking out acorns and nuts. The pintail also visits stubble fields, but less so than the common mallard. The blue-winged teal occasionally utilizes such stubble fields. This adaptation is no doubt partially, if not completely, responsible for the relative success of such species as the mallard, pintail, and Canada goose.

The diving ducks, however, have not fared so well. The placement of the legs on diving ducks is well back to enable them to swim well when under water, and as a result they have difficulty walking, which severely limits their use of plant resources on land. The diving ducks generally frequent larger inland bodies of water than surface feeders. They feed by diving, often seeking their food at considerable depth. They require a specialized habitat characterized by abundant aquatic food plants, and as a result have declined in numbers with the present-day alteration of the Mississippi bottomlands. The following species of ducks can be classed as divers: canvasback, redhead, ringneck, lesser scaup, ruddy duck, mergansers (three species), and the bufflehead. Of these nine species, the ringneck seems to prefer the marshes and sloughs to the open lakes and streams, and is less common in the broad open waters than such "rafting" species as the lesser scaup and canvasback. The term "rafting" refers to the tendency of these species to collect in large dense flocks on broader waters where they rest for hours at a time during the day.

Having discussed the seasonal movements, feeding habits, habitat preferences, and relative abundance of the species of waterfowl that utilize the Mississippi flyway, and having classed the species according to such criteria, we can now compare these species with those represented at the archaeological sites.

Table 17 lists the various species of ducks, geese, and swans represented at the seven sites being studied. The relative extent to which each species was exploited at each site is measured by two variables: the number of birds represented, and the projected meat yields of each species. At the Banks site, for example, there was a minimum of eleven Canada geese (see Appendix B), which represented 11 percent of the total minimum number of waterfowl, and 24 percent of the waterfowl meat yield from the Banks site.

From Table 17 a number of observations and comparisons can be made concerning the exploitation of waterfowl populations by Middle Mississippian groups.

The only two species of ducks represented at the Gooseneck site are the wood duck and the hooded merganser. Both species have wide ranges, including the wooded timberlands that surround ponds and streams, and may be year round residents of the Current River area, although winter populations, if any, would be small. Since the Current River lies at the extreme western edge of the flyway, and its oxbow lakes are smaller and fewer in number than the lowland rivers to the east, migrating duck populations exist in much smaller numbers. It is, therefore, not surprising that only these two very common species are represented at the Gooseneck site. The small number of waterfowl skeletal elements at the Gooseneck site is not the result of poor preservation or recovery techniques, but is, rather, an accurate reflection of an exploitation pattern which concentrated upon larger land animals.

The Banks site and the Lilbourn site have much higher species counts, minimum number of individuals represented counts, and poundage estimates than the other sites. This may be in part because of poor preservation at the

TABLE 17

RELATIVE IMPORTANCE OF WATERFOWL AT SEVEN MIDDLE MISSISSIPPI SITES, BY PERCENTAGE OF THE TOTAL MINIMUM NUMBER OF DUCKS, GEESE, AND SWANS AT EACH SITE (MN), AND BY PERCENTAGE OF THE TOTAL PROJECTED WATERFOWL MEAT YIELD (M)

SPECIES	CHUCALISSA		BANKS		LILBOURN		SNODGRASS		TURNER		POWERS FORT		GOOSENECK	
	MN	M	MN	M	MN	M	MN	M	MN	M	MN	M	MN	M
Whistling Swan			1	4										
Trumpeter Swan			1	7	.6	6								
Canada Goose	25	53	11	24	7.3	23	33	64	25	50				
Blue/Snow Goose	9	13	4	7	2.4	6								
Mallard/Black Duck	21	16	55	44	28	33	33	24	50	40	50	66		
Pintail			8	4	4.8	4								
Blue-winged Teal			1	.2	11	3								
Green-winged Teal			2	.4	9	2								
Gadwall			1	.4										
Baldpate			3	.4										
Shoveler	4	1.6			10	7								
Wood Duck	21	8	3	1	9.5	6	33	12	25	10	50	33	50	50
Lesser Scaup			2	.8										
Goldeneye					4.5	3								
Bufflehead			1	.4	2.4	1.5								
Hooded Merganser	21	8	6	2.5	7	4							50	50
Mergus sp.			3	2.5	.6	.8								
Common Coot			1	.4	2.4	1.5								

lowlands sites of the Powers Phase, but it also reflects the excellent accessibility to the migrating duck populations of the Banks and Lilbourn sites. As the migrating waterfowl populations move south into the central section of the flyway, they land on the numerous oxbow lakes and backwater areas to feed, rest, or stay the winter. Both the Banks site, which was situated directly adjacent to a large permanently flooded oxbow lake, and the Lilbourn site, which was quite close to a number of oxbow lakes, were within this zone of unparalleled waterfowl habitat. It is not surprising, then, that more types of waterfowl, in greater numbers, occur at these two sites.

The Chucalissa site had fewer species represented, and only three strongly migratory species occurred in the sample (blue/snow goose, and shoveler). This suggests that the location of the Chucalissa site on the eastern bluffs of the Mississippi River did not allow easy access to oxbow lakes in the Mississippi valley. This inaccessibility to oxbow lakes is also suggested by the high proportion of species that would be expected to occur along the upland streams (i.e., the wood duck and hooded merganser). It is also interesting to note that the three migratory species represented at the Chucalissa site, will all exploit available land food sources as well as the aquatic vegetation of shallow water areas, and are more apt than other species to occur in areas away from oxbow lakes.

Because of poor preservation, only small samples of waterfowl skeletal elements were recovered from the lowland sites of the Powers Phase, and it is difficult to accurately estimate the dietary contribution of waterfowl to the Powers Phase populations. Since the Powers Phase area is located at the extreme western edge of the Mississippi flyway, where waterfowl habitat is less impressive, ducks and geese were probably much less abundant than at the Banks and Lilbourn site locales. Canada geese, mallards, and the ubiquitous wood duck occur at all lowland Powers Phase sites, and also constitute a high percentage of the waterfowl samples at the more eastern sites.

The Canada goose and the mallard/black duck represent from 56 to 90 percent of the waterfowl meat yield at six of the seven sites being considered. These two species are very abundant in the flyway today, and their high representation in these prehistoric samples may well reflect their long-standing domination of the flyway, rather than selective exploitation on the part of Middle Mississippi hunters.

The wood duck, which occurs in significant percentages only in the small samples recovered from the Gooseneck and Powers Phase sites, is nonetheless the only species which was recovered from all seven sites. Although it never reaches the density levels of some of the other migrating species, the wood duck was no doubt present throughout the valley from March through November, and its broad distribution reflects its wide niche status.

There is a high correlation between the exploitation of different species of waterfowl and their respective feeding habits. The diving ducks are represented in very low percentages, except for the hooded merganser, which occurs over large areas of the Mississippi valley through most of the year. In particular, the lesser scaup duck, which is the second most abundant species within the flyway today, is represented in very low percentages in the prehistoric samples. Both difficulty of exploitation and low density levels probably functioned to keep representation of diving ducks at a low level in the Middle Mississippi samples.

It is also interesting to note that those species that were most heavily exploited (Canada goose, blue/snow goose, mallard/black duck, wood duck) are species that today eat the leftover grain and corn from farmers' fields. These are the species that would be most apt to be attracted to and captured by dry land snares or traps baited with foods such as corn and acorns. It is impossible, of course, to determine to what extent such capturing techniques were employed.

Since those species of waterfowl that were most intensively exploited, except for the wood duck and the hooded merganser, wintered in the central section of the flyway in large numbers, it is not possible to define the seasonal nature of exploitation of waterfowl populations to any more narrow a time range than the period November through February. The probable period of exploitation can be narrowed, of course, for those species which were present only during the fall and spring migration periods (Fig. 9).

Middle Mississippi groups situated in such optimum locations as the Lilbourn site and the Banks site could have intensively and continually exploited waterfowl populations in rather small geographical areas throughout the winter, perhaps concentrating on only a few oxbow lakes. This localized exploitation was possible since waterfowl populations were not a stable, eventually exhaustible food resource, but one which would have been constantly replenished as ducks and geese moved into oxbow lake areas as quickly as they were harvested. At the same time, winter predation by Middle Mississippi groups on waterfowl populations was too light to have had many unfavorable effects on the waterfowl populations, judging from a comparison of the prehistoric level of predation (indicated by waterfowl remains recovered from the sites being considered) and the level of predation that migratory waterfowl populations can support today.

WILD TURKEY (*Meleagris gallopavo*)

Judging from the occurrence of skeletal elements of the wild turkey in archaeological sites, it was an important food source during much of the prehistoric period in the eastern United States. It was never domesticated in the eastern half of its range, however, as it was in the southwestern United States and Mexico. The numerous early accounts of domestication of the eastern wild turkey by Indian groups of the southeast (Du Pratz, 1758:125; Membre, 1852) were no doubt based on the reported practice of raising wild poults, rather than any true success at domestication (Barton, 1805; Swanton, 1946).

America's largest upland game bird has been intensively studied throughout its range, and its seasonal shifts in flock composition, food preference, etc., can thus be described with a good deal of accuracy.

The breeding season in the southeast Missouri area begins during the last week of March, peaks between April fifteenth and thirtieth, and then gradually decreases, ending by the first of June. During the breeding season dominant males usually establish gobbling territories. Ellis and Lewis, in their study of the Lake Springs, Missouri, turkey population, found, however, that dominant males defended the hen flock rather than an established geographical area (1967:580). Most of the actual breeding is done by dominant males, with submissive adult males and juvenile males denied access to the hens by the more dominant individuals.

After an incubation period of 28 days, the peak of the hatching season occurs between May twentieth and June tenth. Missouri nests contained an average of 11 eggs, with hatched broods in June averaging 9.6 poults (Dalke et al., 1946:50). Brood mortality rates during the summer averaged about 20 percent, so that September broods averaged 7.7 poults (Ibid.:51). The poults are almost full grown by late September.

Except during the breeding season, there is a strong segregation between females and adult males. Individual flocks consisting of a hen and her poults are maintained through the summer, with broods and unmated hens joining to form gradually larger flocks as the year progresses. Adult males remain in small groups during the summer and early fall. Larger winter flocks begin forming in late November and early December, with hens and juveniles forming separate flocks from adult males. The adult male flocks are smaller and less stable.

The following mean winter flock sizes were reported for the Lake Springs turkey population during 1965-66: Flocks consisting of hens and young/flocks consisting of adult males–November 13.0/5.0, December 48.0/7.0, January 32.5/6.8, February 23.7/4.2, March 22.0/1.8 (Ellis and Lewis, 1967:375). Juvenile males will quite often break off from female flocks during the winter months, forming entirely separate flocks. Larger winter groupings (droves) consisting of two or more flocks occasionally occur in common feeding areas for short periods of time. Winter flocks break up with the onset of the breeding season in late March. Turkeys also reach their annual peak weights just prior to the breeding season. Average weights of male turkeys killed during the spring hunting season in Missouri are 20.8 pounds (adult male) and 14.2 pounds (juvenile male) (Lewis, 1962).

Wild turkeys eat a wide variety of seasonally available plant and animal species, with the specific plants exploited varying from region to region. Of the seventy-three genera of plants identified by Dalke et al., (1942) as being eaten by Missouri turkeys during the spring and summer, 73 percent were used in low frequencies, indicating a diverse utilization of the vegetation from a number of habitat areas. Their feeding habits include stripping the seed heads of grasses and sedges, browsing on the fruits of a number of species, and scratching for insects and oak mast. Oak mast utilization is low during August and September, rises to a peak in January, then falls off gradaully to a mid-summer low.

In his study of turkey food habits in the White River bottomlands of southeastern Arkansas, Meanley (1956) found seasonal use of food resources from a number of habitat zones. During the summer and fall, turkeys were found to use intensively the grasses, sedges, and other herbaceous vegetation of dry oxbow lake beds. The sandbar areas along the White River were also intensively used during the late summer and fall, with turkeys stripping the seed heads of numerous species of grasses. Since oxbow lake beds were often in close proximity to sand bar areas, turkeys would work back and forth between the two areas. Densities along sand bar areas were found to be quite high during the fall low water stages, with 112 turkeys (ten separate broods) recorded along a twelve mile stretch of the White River in August of 1954 (Ibid.:307). The better drained areas of the first bottoms when not under water were also widely used by foraging turkeys. During the winter and early spring, turkeys were found to concentrate their feeding on rarely flooded first bottom ridges. Meanley considers these ridges, where sweet gum, sweet pecan, and southern red oak predominate, as the best habitat type for turkeys, providing sweet pecan and oak mast, sugarberry fruit, and poison ivy fruit and seeds.

The daily feeding movements of turkey flocks do not follow easily predictable patterns (Korschgen, 1967:140). Turkey flocks may spend hours in a small area when feeding on mast, or may cover fairly great distances in short periods of time, feeding along the way. Feeding is most intensive during the early morning and late afternoon.

Flocks of eastern wild turkeys (*M.g. silvestris*) rarely have permanent roosting sites, but rather roost wherever they are at nightfall. Rather than roosting in a single tree, a flock will occupy a number of trees in close proximity to each other; each tree rarely holds more than three individuals (Bailey and Rinell, 1967:94).

The mean minimal annual range of turkeys in the Lake Springs area was found to be 1106 acres for males, and 1366 acres for females (Ellis and Lewis, 1967:577). This annual range value of approximately two square miles is a minimum value, with poor mast years forcing greater winter movements.

Ellis and Lewis were also able to define distinct winter ranges for four large turkey flocks. The flock ranges were mutually exclusive in nature, except for the overlapping of three of the four ranges at a centrally located thirty acre bottomland cornfield and two adjacent wooded ridges. A number of flocks used this excellent food source area each winter, and most of the large droves were observed here (Ellis and Lewis, 1967:571). Dalke et al. noted similar overlapping of winter flock ranges, especially in bottomland cornfield areas (1946:25). The relative density of turkey populations has been estimated for a number of areas in Missouri. Dalke et al. found a density of 20.4 birds per square mile in the 7.18 square mile Drury Refuge and a density of 15.7 birds per square mile in the 8.6 square mile Caney Mountain Refuge during March of 1944. Ellis and Lewis recorded a density of 25.6 birds per square mile on the central 4,400 acres of the Lake Springs study area during the winter of 1957 (1967:571). These relatively high density figures do not, however, remain constant throughout the year.

Turkeys are more evenly dispersed over large ranges during the late spring, summer, and early fall, with individual family groupings using a wide variety of plants that occur in small quantities over large areas. The larger flocks that start to form in the late fall and last until the end of March are the result of a seasonal shift in food dependence. Winter food sources (agricultural crops, oak and pecan mast, etc.) occur in great quantities in more restricted areas. This shift to much more localized food sources creates higher population densities.

Using this background information about modern turkey populations in Missouri and Arkansas, a discussion of the exploitation of turkey populations by the Middle Mississippi groups can now be undertaken.

Meanley's study of a turkey population in the first bottom areas of the White River (1956) suggests that the bottomland areas directly adjacent to the Chucalissa, Banks, and Lilbourn sites represented excellent range for turkey populations. The seasonal food preferences and movements of turkey populations during the Mississippi period can be assumed to have been similar to modern patterns in these first bottom areas, with drying oxbow lake beds and riverside sand bars being used during the late summer and fall, while feeding shifted to first bottom ridges during the winter and spring.

Similarly, based on the work of Dalke, et al. (1942, 1946), and Ellis and Lewis (1967), we can assume that the upland oak-hickory forest area east of the Mississippi valley, as well as the Powers Phase area, would have supported turkey populations at least as large as those reported today.

In both the lowland and upland areas the seasonal composition of flocks, breeding cycles, and variation in seasonal density was similar to the patterns already described for modern populations.

Population densities during the winter months (November-March) could have easily reached twenty to twenty-five individuals per square mile on the oak-hickory ridges of the Powers Phase area, and been somewhat higher on the first bottom ridge areas of the lowlands. Density values through the rest of the year were probably quite a bit lower as the individual family groupings dispersed more evenly over the range, averaging perhaps ten turkeys per square mile. This rather conservative spring breeding population estimate of ten turkeys per square mile is combined with an average edible meat yield per individual value of 8.5 pounds and a hatched brood average of 9.6 to obtain a potential annual meat yield for the species of 408 pounds of edible meat per square mile (10 x 4.8 x 8.5). The fall–winter biomass level is projected as 170 pounds of edible meat per square mile (20 turkeys per square mile x 8.5).

Although there is no direct archaeological evidence on either seasonality of turkey hunting, or the possible techniques employed by Middle Mississippi hunters, the following seems most likely.

The winter months would seem to be the most advantageous time of year for hunting turkeys, because of both the larger winter flocks and the higher population densities during the period November-March.

Schorger has a lengthy discussion of the turkey hunting techniques used by historical Indian tribes and early settlers in the eastern United States (1966:377-408). Almost all of Schorger's accounts which give either specific or indirect information concerning the time of year hunting took place, indicate fall-winter hunts.

A number of the methods described by Schorger are quite interesting. Turkeys usually evade danger by rapidly scattering on foot. Such a reaction makes pursuit and capture quite difficult. If the flock can be forced into flight, however, they will usually come to roost in nearby trees, allowing hunters to shoot at stationary targets. Such a method of driving turkeys into trees was used widely in the eastern United States, with Indian hunters rapidly rushing the flocks when they first sighted them, yelling and trying to force them into flight. Schorger cites accounts of Indian groups using this technique in Indiana and along the Ohio River (1966:378).

The most common method of turkey hunting during the contact period was for hunters to wait in feeding areas where turkey sign was abundant, or to use a variety of decoys or calls. Schorger states that while Joutel was in the Mississippi valley in 1687, he noted that Indians used the head of the turkey as a decoy (1966:379).

In addition to shooting turkeys from roosting trees, and using still hunting and decoy techniques, Middle Mississippi hunters may have used snares (Ibid.:378), or traps (Ibid.:391).

The flocks consisting entirely of juvenile males, would seem to be the most susceptible to hunting by any technique because of their inexperience (see Latham, 1967:543). If the legendary ability of experienced adult gobblers to evade hunters were true in the Middle Mississippi period as well, adult male turkeys should be represented in lower percentages in the harvests than in the turkey population.

The most obvious indicator of sex in turkeys is the spur, a stiff horny process located on the posterior surface of the tarsometatarsus. Spurs, appearing as buttons during the first year in both sexes, are fully developed only in adult males. A few rare occurrences of fully developed spurs on females have, however, been recorded. The tarsometatarsus fragments of *Meleagris gallopavo* from each of the seven sites being considered were examined to see if they exhibited the fully developed spur cores of adult males. Those fragments which did not have fully developed spur cores were classed as hens or juveniles. Table 18 shows the tarsometatarsus counts from each site, classed as either adult male or hen/juvenile. The counts consistently indicate more juveniles and hens represented than adult males, indicating that hen and juvenile flocks contributed more to the Middle Mississippi kill than adult male flocks. Only 23 percent of the total sample of 83 tarsometatarsi represented adult males. This ratio of adult males to hens and juveniles in the prehistoric harvest corresponds fairly closely to both the composition of present day turkey populations, and modern turkey harvests. In a census of 6,064 turkeys harvested in Virginia during the years 1958-1963, adult males made up only 18.9 percent of the total kill (Gwynn, 1964).

Judging from a comparison with modern turkey populations, the low representation of adult males in the prehistoric harvest is most likely largely a function of their low representation within the turkey population, rather than a result of any deliberate selection on the part of Middle Mississippi hunters of the seemingly more vulnerable flocks of hens and juveniles.

TABLE 18

RATIO OF FULLY DEVELOPED SPUR CORES TO UNDEVELOPED SPUR CORES IN SEVEN MIDDLE MISSISSIPPI SITES.

	NUMBER OF TARSO-METATARSI WITH FULLY DEVELOPED SPUR CORES PRESENT–ADULT MALES	NUMBER OF TARSO-METATARSI WITH FULLY DEVELOPED SPUR CORES ABSENT–HENS/YOUNG	TOTAL
Chucalissa site	2	16	18
Banks Village site	13	31	44
Lilbourn site	1	8	9
Snodgrass site	1	3	4
Turner site	0	2	2
Powers Fort	1	0	1
Gooseneck site	1	4	5
Total	19	64	83

BEAVER (*Castor canadensis*)

The beaver is the largest rodent in North America. Its original distribution included most of North America, extending from coast to coast and from above the arctic circle to below the Mexican border, covering a wide variety of aquatic habitats. The beaver, exterminated in most areas of the eastern United States, survives today in protected forest areas, including portions of the Missouri Ozarks.

Remains of *Castor canadensis* have been recovered from most of the archaeological sites in the eastern United States, but rarely are more than a few individuals represented at any single site.

The most conspicuous evidence of active beaver colonies is the dams of tree branches and mud that are constructed across small streams of low gradient. Such dams serve a number of important functions: the resultant beaver ponds provide water of sufficient depth to allow construction of lodges and offer protection to the beaver, as well as providing an important avenue of transportation, and encouraging the growth of aquatic plants, which are important in the beaver's summer diet. Stated in more simple terms, beaver dams function to alter the habitat, making it more conducive to occupation by this species, and are, therefore, constructed only in locations that require such alteration. In situations such as lakes, sloughs, or large streams, where the water is already of sufficient depth to provide transportation and protection, beavers do not built dams, and limit their building activities to the construction of either lodges (in still water situations) or bank burrows (in swift moving water situations).

Thus most beavers occupying larger streams in Missouri do not construct either dams or lodges, but rather occupy stream or slough bank burrows near areas of permanent deep water. This is because of the depth and swiftness of many Missouri streams, their tendency toward unpredictable and severe floods, and large-scale fluctuations in water levels (Schwartz and Schwartz, 1959).

Beavers are semi-aquatic and nocturnal in nature, rarely appearing during the day except in the fall when they must gather food for winter.

Beavers are primarily bark eaters, consuming mostly the bark of tender twigs and the new growth (cambium layer) of larger branches and trunks. Although the beaver prefers certain species, it will use the bark of practically any deciduous tree. Preferred species in lowland areas of the Mississippi valley are cottonwood and willow, while a much greater variety of species, including blue beech, white oak, alder, hickory, flowering dogwood, elm, sycamore, black gum, red maple, red and black oak, and birch are taken in the Ozark uplands (Schwartz and Schwartz, 1959). During the summer months, when beavers feed more on a variety of aquatic plants, tree cutting and movement onto dry land is at a minimum (Bradt, 1938; Townsend, 1953).

Beavers must sometimes travel fairly great distances from water to obtain food, when trees closer to the water, their first preference, have been harvested.

Beavers mate in January or February in Missouri, with the single annual litter being born in April, May or June. Litters vary in size from one to eight, with an average of three to four (Swank, 1949; Bradt, 1938). This represents a potential annual productivity of 3.5 young/adult female. Beavers rarely breed until the spring of their third year.

Juvenile mortality is quite low in present day beaver populations, partly because of the lack of potential natural predators such as coyotes, bobcats, otters, and mink.

As Bradt noted in 1938, the logical unit of study in beaver populations is the colony,

> a group of beavers occupying a pond or stretch of stream in common, utilizing a common food supply, and maintaining a common dam or dams. They may or may not be living in the same lodge or burrow. . . . Beavers appear to maintain a system of territorial rights, and there is no evidence of overlapping of the colonies (p. 145).

Colonies typically consist of an individual family, including the two parents, the yearlings born the previous year, and the kits of the current year (Townsend, 1953). Colonies are thus limited to a size of ten to sixteen individuals, and rarely exceed twelve. Three age classes are represented in the colony (two adults, four to six yearlings, and four to six kits). This constant colony size is maintained by the "budding off" of two-year-old young. As young beavers approach sexual maturity at the end of their second year, they leave or are forced out of the colony, usually in the spring, shortly before the birth of a new litter of kits (Bradt, 1938). This limitation of colonies to ten to sixteen individuals "prolongs the period of occupation for each site, as the addition of other mature beavers would materially increase the rate of tree cutting for food, and would exhaust the accessible food supply more rapidly" (Bradt, 1938:160). Since two-year-old individuals are forced from the colony, and cannot enter territories already occupied by other colonies, such emigration results in the systematic dispersion of beavers into unoccupied areas.

As the available food supply of a colony's territory is gradually used up, the colony is forced to relocate. Such dispersal occurs most commonly in the fall. The length of time an area will support a colony depends upon both the quantity and the quality of food available. An adult pair introduced into a ten acre lake in Michigan eventually produced a colony of twelve, which had almost completely exhausted the available food supply within 500 feet of the lake edge within a period of five years after the initial introduction, and subsequently moved to a new location (Bradt, 1938).

Density estimates and potential annual productivity values for prehistoric beaver populations for the four environmental zones being considered will not be projected for a number of reasons. Although Schwartz and

Schwartz (1959) estimated an original population density of perhaps fifty beavers per square mile in favorable habitat areas of Missouri, there has not been any good research done on this species in the Mississippi valley area. This lack of research, and the shifting nature of beaver colonies, make it impossible to estimate the beaver carrying capacity of the various environmental zones.

Beaver dams and lodges could be expected in the low gradient areas of smaller streams, with colonies in the larger, swifter rivers using bank burrows. Such "bank beaver" colonies characteristically have fewer members, are more difficult to locate, and shift their location more often.

The oxbow lakes and sloughs within the meander belt that were deep enough throughout the year (such as Lake Wapanocca, adjacent to the Banks site) probably supported sizable beaver populations, but it is not possible to project either density or productivity estimates.

Possible techniques of exploitation of beaver colonies by Middle Mississippi populations include: (1) capturing out of water, (2) submerged trapping, and (3) capturing in lodges or burrows.

The fall of the year would have been the most opportune period for capturing beaver out of the water either by trapping or by stalking, and beaver landing areas would have been the most logical sites of capture.

Beavers leave the water infrequently during the summer months, when aquatic plants form a large part of their diet, and construction activities are at a minimum. With the shift in their food preference to dry land species during the fall, and the increase in tree cutting activity, both for dam and lodge construction and for stockpiling of winter food, beavers spend an increasing amount of time on dry land. During this fall period of intensive activity, which peaks during late September, October, and November, beaver make daytime excursions onto dry land, rare for this usually nocturnal species.

Beavers consistently enter and leave the water at established landing sites, but the size and strength of beavers would have made trapping difficult, as would their extreme suspicion of strange objects above the surface, and the high probability of a snare or trap being sprung by branches carried by the prey (see Bradt, 1938, for a discussion of these problems).

Submerged baited or unbaited traps, on the other hand, would have been quite successful if strong enough, for beavers are quite oblivious to anything beneath the surface.

Middle Mississippi groups could also have captured beavers by digging down through the top of lodges or burrows. Attempting to capture beavers by digging them out of lodges or burrows would have been a difficult procedure, however, since the underwater entrances, usually four to six feet below the surface, would have had to have been located and blocked prior to any attempt to dig down from the top.

Ethnohistorical information concerning seasonality of exploitation and possible techniques of procurement used by Indian groups in the southeast United States is unfortunately lacking.

Castor canadensis skeletal elements occurred in fairly low frequencies in the seven Middle Mississippian sites being considered; a total of only twenty individuals were represented. There does not seem to be any variation between sites in utilization of this species.

A number of osteological criteria can be employed in determining the age of beavers (Friley, 1949; Robertson and Shadle, 1954). A method for aging beavers on the basis of eruption, degree of root closure, and deposition of annual cementum layers on mandibular teeth, developed by Van Nostrand and Stephenson (1964), and subsequently modified by Larson and Van Nostrand (1968), is used here. A total of seven beaver mandibles recovered from the sites being studied were complete enough to be assigned to age classes according to these criteria (Table 19).

Because this sample of beaver mandibles is so small, only two points will be made concerning it: (1) It appears that there was no consistent selection of only adults or only juvenile beavers by Middle Mississippi populations. (2) The three mandibles representing kits (½ to 1 year old) indicate that beavers were probably exploited during the period October-May. It is not possible to narrow the season of exploitation any further than this seven month range on the basis of archaeological data, but our discussion of beaver habits suggests that the most advantageous period for successful exploitation would have been during the fall period of intensive beaver activity, which peaks during late September, October, and November.

TABLE 19

AGE COMPOSITION OF THE BEAVER HARVEST FROM 4 MIDDLE MISSISSIPPI SITES (BASED ON DENTAL AGING CRITERIA OF VAN NOSTRAND AND STEPHENSON, 1968)

SITE	AGE
Chucalissa Temple Mound	½ to 1 year
Banks Village Site	½ to 1 year
Banks Village Site	1½ to 2 years
Banks Village Site	3½ to 4 years
Turner Site (pit 8)	2½ to 3 years
Turner Site (pit 34)	½ to 1 year
Powers Fort (structure 1)	3½ to 4 years

If the quality of the beaver pelt was of major importance, however, the period of exploitation may have been later in the year, since beaver pelts do not become prime until December.

Judging from the low representation of *C. canadensis* at the sites being studied, it is clear that the species was not intensively harvested by the Middle Mississippi groups, and was not a common item in their diet.

OPOSSUM (*Didelphis marsupialis*)

The opossum is the only marsupial in the Mississippi valley today. Its geographical distribution has gradually expanded during the historic period, because of the extensive human alteration of the environment. It has moved northward into Illinois, east into New York, and west into Kansas, and has been introduced west of the Rocky Mountains (Guilday, 1958).

The opossum is quite often represented in archaeological sites in the eastern United States, but usually in low numbers.

The preferred habitat of opossums is wooded regions with abundant open water areas such as small streams, ponds, and swamps. Opossums are not found in densely forested areas that lack open water. They avoid open areas, and rarely venture very far from forest cover. The forest type most favored by opossums is mixed age class timber along small streams.

The opossum's affinity for water has been noted by a number of authors. In his study of opossum populations in east Texas, Lay (1942) indicated that the distribution of opossums was highly correlated with the distribution of open water; in Reynolds's study of opossums in central Missouri (1945), 83 of 116 captures of opossums occured within 100 feet of water.

Opossums are an unusually shy and secretive species, and are strictly nocturnal. In over a thousand days in the field, Fitch and Sandidge observed only four opossums active during the day, and all four cases involved individuals forced into daytime foraging immediately after prolonged winter cold spells had necessitated a long period of inactivity (1953:315).

Although opossums are omnivorous, they display "a distinct preference for animal material, particularly for insects" (Reynolds, 1945:373). Insects were eaten throughout the year, even during the winter, when we would expect them to be unavailable as a food source. Reynolds found that remains of 25 different species of insects were the most common item in analyzed droppings and stomachs; ground beetles (*Larabidae*), lamellicorn beetles (*Scarabaeidae*), short-horned grasshoppers (*Locustidae*), squashbugs (*Coreidae*), and stink bugs (*Pentatomidae*) were of prime importance.

Among the twelve species of mammals that Reynolds found to have been eaten by opossums, the cottontail rabbit (*Sylvilagus floridanus*) occurred with the greatest frequency. The inclusion of these larger species in the diet of Missouri opossums was most likely a result of feeding on carrion rather than active hunting by the opossum. Accounts do exist, however, of opossums killing young cottontails which are still in the nest.

A wide variety of fruits, including pokeberry, wild grape, persimmon, and blackberry were also eaten, especially during the fall and early winter (Reynolds, 1945:372).

Opossums habitually follow creeks, gullies, and pond or lake margins in their night foraging, since these routes provide more abundant food sources than the adjoining habitat (Fitch and Sandidge, 1953:317). Their nightly movements in search of food are sometimes much less structured, however; they seem to wander at random, following an extremely circuitous and erratic route (Fitch and Sandidge, 1953:316).

Opossums use a wide variety of daytime dens, including cavities in trees, horizontal logs, rocky slopes, abandoned ground burrows of other animals, etc.–almost any place that is dry, sheltered, and safe. They often use many different den sites, some for only a few days.

Although a number of studies, including that done by Reynolds (1945), concluded that opossums were nomadic in nature and did not have established home ranges, more controlled studies, such as those done in east central Illinois (Sanderson, 1961; Holmes and Sanderson, 1965) indicate that opossums have well-defined home ranges. Home range estimates for opossums range from a low of 11.5 to 38.4 acres (Lay, 1942) to a high of 134 to 206 acres (Verts, 1963). Fitch and Sandidge (1953) estimated the average home range of opossums in northeast Kansas to be approximately 50 acres. The variation in these home range estimates probably reflects the difference in habitat of the study areas.

A similar variation exists in the density estimates that have been obtained for opossum populations by different researchers. Hamilton (1958) estimated the opossum population density of the 2000 acre Montezuma National Wildlife Refuge in New York to be about twenty per square mile. Fitch and Sandidge estimated the fall population density on a 590 acre area of relatively low quality habitat in northeastern Kansas to be about 1 per 20 acres (32 per square mile), and the spring population density to be about half that large (1953:312,335). Holmes and Sanderson's (1965) population figures for a 1600 acre, high quality opossum habitat area in east central Illinois indicate a mid-summer adult breeding population that varied from 42 to 62 individuals per square mile over a four year period.

The onset of the breeding season for opossums in Missouri is the first of February. Breeding continues through the first three weeks of February, with the peak coming during the second week of the month. The gestation period is only 13 days, so that most of the first litters are born toward the end of February (Reynolds, 1945). A second breeding period occurs soon after the young of the first litter leave the pouch, and the second litters are born in late May or early June. Estimates of average litter size vary from 6.8 (Lay, 1942) to 8.9 (Reynolds, 1945). Female opossums can have young their first year. Little information is available on the percentage of female opossums that bear two litters each year, but Holmes and Sanderson thought that virtually all adult females gave birth to at least one litter per year (1965:290). We will assume that 1.5 litters per year was the average, and that the average potential yield of a female opossum is, therefore, approximately twelve young.

The size of an opossum population usually fluctuates drastically through a yearly cycle. In the study by Holmes and Sanderson, the opossum population on July first of 1959 was 419 per square mile. Approximately 42 opossums per square mile were present the following spring (1965: 290).

Mortality rates are quite high for both juveniles and adults, and life expectancy is short. Few individuals live beyond two years of age, and an annual turnover in the breeding population of 95 percent is not uncommon. The juvenile to adult ratio, which is about 4:1 during the summer months, remains fairly constant through the fall, and gradually increases thereafter, since few adults survive through the winter of their second year.

The rather limited data available concerning seasonal variation in feeding habits, movements, density, etc., does not suggest any single time of the year that opossums would be more susceptible to exploitation by Middle Mississippi groups.

Because of their nocturnal nature, opossums were probably caught either in traps or snares placed along the margins of small streams or other bodies of water, or by seeking out their dens during the day. As was already mentioned in reference to the hunting of raccoons, it is doubtful if night hunting, either with or without dogs, was employed during the Mississippi period.

Either of the techniques mentioned above would have been less successful in obtaining opossums than it was for other species such as the raccoon. While it is true that the opossum has an affinity for water, and often follows foraging routes along streams or pond margins, such movement patterns are not as habitual as they are in the raccoon. The opossum follows a random, erratic foraging route much of the time, and thus would be less susceptible to snares or traps placed along known or obvious routes of movement. Similarly, it uses a much wider variety of denning situations than does the raccoon, and rarely occupies a single den for more than a few days at a time; it would thus be less susceptible to exploitation.

Ethnohistorical descriptions of the exploitation of opossums by Indian groups in the southeastern United States are restricted to brief mention of the species as being hunted, and nothing more.

The opossum was represented at each of the sites being considered, but occurred in very low numbers. Table 20 lists the minimum number of individuals represented at each site. The total number of individuals represented at the seven sites is less than the number of young that four female opossums could produce in a single year.

A number of different age criteria have been recognized for opossums, including the rate of eruption of permanent dentition (Petrides, 1949). Petrides found that during the first ten months of life the number of mandibular and maxillary teeth is increased regularly by additions from the rear until the full complement of three premolars and four molars is attained. A mature set of fifty teeth is present with the emergence of the fourth molar, at the age of 9½ to 10 months (1949:373). Thus it is possible to separate opossums into two age categories: less than ten months (juvenile), and older than ten months (adult).

Each mandible and maxilla fragment recovered from the sites being considered was examined and, if complete enough to allow aging, was classed as either juvenile or adult. The number of mandibles and maxillas assigned to each class for each site is presented in Table 21. All individuals classed as juveniles were from 7 to 10 months old (Petrides, 1949:374). Of the specimens classed as representing adults, a few exhibited extremely worn

TABLE 20

THE MINIMUM NUMBER OF OPOSSUMS (*Didelphis marsupialis*) REPRESENTED AT SEVEN MIDDLE MISSISSIPPI SITES

SITES	MINIMUM NUMBER OF INDIVIDUALS
Chucalissa Village Midden	10
Chucalissa Temple Mound	0
Banks Village Site	15
Lilbourn Site–Structure 9	2
Lilbourn Site–Structure 12	1
Lilbourn Site–Structure 25	1
Turner Site	3
Snodgrass Site	5
Powers Fort	2
Gooseneck Site	1
Total	40

dentition, and were clearly older than one year. These specimens were classed as "old adults" in Table 21.

As Table 21 indicates, opossums less than ten months old occur in very low percentages in the prehistoric samples, with specimens aged seven to ten months accounting for only 6.4 percent of the mandibles recovered, and 9 percent of the maxillas. No specimens younger than seven months were recovered. This contrasts with the situation that exists in modern populations, where young of the year comprise a significant proportion of the population throughout the year (Fitch and Sandidge, 1953:331).

This marked difference between the age composition of the prehistoric samples and modern opossum populations can probably be explained by one of the following:

TABLE 21

AGE COMPOSITION OF THE OPOSSUM HARVEST FROM 7 MIDDLE MISSISSIPPI SITES. (BASED ON DENTAL CRITERIA OF PETRIDES, 1949)

SITE	MANDIBLES			MAXILLAE		
	JUVENILE	ADULT	OLD ADULT	JUVENILE	ADULT	OLD ADULT
Chucalissa Site	1	15	2	1	5	2
Banks Site	2	16	3	0	0	0
Lilbourn Site	0	1	0	0	0	0
Turner Site	0	1	0	0	0	1
Snodgrass Site	0	2	1	0	1	1
Powers Fort	0	3	0	0	0	0
Gooseneck Site	0	0	0	0	0	0
Total	3	38	6	1	6	4
Percentage	6.4%	80.8%	12.8%	9%	55%	36%

TABLE 22

AGE COMPOSITION OF A MODERN WINTER OPOSSUM POPULATION (FROM FITCH AND SANDIDGE, 1953:331)

SUMMER YEARLINGS	SPRING YEARLINGS	OLD ADULTS
14.2%	56.6%	29.2%

(1) Differential preservation or recovery of mandible and maxilla specimens resulting in the under-representation of juveniles. This possible source of bias is rejected on the basis of the excellent state of preservation of the juvenile specimens in the sample.
(2) Differential selection of opossums by Middle Mississippi groups. It is possible that Middle Mississippi hunters deliberately spared young opossums for some reason. If such a conservation measure was in effect for any animal species, it would be most difficult to infer from the archaeological record. It would have been difficult also to differentiate young of the year from adult opossums once they had attained small adult size, around November first. This unlikely source of bias is rejected in favor of the third possibility.
(3) Seasonal exploitation of the opossum population by Middle Mississippi groups. The first litters of opossums are born in late February and early March in Missouri. Eruption of permanent dentition is complete by the middle of December. After this date, spring-born yearlings cannot be distinguished from older individuals on the basis of the degree of eruption of permanent teeth alone. Yearlings born in late May and early June can be distinguished on the basis of tooth eruption up until the middle of March, after the first litter of the following year has been born. Spring-born were found to outnumber summer-born yearlings in a study of a winter opossum population by a ratio of four to one (Table 22) (Fitch and Sandidge, 1953). If we assume that the prehistoric harvest occurred after the middle of December and before the first of March, spring-born yearlings would exhibit dentition of adults (over ten months of age), while older individuals would have characteristically well worn teeth, and summer born yearlings would not yet have a full set of permanent teeth. Thus if exploitation of opossums by Middle Mississippi hunters took place primarily during the winter, this would explain in large part the seeming low representation of juveniles in the prehistoric harvest.

In estimating the potential annual meat yield and fall–winter biomass values for opossum populations during the Mississippi period, an average edible meat yield per individual value of 8.5 pounds is combined with a mean spring breeding population estimate of 42 opossums per square mile (a fall-winter population estimate of 62 opossums per square mile) and an estimated number of young per female of 12. The potential annual meat yield for the species is therefore 2142 pounds of edible meat per square mile (42 x 6 x 8.5). The fall–winter biomass level is projected as 527 pounds of edible meat per square mile (62 x 8.5).

EASTERN COTTONTAIL (*Sylvilagus floridanus*)

SWAMP RABBIT (*Sylvilagus aquaticus*)

Two species of lagomorphs occur in the Mississippi valley area, and both were used to a limited extent during the Mississippi period. Both of these species will be considered in this section.

Although the cottontail rabbit and the swamp rabbit are quite similar in a number of ways, including physical appearance, they differ considerably in their distribution and their habitat requirements.

The swamp rabbit, as the name implies, is found only in a specific micro-environmental zone of the valley: directly adjacent to and within flooded areas of the Mississippi lowlands. The cottontail rabbit, on the other hand, occurs in a wide variety of suitable dry land habitat situations.

Although the cottontail is highly adaptable, and does occur in small numbers within closed canopy climax deciduous forests, it is most abundant from five to twleve years after timber is cut (Halls and Stransky, 1971:13). Small farms with overgrown fencerows and old orchards provide prime cottontail habitat. A most important habitat requirement for the cottontail is access to the escape cover offered by thickets, weed patches, and dense high grass, which is provided in the early successional stages of fields and forests. They prefer, therefore, an open brushy or forest border habitat with generous amounts of shrubby vegetation and small open sites.

A cottontail usually spends his days, when not feeding, in well worn depressions or "forms": resting places concealed in suitable cover such as thickets, dense high grass, or brush piles. The home range of any cottontail will contain a number of these forms, each of which is used by many cottontails. Forms are usually connected by a variety of well-traveled, well-known escape routes. It is difficult to flush a cottontail from its form; one can approach quite close to such hiding places without forcing the rabbit into the open.

The food preference of cottontails in Missouri shifts according to the seasonal availability of various plant species. During the winter they subsist on dried herbs and grasses, fruits and berries, etc. Almost their entire diet during the growing season consists of the leaves, stems, and flowers of grasses (primarily orchard grass, timothy, and nodding wild rye), herbs, and sedges (Schwartz and Schwartz, 1959). These plant species occur primarily in open areas and along forest margins.

Cottontails are most active at night and in the early morning hours. Most feeding takes place three to four hours after sunrise, and then again from late afternoon until after sunset (Schwartz and Schwartz, 1959:101). They are active throughout the year, except during the very coldest weather. Schwartz (1941) has estimated the average minimum home range of cottontails in an excellent habitat situation in central Missouri at about 1.4 acres for males, and 1.2 acres for females. Haugen's study of Michigan cottontails (1941, 1942*a*, 1942*b*) under poorer range conditions gives much higher minimum home range values, with females having average home ranges of 14 to 15 acres during the fall and winter. During the spring and summer breeding season this minimum home range expands to an average of 22.5 acres. The home range of the male cottontail expands even more significantly during the breeding season as adult breeding males roam in search of females. Territoriality exists only insofar as dominant males (see below) defend an area surrounding the females in a breeding population (Marsden and Holler, 1964:35).

Conaway, Wight, and Sadler noted that the breeding season began during a limited period in early February (1963:173). The onset of the breeding season has been observed to vary, however, by as much as six weeks.

This initial synchrony of conception continues through the seven-month-long breeding season. The controlled pattern of group births is a result of a stable gestation period of twenty-six or twenty-seven days (Marsden and Conaway, 1963) and the high occurrence of "postpartum conceptions." Immediately after giving birth (parturition), female cottontails enter a short estrus period (postpartum estrus) and postpartum conceptions usually occur. Because of stable linear dominance hierarchies among the adult males of cottontail breeding groups, the dominant (alpha) male is responsible for the majority of copulations (Marsden and Holler, 1964). Most adult female cottontails have from six to eight litters a year, with the majority of births being closely grouped at approximately twenty-six day intervals.

The size of litters varies through the breeding season, with peak litter sizes being reached for the second through sixth pregnancies. Conaway et al. estimated the average annual production by females at about 35 young per female (1963:174). Those females that were capable of bearing young at the beginning of the breeding season do not, however, account for the total annual production. It has been estimated that juvenile females, capable of bearing young as early as 2-3 months, contribute 24 to 27 percent of the annual crop of cottontails. A significant percentage of the young do not survive the year. In the same study it was found that the December cottontail population contained 87 percent young of the year (13.4 young per adult female), indicating a juvenile mortality of more than 60 percent during the period from March to December. This high juvenile mortality rate is confirmed by Edwards's estimate of the normal fall age composition of cottontail populations in the Middle West. His 1964 study showed the expected proportion of juveniles in fall populations to be 0.834 plus or minus .005 (95 percent confidence level), a value close to that obtained by Conaway et al. Much of this juvenile mortality can be attributed to predation by a number of species, including great horned owl, bobcat and gray fox. The survivorship curve for cottontails flattens out considerably after the first ten to fourteen months of life (see Lord, 1961:37).

When both the cottontail and the swamp rabbit occur in the same area, a gradation from cottontail to swamp rabbit range can be observed, with a narrow band of overlap existing along swamp margins (Toll et al., 1960:401).

These almost totally separate ranges for the two species are a function of their different food preferences.

The swamp rabbit has a much narrower potential niche than the cottontail, but does occur in significant numbers in floodplain climax forest situations. Swamp rabbits inhabit the backswamp and flooded areas of river floodplains in the southeast United States, and are rarely found outside of this rather narrow micro-environmental zone.

Swamp rabbit forms are found in places where intruders can be observed and where there is access to vegetation or water for escape. The swamp rabbit is an accomplished swimmer, and can use either an aquatic avenue of escape, or one of many well-traveled tunnels through the sometimes dense swamp margin vegetation.

The niche of the swamp rabbit, and that of the cottontail differ in available vegetation. From spring through mid-winter, swamp grass (*Carex lupulina*) makes up a significant portion of the diet of swamp rabbits in southeast Missouri. Large amounts of hazelnut shoots are also consumed during this period. Blackberry (*Rubus Spp*.), hazelnut, deciduous holly (*Ilex decidua*) and spice bush (*Lindera benzoin*) are eaten during the late winter months (Toll et al., 1964). All these species of plants occur within or along the margins of swamps. The use of such emergent aquatic species of plants by the swamp rabbit separates it ecologically and spatially from the cottontail.

The daily feeding periods of the swamp rabbit are similar to those of the cottontail.

Lowe (1958:123) has estimated the average home range of swamp rabbits in Georgia at 18.9 acres, while Toll et al. (1964) observed the average home ranges of swamp rabbits in southeast Missouri to be 5.9 acres for females and 4.6 acres for males. These smaller home range values for Missouri swamp rabbits result from higher density levels, which are also reflected in considerable overlap of home ranges in the Missouri study area (Toll et al., 1964:406). Lowe's study estimated the density of the swamp rabbit population in question at about one rabbit per 18 acres, while Toll et al. found a population density of one rabbit per 1.5 acres (1964:406). The smaller average home range and higher density values determined for swamp rabbits in southeast Missouri are, of course, a function of a better quality habitat situation.

The onset of the breeding season in Missouri swamp rabbit populations occurs in March, and lasts through September. Patterns of postpartum estrus and conception, as well as linear dominance hierarchies among adult male swamp rabbits are similar to those described for cottontails.

Because of a longer gestation period (39-40 days) swamp rabbits have slightly fewer litters per breeding season, probably five to six (Marsden and Holler, 1964, Table 7). Toll et al. (1964) have estimated the size of the average litter to be two to six, with a 3.7 average. Thus the average annual production per breeding female would be approximately 19 to 23 young.

Infant mortality is quite high in swamp rabbit populations. In their study of swamp rabbit population in southeast Missouri, Martinson et al. (1961) found that young of the year composed 63 percent of the January-February population. This 0.63 juvenile/total January population ratio represents 3.4 young per adult female, and when compared with the annual production estimate of 19-23 young per female, it indicates a higher level of juvenile mortality than for cottontails, though this may be in part a result of both the later census date of the swamp rabbit study and the high density level of the swamp rabbit population. The extent to which predators account for first year mortality in swamp rabbit populations is not known, but, because of better cover situations, swamp rabbits may be less susceptible to predation than cottontails.

These two species are quite similar in many ways: their physical appearance is comparable, except for the swamp rabbits' somewhat larger size, and comparable patterns of social behavior have been observed in each species (Marsden and Holler, 1964).

The average annual production figures for both species are quite high, because of long breeding seasons, postpartum estrus, and short gestation periods. High juvenile mortality rates, on the other hand, are also characteristic.

In terms of their respective niches within the ecosystem, however, the cottontail and the swamp rabbit are quite different. They are separated spatially by the distribution of the plant species eaten by each. The swamp rabbit is a narrow niche species that is most abundant in undisturbed, climax floodplain forest situations (primarily cypress-tupelo swamps and margins). The cottontail, on the other hand, is more flexible than the swamp rabbit in terms of habitat use, but prefers a successional forest, or areas where the closed canopy of the climax forest has been disturbed, resulting in grassy open areas and abundant forest margins.

The extent to which each of these two species was present in each of the four environmental zones being considered can be generally discussed, but quantitative estimates of density are more difficult to establish. The cottontail was no doubt present in upland areas to either side of the valley, and within the valley itself, with its abundance directly dependent upon the occurrence and distribution of open areas in the forest canopy. The Sikeston ridge prairie–forest interface area north of the Lilbourn site would have been excellent cottontail habitat, as would those channel cutoff areas of the Mississippi River that were dry through much of the summer. And in clearing the forest for agricultural crops, Middle Mississippi groups would have increased the carrying capacity of the immediate area for cottontails. While cottontails would also have been present in those areas where the forest canopy was largely closed, the density levels would have been very low. The swamp rabbit would have been restricted in distribution to swamp areas, and the density values would have varied according to the quality of the swamp habitat, with quality and availability of food being the most important limiting factor.

The cottontail rabbit population of any specific area can vary markedly from year to year, and from season to season. Perhaps because of this variability, few density estimates of cottontail populations exist in the literature. In the absence of any other density estimates for Missouri cottontails, the fall-winter figure of one rabbit per 4½ acres given by Bennitt and Nagel (1937:93) will be employed herein as the projected estimate of the density of the prehistoric cottontail breeding population. As previously mentioned, density estimates for swamp rabbits vary from 1 per 18 acres (Lowe, 1958) to 1 per 1.5 acres (Toll et al., 1964). Because it is well within this observed range of variation in density levels for the swamp rabbit, the value of one rabbit per 4½ acres will also be applied to this species. These density estimates are little more than educated guesses, but they must suffice, given the general lack of data on this point.

Because of the mutually exclusive distribution of these two species, the prehistoric breeding population of both species combined can be expressed as 142 rabbits per square mile (1 per 4½ acres), with the representation of each species in any area depending upon the occurrence of swamp or dry land habitat. In estimating the potential annual meat yield and fall-winter biomass values for rabbits, an average edible meat yield per individual value of 2.5 pounds is combined with a mean spring-summer breeding population estimate of 142 rabbits per square mile (a fall-winter population estimate of 180 rabbits per square mile) and an estimated number of young per female of 25. The potential annual meat yield for the species is therefore 4,437.5 pounds of edible meat per square mile (142 x 12.5 x 2.5). The fall–winter biomass level is projected as 450 pounds of edible meat per square mile (180 x 2.5).

Rabbits were probably caught by putting snares or traps along their easily identifiable paths or tunnels. Because rabbits refuse to "flush" unless approached very closely, communal rabbit drives and individual stalking methods were not likely to be successful (cf. Flannery, 1966:803).

Among the few ethnohistorical descriptions which mention the techniques employed by Indian populations of the southeast United States or indicate seasonality of exploitation, is the following:

> Another sort of trap, used by DeSoto's followers in the winter of 1541-42 in catching "conies", i.e., Rabbits, was borrowed from Indians west of the Mississippi, probably in what is now Arkansas. They were snared by means of stout strings which lift the feet off the ground and a noose of strong cord fastened to which is a joint of cane, which runs to the neck of the Rabbit, so that it can not gnaw the cord. (Swanton, 1946:330)

Table 23 lists the minimum number of individuals of both species of rabbits represented at each of the sites being considered. When compared with the potential annual production of each species (cottontail–35 young/adult female, swamp rabbit–19-23 young/adult female), these values indicate clearly the very limited extent to which rabbit populations were exploited by Middle Mississippi groups. The combined minimum individual counts from all of the sites for each species, is little more than the potential annual production of two female rabbits of each species. There are a few additional points of interest in Table 23:

a) As expected, the swamp rabbit is not represented at the Gooseneck site, because the lack of appropriate habitat,
b) As expected, the swamp rabbit is more abundant than the cottontail at the two meander belt sites, while the cottontail is more abundant at the Chucalissa site and the sites of the Powers Phase,
c) The high representation of swamp rabbit at the Chucalissa site indicates use of the floodplain habitat for hunting.

The age composition of the rabbit harvest at the sites being considered differs markedly from the age structure of modern rabbit populations, which have already been mentioned. Among the criteria which can be employed for aging cottontail and swamp rabbits is the presence of epiphyseal cartilage in

TABLE 23

MINIMUM NUMBER OF INDIVIDUALS OF TWO SPECIES OF RABBITS REPRESENTED AT EACH OF SEVEN MIDDLE MISSISSIPPI SITES.

SITES	*Sylvilagus floridanus*	*Sylvilagus aquaticus*	TOTAL
Chucalissa Village	22	10	32
Chucalissa Temple Mound	1	1	2
Banks Village Site	13	17	30
Lilbourn Site–Structure 9	7	5	12
Lilbourn Site–Structure 12	3	3	6
Lilbourn Site–Structure 25	2	10	12
Turner Site	3	1	4
Snodgrass Site	11	1	12
Powers Fort	3	1	4
Gooseneck Site	1	0	1
TOTAL	66	49	115

long bones, such as the humerus, radius and ulna. The completion of epiphyseal closure occurs at ten to eleven months in swamp rabbits (Martinson et al., 1961) and at nine months in cottontails (Hale, 1949:221). This epiphyseal closure criteria was employed in the analysis of the age composition of the rabbit harvest at each of the sites being considered.

Each recovered humerus, radius, or ulna that was identified as from either cottontail or swamp rabbit, and on which the appropriate epiphyseal area was intact, was classed as representing either a juvenile or an adult. The data for each skeletal element for each site is shown in Table 24. While the

TABLE 24

ADULT/JUVENILE RATIO OF PREHISTORIC RABBIT HARVESTS, BASED UPON THE DEGREE OF EPIPHYSEAL CLOSURE IN SELECTED SKELETAL ELEMENTS. (HALE, 1949; MARTINSON ET AL., 1961)[1]

	HUMERUS		RADIUS		ULNA		TOTAL	
	OPEN	CLOSED	OPEN	CLOSED	OPEN	CLOSED	OPEN	CLOSED
Chucalissa Site	6	12	2	3	1	3	9	18
Banks Site	3	9	0	4	0	3	3	16
Lilbourn Site	0	1	0	0	0	0	0	1
Turner Site	0	0	0	0	0	0	0	0
Snodgrass Site	1	2	0	0	0	1	1	3
Powers Fort	0	1	0	0	0	1	0	2
Gooseneck Site	0	0	0	0	0	0	0	0
Total	10	25	2	7	1	8	13	40
				Sylvilagus floridanus				
Chucalissa Site	1	3	1	2	1	4	3	9
Banks Site	4	5	0	2	1	1	5	8
Lilbourn Site	1	3	0	1	0	0	1	4
Turner Site	0	0	0	0	0	0	0	0
Snodgrass Site	0	0	0	0	0	0	0	0
Powers Fort	0	1	0	0	0	0	0	1
Gooseneck Site	0	0	0	0	0	0	0	0
Total	6	12	1	5	2	5	9	22
				Sylvilagus aquaticus				

1. Open indicates juvenile rabbit, closed indicates adult.

sample sizes for each individual site are too small to justify more than a gross interpretation, the total values listed at the bottom right of each table suggest a pattern that is consistent throughout, and is quite interesting. The number of skeletal elements representing adults consistently outnumber those representing juveniles, with 24 percent of the total cottontail sample, and 29 percent of the swamp rabbit sample being juveniles. It should also be noted that it is possible to determine if rabbits are less than one month old by the progressive eruption of mandibular dentition (Dice and Dice, 1941). No mandibles representing individuals less than one month of age were recovered.

This prehistoric pattern is in direct and striking contrast to the age structure of modern winter rabbit populations, in which juveniles make up 87 percent (cottontail) and 63 percent (swamp rabbit) of the population, even after a period of high juvenile mortality.

The low representation of juvenile rabbits in the sample recovered from seven Middle Mississippi sites was probably the result of one of the following four factors: (1) differential preservation and/or recovery, (2) deliberate selection of adult rabbits by Middle Mississippi populations, (3) low seasonal representation of juveniles in prehistoric rabbit populations, (4) undeliberate selection of older individuals. Of these four possibilities, the last two are the most probable.

Although juvenile rabbits, especially those less than a month old, have skeletons that are more delicate and thus less likely to be either preserved or recovered from an archaeological site, recovery techniques and preservation were adequate enough at a number of sites to rule out this possibility. The hypothesis that Indians deliberately selected adult rabbits is equally untenable, since the rapid growth of juveniles makes it impossible to distinguish them from adults on the basis of external physical attributes as early as four months after birth.

It is possible that infant mortality within rabbit populations due to nonhuman predation may have been higher during the Mississippi period, resulting in much lower survival rates of young of the year into the late fall-winter period, with this lower seasonal representation of juveniles showing up in Middle Mississippi harvests. Thus one possible explanation for the low percentage of juveniles in the human harvests is a late fall-winter hunting season, combined with more intensive exploitation of young of the year by nonhuman predator populations prior to the season of human exploitation.

If the rabbit populations were exploited during the breeding season, on the other hand, and the method of capture employed was snares or traps set along routes used by rabbits, the low representation of juveniles in the harvest could be explained by the relative movement of juvenile and adult rabbits during this time of the year. This explanation is based on the assumption that those individuals that have larger home ranges, and that move over greater distances more consistently, have a greater probability of being captured by traps or snares. Haugen noted the significant increase in the home range of cottontails during the breeding season (1942*a*), and stated that as the animal grew older, the distance that it moved, and the size of its home range, also increased. Similarly, Marsden and Holler observed that:

> In male cottontails, exploring appeared to involve searching for receptive females, and was mainly a behavior of dominants. In male swamp rabbits exploring was even more obviously sexually oriented. Dominant males were the principal explorers. . . . exploring by females in both species was most conspicuous during apparent searches for nesting sites (1964:9).

Thus dominant (and necessarily adult) males, and nest-seeking females tend to explore significantly more, and over wider areas, than subordinate juveniles, and would therefore be more prone to capture. This effect would be especially significant during the first four months of the breeding season (March, April, May, and June).

During this four month period the ratio of "mobile" (four to nine months of age) juveniles to adults would be the lowest of any point in the yearly cycle. The young of the year would all be less than four months of age, and exploring very little (Lord, 1961:37), while those individuals born the previous year that were still less than nine months of age (and classed as juveniles according to the criteria of epiphyseal fusion) would be relatively few in number (Ibid., Table 1).

Thus, the age composition of these Middle Mississippi rabbit harvests could result from either a late fall–winter or a spring season of exploitation. It is difficult to select between these two projected seasons of exploitation.

The swamp rabbit would also have been vulnerable to predation by Middle Mississippi hunters during the high water periods of late winter–spring. During these spring flood periods, swamp rabbits would have been forced to seek the limited areas of high ground (Lowe, 1958:117, 123; Toll et al., 1960:409; Martinson et al., 1961:279). The spring flood stage may have restricted their movements for as long as two months, and occasional high water levels in December would also have restricted their movements, making it much easier to locate and capture them.

COMMON SNAPPING TURTLE (*Chelydra serpentina*)

ALLIGATOR SNAPPING TURTLE (*Macroclemys temmincki*)

Two species of turtles belonging to the family *Chelydridae* occur in the Mississippi valley area today: the common snapping turtle, and the alligator snapping turtle. While the common snapping turtle is a common species in archaeological sites in eastern North America, the alligator snapper has been reported from only a few sites, and only two of the sites being considered in the present study. This low representation in prehistoric samples corresponds to its present rarity. Although many other species of turtles, including the ubiquitous box turtle, are represented at the sites being considered, these two species are the only reptiles large enough to contribute any significant amount to the diet of the Middle Mississippi groups in question. The alligator snapper is the larger of the two species, sometimes attaining a weight of over 200 pounds although the average weight is much lower, while the common snapper has an average weight of sixteen pounds, and rarely exceeds thirty pounds.

Because information concerning these two species is extremely limited, the following discussion will be both brief and general in nature.

Both species share a number of similar traits, including physical appearance, habits, and habit preference. Snapping turtles occur in a wide variety of aquatic habitat situations, including streams, larger rivers, lakes, ponds, swamps, and seasonally flooded areas. Both are aquatic species, rarely sunning themselves, and leaving the water only to lay eggs or escape drying ponds. A preference for muddy water has been mentioned by a number of authors, but snapping turtles also occur in clear water situations (Anderson, 1965).

Both common and alligator snapping turtles are bottom-dwelling species that swim infrequently, spending most of the time lying in wait for unwary fish on muddy stream or lake bottoms, where they are effectively camouflaged.

Lagler's study of turtle food preferences in Michigan showed that common snapping turtles were omnivorous. Plants were the principal food (36.2 percent), with fish accounting for 34.2 percent, carrion 19.6 percent, invetebrates 7.8 percent and miscellaneous vertebrates 2.2 percent (1943) of their diet. The diet of the alligator snapper appears to be generally similar to that of the common snapping turtle (Anderson, 1965:10).

The mating season for common snapping turtles in Missouri extends from April through May. Egg laying occurs during the month of June for common snappers, and late June or July for alligator snappers. Twenty to thirty eggs are deposited in a dry land nest that may be quite distant from water (Smith, 1961). Hatching takes place during August and September (Anderson, 1965), and hatchlings make their way back to water areas at this time.

Snapping turtles hibernate during the winter months in submerged mud and in muskrat tunnels. The exact dates of hibernation are not known, however. Large numbers of snapping turtles are often found hibernating together, and are harvested by modern turtle hunters during this winter period of inactivity.

Unfortunately, information concerning home ranges, density, and population dynamics was not available for these two species, and as a result, potential annual productivity values cannot be estimated.

There would seem to be three periods of time during the year that prehistoric human populations could have collected snapping turtles with a minimum of effort.

1) June egg laying season—female snapping turtles could have been easily collected as they moved onto dry land to lay eggs;
2) summer dry season—snapping turtles could have been collected as they moved out of ponds and temporary flooded areas that were gradually drying out;
3) winter period of hibernation—since snapping turtles often hibernate in groups, they could have been harvested in large numbers during this period of winter inactivity, if they could have been located.

The first two of these periods of increased vulnerability are a result of the turtles becoming more susceptible to predation as they move on to dry land, while in the third period greatly increased snapping turtle density made hunting more productive.

It is impossible to test any of these hypotheses about seasonality of exploitation at the present time, but archaeological evidence could indicate which of these possibilities was the most probable, when further data become available.

It is entirely possible, of course, that snapping turtles, and other species of aquatic turtles, were never deliberately hunted, but rather were collected along with fish during the continual summer harvest from ever-diminishing shallow backwater lake areas.

It was hoped that sectioning of long bones of snapping turtles, and other species of turtles, would allow aging of individuals and provide the age composition of turtle harvests. The annular rings in turtle long bones reported by Mattox (1935) were unfortunately not observed in the long bones that were sectioned in the present study.

ABORIGINAL DOG (*Canis familiaris*)

Of all the animal species eaten by the prehistoric human populations of North America, the domestic dog (*Canis familiaris*) has been the subject of perhaps the earliest (Cope, 1893) and certainly the most detailed analysis and interpretation (Allen, 1920; Haag, 1948; Potter and Baby, 1964; Lawrence, 1967, 1968; Colton, 1970; McMillian, 1970; Guilday, 1971; Parmalee, et al., 1972). This continuing scholarly consideration of *Canis familiaris* is not, however, a result of the importance of this species as a source of sustenance for prehistoric groups, but rather has occurred largely because of interest both in determining the dog's first occurrence in different geographical areas in North America, and in defining the subsequent development of temporal and geographical varieties. W. G. Haag's osteometric analysis of aboriginal dogs (1948), which included measurements of a sample of *Canis familiaris* remains from nine Mississippi period sites, is the only published study which considers Middle Mississippi dogs. Not surprisingly, the results obtained from the osteometric analysis of the dog elements recovered from the Banks, Chucalissa, Lilbourn, and Powers Phase sites are similar to the results obtained by Haag. The measurements of those cranial, dental, and postcranial elements of *Canis familiaris* recovered from the sites being studied which were complete enough to be measured are presented in Tables 25, 26, and 27. The measurements follow Haag (1948). The ranges and mean values obtained by Haag for his Mississippi sample are presented at the bottom of the tables for comparison.

With the exception of measurement 25 (Alveolus I_1-M_3) the standard deviation (SD) values obtained for each measurement are smaller in the present sample. That the present sample displays less variation than Haag's is, no doubt, because it was drawn from a much smaller geographical area, with most of the measurements coming from Banks and Chucalissa specimens. These low standard deviation values, however, are also indicative of a quite homogeneous population, considering the "domestic" status of the dog. A number of data points for measurements 1,8,23,25,27,28,29,30, and 32 fall outside of the range observed by Haag for his Mississippi sample. They all fall within his range values, however, for the pooled Woodland-Mississippian group (1948:226). The only statistically valid differences observed between the present sample and the results obtained by Haag occur in the dental (mandibular) measurements (numbers 25-32). The means and ranges obtained indicate slightly shorter mandibles in the present sample. While few in number, the maxillary measurements (19-23) also suggest that the presently studied population had slightly shorter snouts than those studied by Haag. Even though a few other cranial and postcranial elements measured in the present study seem to differ from Haag's results, the small samples do not allow any further comparison or discussion.

The largest sample of dog remains was obtained from the Banks site. The sample of 95 bones fragments, representing a minimum of eighteen individuals, was recovered almost entirely from refuse midden areas, with few elements being recovered from either excavated house patterns or from human burials. It is doubtful if any of the dog remains represented intentional burials, and no articulated skeletons were found. Although butchering marks were not observed, the disarticulated nature of the skeletal elements, their occurrence in refuse areas, and the low occurrence of complete long bone elements strongly suggests that they were eaten. Of the eighteen individuals represented, five were juveniles.

A total of 212 skeletal elements representing a minimum of eight individuals were recovered from the Chucalissa site. Two articulated dog skeletons were recovered from the main village area north of Mound A, and,

TABLE 25

DENTAL MEASUREMENTS OF MIDDLE MISSISSIPPI DOGS FROM 6 SITES, COMPARED WITH HAAG'S MEASUREMENTS[1]

SITE	CATALOG NUMBER	ALVEOLUS I^1-M^2 (19)	ALVEOLUS C-M^2 (20)	ALVEOLUS P^1-M^2 (21)	ALVEOLUS P^2-M^2 (22)	ALVEOLUS M^1-M^2 (23)	LENGTH CARNASSAL (24)	ALVEOLUS I_1-M_3 (25)	ALVEOLUS C-M_3 (26)	ALVEOLUS P_1-M_3 (27)	ALVEOLUS P_2-M_3 (28)	ALVEOLUS P_3-M_3 (29)	ALVEOLUS P_4-M_3 (30)	ALVEOLUS M_1-M_3 (31)	LENGTH CARNASSIAL (32)
Banks	1	84.5	68.5	57.0	49.5	18.0	17.2								
Banks	2			61.9	51.0	18.2	17.0								
Banks	3	79.0	66.6	55.5	48.6	17.2	16.5								
Banks	4					16.5	15.0								
Banks	5			58.5	52.0		18.4								
Banks	6					17.0	17.9								
Banks	7					17.5	16.9								
Banks	8						16.5								
Banks	9														19.5
Banks	10							91.8	86.4	71.0	66.2	50.2	41.2	31.0	20.2
Banks	11							85.5	80.0	66.0	60.9	56.0	45.5	34.6	20.5
Banks	12												43.6	33.3	20.7
Banks	13							82.0	81.2	69.1	64.0		44.0	32.8	19.8
Banks	14									65.0	58.9	49.5	39.3	29.5	19.0
Banks	15							78.0	79.3	61.7	56.8	47.8	38.9	29.0	18.0

1. Description of measurements can be obtaind from Haag, 1948; measurements are in mm.

		19	20	21	22	23	24	25	26	27	28	29	30	31	32
Banks	16									61.0	56.6	48.0	39.0	30.3	18.5
Banks	17									67.0					
Banks	18													32.9	20.0
Banks	19							93.9		68.3	64.0	54.5	44.0	33.9	
Banks	20							88.0		67.9	63.8	49.0	39.3	32.9	19.6
Banks	21							78.6		62.0				31.7	18.0
Banks	22									62.5	57.8	49.2	39.2	31.7	18.2
Banks	23							78.9		60.8	56.6	49.6	40.0	31.3	18.3
Banks	24									59.9	56.5	48.9	39.6	30.0	18.2
Banks	25							84.4		63.7					
Banks	26							81.0		62.5			41.3	31.9	18.9
Banks	27									64.5	56.0	46.8	39.0	32.5	18.3
Banks	28									59.5	60.5	52.0	41.5	32.0	20.2
Banks	29											54.3	43.2	31.5	20.2
Banks	30							88.6	83.5						
Banks	31									69.5	59.0	50.5	41.3	31.5	20.1
Banks	32									59.4					19.0
Mean								84.6	82.8	64.2	59.8	50.4	41.1	32.3	19.2
Variance								5.2		3.8	3.3	2.3	4.4	1.6	1.1
Chuc.	1493						17.8								
Chuc.	1129						16.5								
Chuc.	778						16.2								
Chuc.	765							80.5	75.5	64.0	59.5	50.0	40.8	31.2	18.2
Chuc.	1811							80.0	74.5	64.2	60.0	52.0	42.0	32.5	20.0
Chuc.	907									65.0	61.0	51.0	41.0	30.5	18.5
Chuc.	946										61.2	51.0	40.9	32.0	20.0
Chuc.	795														20.0
Snod.	45						17.1								

TABLE 25 (Continued)

		19	20	21	22	23	24	25	26	27	28	29	30	31	32
Snod.	84													29.9	19.5
P.F.	Surf												43.8	32.7	19.7
Turn.	44									66.0	60.0	50.0	41.2	31.3	19.4
Lilb.	681				48.5	16.2	18.0								
Sample Size		2	2	4	5	7	13	13	7	23	19	19	23	26	27
Range	low	79.0	66.6	57.0	48.5	16.2	15.0	78.0	74.5	59.4	56.0	46.8	38.9	29.0	18.0
	high	84.5	68.5	61.9	52.0	18.2	18.4	93.9	86.4	71.0	66.2	56.0	45.5	34.6	20.7
Mean				58.2	49.5	17.2	17.0	83.9	80.0	64.1	59.9	50.5	41.2	31.7	19.3
Standard Deviation				2.4	1.4	.8	.9	4.9	3.9	3.4	2.8	2.1	1.9	1.5	1.1
Variance				5.6	2.1	.6	.8	24.1	15.9	12.0	8.3	4.1	3.6	2.3	1.2
Haag's Measurements Range	low	79.0	65.5	54.0	47.8	14.0	15.0	79.0	74.5	61.9	56.7	48.5	39.2	29.0	18.1
	high	87.0	76.0	63.0	56.4	17.9	18.5	94.0	88.2	74.7	71.5	61.0	48.8	37.0	22.2
Standard Deviation		2.9	3.3	2.8	2.8	1.0	1.1	4.6	4.4	4.0	3.8	3.1	2.5	1.9	1.1
Mean		83.9	70.4	58.0	52.2	16.2	17.2	87.0	81.4	67.6	63.8	54.1	43.5	32.6	19.8

TABLE 26

POSTCRANIAL MEASUREMENTS OF MIDDLE MISSISSIPPI DOGS.

		MEASUREMENTS						
SITE	CATALOG NO.	35 HUMERUS LENGTH	36 HEAD DIAMETER – HUMERUS	37 TRANSVERSE DIAMETER – HUMERUS	38 LENGTH RADIUS	39 LENGTH ULNA	40 ULNA NOTCH LENGTH	42 TIBIA LENGTH
Chucalissa	61	122.0	33.0	24.2				
Chucalissa	63	122.3	33.0	24.0				
Chucalissa	42				122.6			
Chucalissa	2342					148.2	126.3	
Chucalissa	1569	130.0						
Chucalissa Mound								131.2
Banks	33				120.4			
Banks	34				126.3			
Banks	35				129.5			
Haag Measurements Range		115.0–147.0	31.7–39.9	24.0–31.5	120.0–147.0			125.0–156.0
Mean		129.6	35.4	26.8	133.0	154.0	132.0	139.0

TABLE 27

CRANIAL MEASUREMENTS OF MIDDLE MISSISSIPPI DOGS (DATA AVAILABLE FROM BANKS SITE ONLY).

BANKS SITE CATALOG NUMBERS	1 OCCIPITAL LENGTH	2 BASAL LENGTH	3 CONDYLO-BASAL LENGTH	4 PALATAL LENGTH	5 WIDTH AT M^1	6 WIDTH AT CANINES	7 WIDTH AT MASTOIDS	8 WIDTH AT OCCIPITAL CONDOYLES	16 LEAST CRANIAL WIDTH	17 MAXIMUM CRANIAL WIDTH
1	172.9	150.5	160.5	81.0	56.2	34.2	63.6	32.7	36.5	57.3
2					56.0		59.5	33.0	36.5	56.0
3							63.2	35.0		
4								36.8		
5							56.1	31.2		
6							62.2	34.5	34.5	59.4
7							56.2	32.2	35.5	54.5
Mean					56.1		60.1	33.6	35.7	56.8
SD					1.3		3.1	1.7	.9	1.7
Haag Measurements										
Range	158.0	138.0	145.0	77.0	53.0	28.7	54.3	32.0	31.7	52.5
	170.0	153.5	161.8	83.7	60.0	34.5	66.0	39.0	40.0	60.5
Mean	162.7	145.5	153.2	80.3	56.5	32.2	61.4	35.1	34.3	57.0

although not complete, may represent intentional burials. The first of these possible burials, contained an almost complete skeleton (63 fragments) of an individual five to seven months old. The second skeleton consisted of a headless individual with fragments of all four legs, pelvis, and vertebral column present (32 fragments). The 117 remaining skeletal elements recovered from the main village midden area were scattered, non-articulated, and largely fragmentary in nature (five of thirty-five long bone elements were complete). No butchering marks were observed. Except for the single juvenile, all the recovered elements represented mature individuals.

The remaining five sites all yielded very few skeletal elements assignable to *Canis familiaris*. A total of only three fragments, representing a minimum of two individuals, were recovered from the three structures analyzed at the Lilbourn site. Butchering marks were observed on one of these (transverse cuts on the lateral surface of the distal end of a right tibia).

Powers Phase sites yielded a total of only twenty-four skeletal elements, representing a minimum of six individuals (all mature). A series of transverse cuts, observed on the lateral surface of the ascending ramus of a mandible recovered from structure 32 at the Turner site, were the only evidence of butchering on the skeletal elements recovered from Powers Phase sites. No dog remains were recovered from the Gooseneck site.

The tightly flexed, articulated skeleton of a dog was found associated with burial 15 from the Turner site. Unfortunately, osteological measurements were not taken in the field, and most of the fragmentary remains were later lost. The intentional interment of *Canis familiaris*, a common practice during the Archaic period, is less common during the Woodland period, and is exceedingly rare during the Mississippi period. The dog burial associated with burial 15 at the Turner site is one of the few ever recorded for the Mississippi period. Two dog burials were recovered from mound C at the Etowah site (L. H. Larson, personal communication), and one from the Lilbourn site during the 1972 season.

It is significant that out of the great quantities of animal bone recovered from the seven Middle Mississippi sites being considered, evidence was recovered for a minimum of only thirty-four dogs. The three structures at the Lilbourn site, where both preservation and recovery were quite good, produced a minimum of 191 small mammals (twenty-four species represented), of which only two were dogs. The use of dogs as a food source was clearly quite limited, not only at the Lilbourn site, but at Middle Mississippi sites in general. The dietary position of *Canis familiaris* at the Middle Mississippi sites being considered was no doubt quite similar to that described by Guilday (1971:11) for a peripheral Fort Ancient site (Buffalo Village 46-Pu-31). Swanton's description of the limited use of the dog by early historic Indian groups of the southeastern United States:

> The dog was utilized in hunting to a very limited extent. The flesh does not seem to have been a regular article of diet anywhere, but it was consumed at certain feasts of a social or ceremonial character. (1946:251),

was applied by Guilday to the Buffalo Village site, and seems equally applicable here.

The almost total lack of evidence for intentional interment of dogs at Middle Mississippi sites suggests that dogs were not held in much esteem within the villages. Ethnohistorical evidence suggests that the dog played a minor role in hunting activities during the proto-historic period in the southeast. If we accept this minor hunting role as applicable to the Mississippi period, we find an animal that was of little importance either for hunting or as a source of food, and was quite probably held in low estcem. It seems quite possible, then, that the dog in Middle Mississippi villages was less than fully domesticated. The relationship that existed between man and dog might well be considered a symbiotic one rather than a "master-pet" situation. Existing on the margin of the village, where it was protected from predators, and living off the village refuse, the dog population reduced the possibility of disease by effectively removing the supply of offal, and provided a peripheral warning mechanism for the village (see Guilday, 1971:12). Incomplete domestication is indicated by the fact that the dog population was still controlled by natural mechanisms. The size of the dog population was ultimately controlled by their primary source of food: the garbage supply of the village. If this were so, the dog carrying capacity of the village would be determined by the amount of garbage available during the winter months. Mortality would be high for juveniles and for those past the prime of life, producing a mortality curve characteristic of natural populations. Most of the dog population would consist of mature, strong individuals, with few young of the year surviving to maturity, and few individuals living past the prime years. Thus even though the dog population would obtain its food supply from the village, and would be dependent upon the human population for survival, man would not be its master, nor could we consider it truly domesticated.

EASTERN GRAY SQUIRREL (*Sciurus carolensis*)

EASTERN FOX SQUIRREL (*Sciurus niger*)

Two species of sciurids are represented at the Middle Mississippi sites presently being studied, and both will be considered in this section.

The habitat requirements of the eastern fox squirrel and the eastern gray squirrel are approximately the same when only one is present.

If, on the other hand, both species exist in the same preferred mixed hardwood habitat, the distribution of each is significantly reduced (character displacement), with each tending to occur in most abundance in separate and distinctive micro-environmental settings.

The preferred habitat of gray squirrels in such a situation is as follows:

> heavily forested bottomlands and big stands of mature hardwoods with understories of smaller trees and shrubs dense enough for them to travel through the crowns without descending to the ground. (Halls and Stransky, 1971:12)

The gray squirrel is a true "deep forest" species.

The fox squirrel, on the other hand, would be most abundant in upland mixed-hardwood and pine forests and in open bottomland hardwood areas. It prefers mature open groves, often occupies large trees at or near the forest edge, but rarely ranges very far into dense forest situations.

Thus when both species occur in a region, as was the case in the Mississippi valley area during the Mississippi period, and still is today, the fox squirrel should predominate in upland forest situations and along the edge of dense bottomland hardwood forests, while the gray squirrel should be most abundant in the deep bottomland hardwood forest. The distribution of the two species is by no means mutually exclusive, however, as is the case with the cottontail and swamp rabbit, and because of the many similarities between the two species, they will be discussed together.

The diet of these two species consists almost entirely of various plants, but insects and larvae are sometimes taken. Of the seventy-six species of plants used by gray and fox squirrels in Missouri, the six most important ones are hickory, pecan, oak, walnut, elm, and mulberry (Schwartz and Schwartz, 1959). Like most animal species in the Mississippi valley area, gray and fox squirrels shift their feeding habits according to the seasonal availability of various species of plants. During the spring, the buds, seeds, tender stems and flowers of a variety of hardwoods are eaten. Through the summer the fruits of a number of trees, including the mulberry, are important, and by mid-August the emphasis shifts to the yearly mast crop, including unripe walnuts. The mast of oaks, hickories, and walnuts continues to be the dominant source of food for these two species through the fall and winter months (Ibid., 1959:138).

Although the diet of these two species is quite similar, a difference has been observed in their daily feeding habits; gray squirrels have two main periods of daily activity, and fox squirrels three. Gray squirrels feed at sunrise and then again in the late afternoon, while fox squirrels emerge a little later than gray squirrels, feed in the morning, in the middle of the day, and finally in the late afternoon, retiring earlier than gray squirrels.

Gray and fox squirrels construct either internal nests in suitable cavities in older trees, or leaf nests in the forks of trees. Summer leaf nests are constructed in May or June, and a winter nest may be built in September or October if the summer nest has deteriorated.

Except during periods of food shortage, squirrels will rarely move more than a few hundred yards from their nesting tree. The average minimum home range of both gray and fox squirrels is less than three acres (Flyger, 1960; Mosby, 1969; Baumgartner, 1943). Little evidence exists for territoriality in either species.

The density of both fox squirrel and gray squirrel populations fluctuates significantly from year to year, depending largely upon the availability of food (primarily mast) during the winter (see Barkalow et al., 1970). Observed density estimates for the gray squirrel range from a low of twenty-four squirrels per 100 acres (1958 season–Barkalow et al., 1970) to a high of five squirrels/acre (Mosby, 1969), while density values for fox squirrels range from less than fifteen per 100 acres (Baumgartner, 1943:197) to three squirrels/acre (Schwartz and Schwartz, 1959). Part of this variation in density estimates of various squirrel populations is a result of the size of the research area studied; studies done on small tracts of ideal habitat produce higher density values. A combined prehistoric breeding population density value of one squirrel per two acres will be estimated here for both species. This corresponds to average estimates projected for large areas, rather than those for small tracts of prime squirrel habitat. Halls and Stransky (1971) have estimated one fox squirrel per two acres and Baumgartner (1943:197) .8-1.4 per two acres, as the average fall density in a good habitat situation. Similarly, Barkalow et al. (1970) have estimated the average spring density of a gray squirrel population at .98 squirrels per two acres, and the average fall density at 1.06 squirrels per two acres.

Female gray and fox squirrels are sexually receptive for ten to fourteen days during the winter, and for a similar period during the summer. Most gray squirrels in southeast Missouri breed during December, though the season extends into January. The summer estrus period for gray squirrels occurs during the months of May and June. The two breeding periods of fox squirrels in Missouri are usually ten days to two weeks earlier than those of gray squirrels (Schwartz and Schwartz, 1959). After a gestation period of 44 to 45 days, the young of both species are born during late January, February, and March, and during late June, July and August. The average winter litter size of gray squirrels is 2.25 to 3.0; summer litters average slightly higher (Mosby, 1969). Comparable litters have been noted for fox squirrels. Although adult female fox and gray squirrels are sexually receptive twice yearly, they average one litter per year (Mosby, 1969).

In estimating the potential annual meat yield and fall–winter biomass values for squirrels during the Mississippi period, an average edible meat yield per individual value of 1.5 pounds is combined with a mean spring breeding population estimate of 320 squirrels per square mile[1] and an estimated number of young per female of three. The potential annual meat yield for the species is therefore 720 pounds of edible meat per square mile (320 x 1.5 x 1.5). The fall–winter biomass level is projected as 480 pounds of edible meat per square mile (320 x 1.5).

Mosby (1969:70) observed that approximately 43 percent of the young of the year of an unexploited gray squirrel population survived to 0.5 years of age, while Barkalow et al. (1970) estimated that 25 percent of the young of the year (both winter and summer litters) survived until the fall trapping season. The wide variation in these two estimates of juvenile mortality is no doubt a result of the relationship between reproductive parameters and recruitment of juveniles into the breeding population and food conditions, which vary markedly from year to year. Juvenile mortality is quite high during poor mast years. In his nine year study of an unexploited gray squirrel population in Virginia, Mosby (1969) found that the percentage of young of the year in the fall population varied from 23.8 to 52.5, with an average of 35 percent. These modern day juvenile/adult ratios are similar to the age composition of the squirrel harvests at the Middle Mississippi sites.

Exploitation probably occurred mainly in late fall and early winter, when cover was at a minimum, since it would have been much easier during this time of the year to locate the animals themselves, as well as their nests (either the tree cavity or leaf variety). In contrast to many animals, squirrels increase their activity level during the December-January breeding season (Baumgartner, 1943:199), especially the males. Whether the winter breeding season was in fact the period of primary exploitation is unfortunately impossible to determine.

A number of techniques could have been employed by Middle Mississippi populations to harvest squirrels, including snares and traps, as well as climbing up to the tree cavity or leaf nests. The latter of these two nest types could have also been shot at from the ground. Ethnohistorical accounts of squirrel hunting by Indian groups in the southeast United States are unfortunately meager.

The minimum number of gray and fox squirrels represented at each site is shown in Table 28. It is obvious that neither of the species was exploited to any great extent, though both occurred at six out of seven sites.

It is interesting to note that the fox squirrel, an edge and open grove species most abundant in the uplands, outnumbers the gray squirrel 7 to 1 at the Chucalissa site, and a similar situation is suggested in the small samples recovered from the sites adjacent to the western edge of the valley. The ratio

[1] Because the density level, minimum home range, and general habitat requirements of both species are similar, the figure of 320 squirrels per square mile will be employed as the density value of both species combined, without stipulating what percentage of these 320 squirrels per square mile each species represents.

is more evenly balanced, on the other hand, at those sites within the meander belt zone.

It may well be that this seeming variation in exploitation of the two species of squirrels is a function of their relative abundance in the various environmental zones. But the higher representation of the fox squirrel in the prehistoric harvest may also be simply a function of ease of capture. *Sciurus niger* is less cautious, less shy than the gray squirrel, and is more active during the middle of the day, and may have been taken in higher numbers as a result. It is disappointing that there are no osteological indicators of sex in squirrels that could be employed to ascertain the sex ratio of the prehistoric squirrel harvests, since modern studies show that male squirrels are more active and more easily hunted than females.

It is possible to separate adult and juvenile squirrels on the basis of a number of osteological aging criteria, including the presence or absence of epiphyseal cartilage in the humerus, radius, and ulna (Carson, 1961; Kirkpatrick and Barnett, 1957).

Table 29 gives the numbers of adult (nine months and older) and juvenile gray and fox squirrels at each site. The Chucalissa site yielded the

TABLE 28

MINIMUM NUMBER OF INDIVIDUALS OF TWO SPECIES OF SQUIRRELS REPRESENTED AT EACH OF SEVEN MIDDLE MISSISSIPPI SITES.

SITES	*SCIURUS CAROLINENSIS*	*SCIURUS NIGER*
Chucalissa Village	6	48
Chucalissa Temple Mound	2	7
Banks Village Site	20	18
Lilbourn Site–Structure 9	5	10
Lilbourn Site–Structure 12	3	3
Lilbourn Site–Structure 25	9	5
Turner Site	1	3
Snodgrass Site	1	4
Powers Fort	0	0
Gooseneck Site	1	1
Total	48	99

majority of specimens, with only small samples recovered from the Banks, Lilbourn, and Gooseneck sites, and none recovered from the three Powers Phase sites.

Juvenile gray squirrels represented 31 percent of the total prehistoric sample, while 28 percent of the fox squirrel harvest was composed of juveniles. These values are quite close to the average fall juvenile/adult ratio obtained for a modern gray squirrel population by Mosby (1969). If it is assumed that the prehistoric squirrel harvests shown in Tables 28 and 29 represent a true random sample of the squirrel populations at harvesting time,

TABLE 29

ADULT/JUVENILE RATIO OF PREHISTORIC SQUIRREL HARVESTS, BASED ON THE DEGREE OF EPIPHYSEAL CLOSURE IN SELECTED SKELETAL ELEMENTS. (CARSON, 1961; KIRKPATRICK AND BARNETT, 1957)

	HUMERUS		RADIUS		ULNA		TOTAL	
	OPEN	CLOSED	OPEN	CLOSED	OPEN	CLOSED	OPEN	CLOSED
Chucalissa Site	20	53	10	23	2	13	32	89
Banks Site	0	2	0	0	0	1	0	3
Lilbourn Site	4	6	4	4	1	1	9	11
Turner Site	0	0	0	0	0	0	0	0
Snodgrass Site	0	0	0	0	0	0	0	0
Powers Fort	0	0	0	0	0	0	0	0
Gooseneck Site	0	0	0	0	0	2	0	2
Total	24	61	14	27	3	17	41	105
Sciurus niger								
Chucalissa Site	1	4	2	4	0	3	3	11
Banks Site	2	3	1	2	0	1	3	6
Lilbourn Site	1	0	1	0	0	0	2	0
Turner Site	0	0	0	0	0	0	0	0
Snodgrass Site	0	0	0	0	0	0	0	0
Powers Fort	0	0	0	0	0	0	0	0
Gooseneck Site	0	0	0	1	0	0	0	1
Total	4	7	4	7	0	4	8	18
Sciurus carolinensis								

the adult/juvenile ratio of the sample suggests that exploitation was primarily a late fall or winter activity.

BLACK BEAR (*Ursus americanus*)

The black bear is the largest carnivore in the eastern United States. Its original widespread distribution has been greatly reduced by the activities of modern man. The species survives today only at fairly low densities in inaccessible areas of the eastern United States, and as a result, few detailed studies of the species have been done. Because of the lack of hard data concerning *Ursus americanus*, the following description will be rather brief.

The black bear is not a sociable animal. Except during the mating season, which is in June and early July in Missouri (Schwartz and Schwartz, 1959:269), individuals lead a solitary life after weaning. Encounters between adult bears usually elicit antagonistic behavior. While it has not been established if black bears defend strictly defined territories, it is known that female black bears move within a home range approximately ten miles in radius, while the home range of male black bears is somewhat larger, occasionally reaching a radius of fiteen miles (Burt, 1957:58).

Although the black bear is not a true hibernating species, it does go through a period of inactivity from November to April. During this time, a winter den is established in a hollow tree, cave, or some other sheltered spot. The female usually gives birth in late January or early February. The cubs, which weigh less than a pound at birth, gain weight rapidly through the summer and fall, and usually weigh over fifty pounds by the end of the year (Gerstell, 1939:5). By the time they are weaned in August, juvenile black bears are self-sufficient (Erickson, 1959) and quickly adapt to a solitary life. The "family," consisting of a female and her unweaned cubs, is the largest group formed during the year. As black bears increase in age, variation in weight according to sex becomes more pronounced (Harlow, 1961:488).

Black bears are omnivorous in their food habits, consuming a wide variety of grasses, berries, seeds, and nuts, as well as ants, bees, crickets, grasshoppers, fish, frogs, small rodents, fawns, carrion, etc. A study of the fall-winter food habits of the black bear in Florida showed that 93.5 percent of the diet consisted of vegetable matter, and acorns were nearly 50 percent of all foods consumed (Harlow, 1961:490). Like other omnivorous species such as the raccoon and opossum, the black bear is very flexible in its food habits, and tends to take full advantage of any source of food that occurs in abundance.

Because of its extreme flexibility in utilization of a wide variety of plants, animals, and insects, those areas with a corresponding diversity of micro-environmental zones form the best habitat for bears:

> A mixture of flatwoods, swamps, scrub oak ridges, bay heads, and hammock habitats, thoroughly interspersed, makes the best Florida bear range. Bear range consisting of these vegetation types possesses the most varied food conditions in greatest abundance. (Harlow, 1961:491)

This description of ideal bear habitat in Florida could just as well have been applied to the meander belt of the Mississippi River, with its interspersion of a variety of micro-environmental zones. Thus Shelford's statement that the black bear "appears to have been most abundant near large streams" (1963:29) is a function of the diverse nature of the meander belt habitat rather than any selective use of the main channel of large streams by *Ursus americanus*. It is interesting to note that the bend in the Mississippi River just east of the Lilbourn site was known as "Greasy Bend" during the 1800s because of the large amount of bear grease that was processed in New Madrid, Missouri.

Thus while it is obvious that black bears were abundant in the Mississippi valley area during the historical period, and were probably present in significant numbers during the prehistoric period as well, it is quite difficult to reconstruct their niche in any detail. Because of the limited data available on black bears, the parameters of the prehistoric black bear populations in the Mississippi valley can only be sketched in general terms.

The density of prehistoric black bear populations was probably somewhat higher within the meander belt zone than in the other three environmental zones, but in the absence of any detailed population studies, Shelford's density estimate of five bears per ten square miles will be applied to each of the four environmental zones (1963:29). By using this as our estimate of the breeding population, it is possible to estimate the annual potential yield of the black bear population. Since the average litter size of the black bear is 2.2 to 2.4 cubs (Harlow, 1961:488), the potential annual yield would appear to be six individuals per ten square miles (2.5 females x 2.4 young). Since female black bears do not mate while they have cubs, however, they have litters only every other year. This lowers the potential annual harvest to three bears per ten square miles. Theoretically, the prehistoric black bear population could have sustained such an annual harvest on a continual basis with no effect on the breeding population. This is based on the assumption that the number of females in the breeding population remained stable. Since females do not bear young until their third year, the death of a mature female would have significantly reduced the potential annual yield of population.

Based upon limited present day data, the seasonal feeding habits of the black bear would have included exploitation of a variety of plants and animals during the spring and summer months, with the fish populations trapped in shallow water pools being heavily exploited during the middle and late summer. The fall acorn crop would have provided an important food source prior to the beginning of the period of winter inactivity.

This period of winter inactivity, lasting from November to April, would seem to have been the most logical time for Indian populations, both historic and prehistoric, to exploit black bears. Although they most likely did not remain inactive throughout the winter in our area of interest, they still would have been denned up and inactive for much of this period. They could be more easily located, approached, and killed during these periods of inactivity. It is also during this time of the year that bears reach their highest seasonal weight, with much of the increase coming from a thick layer of fat—much prized by historical Indian groups and early settlers.

In his exhaustive study of bear ceremonialism in the northern hemisphere, A. Irving Hallowell notes that it was indeed during this time of the year that the bear was customarily hunted by historic Indian groups:

> Bear hunters in both the New World and the Old show a common tendency toward the adjustment of their hunting practices to the hibernatory habit of the animal. The favorite time to hunt the beast is toward the end of the winter, or in the early spring . . . Sometimes the animal is tracked the previous fall, and its refuge marked, as bears do not usually den until after the first fall of snow. Or the hunters may know the places where the bears of their habitat take refuge year after year. The animal is thus rudely disturbed in its winter sleep before it has a chance to emerge. (1926:33)

In a more specific reference to the southeast United States, Hallowell quotes a letter from Swanton:

> They usually hunted the bear before he came forth from his winter quarters in a hollow tree or cave. In the former case, one hunter threw or dropped fire into the hollow and his companions killed the animal after it had been driven forth. In the latter case, some men would go into the cave bearing a torch. (Ibid.:42)

It is also interesting to note that many eastern woodland Indian groups followed established procedures concerning both the eating of the bear and the disposal of the remains (Ibid.:135-148). The skull was often preserved, usually by placing it upon the branch of a tree in the woods or on a pole. The other parts of the skeleton were usually disposed of in accordance with this taboo:

> Should a dog gnaw or even touch them, the "spirit" or "owner" of the animals will be offended and misfortune or poor luck in hunting will result. (Ibid.:136)

This taboo against allowing dogs to gain access to the skeletal elements of bears is especially interesting in terms of the lack of postcranial skeletal elements of *Ursus americanus* recovered from archaeological sites in the eastern United States. Paul W. Parmalee has suggested numerous times that bear ceremonialism may have existed among prehistoric Indian groups in the eastern United States (Parmalee, 1959*b*, Parmalee et al., 1972). The absence of postcranial skeletal elements of the black bear may indicate that the remains were discarded in places where they could not be found by dogs (or archaeologists).

Skeletal elements of the black bear were recovered from only three of the seven sites being presently considered. Twelve postcranial elements and one maxilla fragment were recovered from the Chucalissa site, while two postcranial elements (one showing evidence of butchering) were recovered from the Banks site, and a maxilla fragment from the Turner site. None of the skeletal elements showed signs of being worked, and no reliable data concerning the age of the animals or the season of death could be obtained. This low representation of the black bear corresponds with the general archaeological situation in the eastern United States, although noteworthy exceptions do occur (Guilday, 1971). Interestingly enough, earlier excavations at the Chucalissa site (see Appendix A) resulted in the recovery of 383 skeletal elements of *Ursus americanus*. It is possible that bear bones were disposed of in a specific location, which was protected from the village dogs, but data concerning the exact location and degree of concentration of these 383 elements is not available.

EASTERN ELK (WAPITI) (*Cervus canadensis canadensis*)

Six forms of american elk, or wapiti, have been defined (Hall and Kelson, 1959). The eastern subspecies, which originally ranged over much of the north central and northeast portion of the United States, was gradually driven to extinction during the expansion of the white man across the eastern United States.

Because the eastern elk is extinct today, it is not possible to reconstruct or even to discuss its prehistoric niche within the Mississippi valley area in any detailed manner.

The pre-Columbian range of the eastern elk, as estimated by Murie (1951) and adapted by Hall and Kelson (1959) probably did not include the lower alluvial valley of the Mississippi River. The following discussion will therefore be quite short, and will be limited to a consideration of its prehistoric distribution, and its relative abundance in archaeological sites within the Mississippi valley.

The sites being presently considered are located on the very edge of the southern boundary of the elk's estimated distribution, as based upon mention of its occurrence in travelers' accounts. The southern extent of its range in the Mississippi valley area derives from three sources: (1) Featherstonhaugh (1835) reported herds of buffalo and elk still roaming in the northeast Arkansas-southeast Missouri area east of the Black River; (2) Old Timer (1898) reported elk as abundant near New Madrid as late as 1859; (3) Rhoads (1897:180) describes elk roaming through the glades and cane breaks of the Mississippi bottoms near Reelfoot Lake in 1849.

While it is obvious that this southern boundary of the distribution of the eastern elk is rather arbitrary, being based solely upon second-hand evidence, it does indicate that the range of the eastern elk did not extend into the lower alluvial valley to any great extent.

Early accounts of the eastern elk in more southerly areas do exist, of course, but they usually refer to higher altitude situations. This restriction to higher altitudes in more southerly areas suggests that while the eastern elk tolerated a variety of habitat situations (judging from its estimated original distribution), its southern expansion was limited by climatic factors. It is generally considered a more northern (Boreal and Transition Zone) species, and southern habitats were evidently not favorable (Murie, 1951:57).

Elk are represented in very low numbers in some Middle Mississippi sites, such as the Cahokia site (eleven skeletal elements), the Hiawassee Island site (fifteen skeletal elements), and the Angell and Kincaid sites, but none of these sites are located within the lower alluvial valley of the Mississippi River. Very few sites within the lower alluvial valley have yielded skeletal elements assigned to this species, and only two skeletal elements identified as elk were recovered from the sites being presently considered. An elk humerus fragment was recovered from the Chucalissa site, and a maxilla fragment from the Snodgrass site.

It is fairly clear that this low representation of elk at sites in the lower Mississippi valley reflects a lack of abundance of the species rather than selective hunting by Middle Mississippi groups, and that the elk was not, in fact, an integral member of the Mississippi valley floodplain biotic community.

Because of the large size of elk, however, the occurrence of a single skeletal element at each of two sites represents a large enough projected meat value to warrant the present discussion. The elk, however, was clearly a species that was exploited very infrequently by any Middle Mississippi group, and should not be considered as an important, reliable source of meat during the Mississippi period.

This almost complete lack of representation of elk at Middle Mississippi sites located within the lower alluvial valley of the Mississippi River contrasts markedly with their representation at Fort Ancient sites that are located farther north, well within the geographic distribution of the eastern elk (Griffin, 1943; Guilday, 1971).

III

PATTERNS OF EXPLOITATION

SEASONAL EXPLOITATION OF ANIMAL POPULATIONS BY MIDDLE MISSISSIPPIAN GROUPS: THE YEARLY CYCLE

THE Middle Mississippi populations under study exploited a wide variety of animal species during the yearly cycle. Not all of the species of animals harvested were of equal importance, however, in the diet of these prehistoric human populations. As was shown at the beginning of Section II, thirteen species/species groups accounted for 92 to 99 percent of the total meat yield represented at each of the seven sites being considered. Each of these thirteen species/species groups was considered in some detail in Section II, and the season of the year during which each was harvested was estimated by combining information concerning the seasonal habits of the prey species with archaeological and ethnohistorical data. The strength of the data concerning seasonality of exploitation varies from species to species, with projected seasons of exploitation for some species being little more than untested hypotheses, while for other species the data allows the season of exploitation to be estimated with a high degree of confidence.

While we must keep in mind that an equal confidence level can not be applied to the estimated season of exploitation of each species, the information concerning seasonality of exploitation will now be summarized, and the yearly cycle of exploitation of animal populations described.

These thirteen species/species groups that were primarily exploited can be logically separated into three groups in terms of season of exploitation, and taxonomic considerations:

(1) fish and turtles,
(2) migratory waterfowl, and
(3) terrestrial species.

It was concluded in Section II that fish were quite probably harvested during two periods of the yearly cycle: the spring spawning run, and the dry summer months when the waters of temporary pools gradually receded. Fish were harvested from backwater areas rather than from main stream or river channels during both periods of exploitation. The spring spawning harvest would have occurred at about the same period each year, while the peak of the summer period of exploitation of fish would have varied from year to year and from area to area, depending upon the original depth and the rate of reduction of backwater pools. During both projected periods of exploitation there were high densities of fish in small areas, under conditions that allowed abundant harvests with a minimum of preparation or equipment.

Species of aquatic turtles, especially snapping turtles, were probably harvested along with the numerous species of fish during the summer period of low water levels.

Fish and aquatic species of turtles were the only major animal species except rabbits that were most likely to be exploited during the summer months.

Migratory waterfowl were available for exploitation during the period from mid-October to mid-April, and were probably exploited throughout that period. Most intensive harvesting of waterfowl no doubt corresponded to the fall and spring peaks in waterfowl population, when migrating flocks significantly swelled the wintering population level of ducks and geese in the oxbow lakes of the central section of the Mississippi valley. Migratory waterfowl, like fish, were apparently exploited most during that period of the year when prey populations occurred in high densities in small geographical areas.

The other eight species of animals being considered were all probably exploited primarily during the winter months, in the period extending from October through February or March.

The projected seasons of primary exploitation for the 11 species/species groups (domestic dog and wapiti excluded) are shown in Figure 10. A number of points should be kept in mind when studying Figure 10: 1) the level of confidence for the projected periods of primary exploitation varies from species to species, depending upon the quality of the available data; 2) the seasonal periods of exploitation charted in Figure 10 do not indicate that individuals of each species were not killed during the rest of the year, but rather that deliberate, concentrated harvesting of the various species took place during the seasons indicated.

The projected yearly cycle of exploitation of animal populations by Middle Mississippi groups can be divided into two basic seasons: a summer season during which various species of fish were the most intensively exploited, with aquatic species of turtles and perhaps rabbits being of secondary importance, and a winter season of exploitation during which a wide variety of terrestrial mammals, migratory waterfowl, beaver and turkey were taken. The white-tailed deer was the most important animal species taken during this winter hunting period.

This rather simple yearly cycle of exploitation of animal populations corresponds closely to the annual economic cycle described for early historic

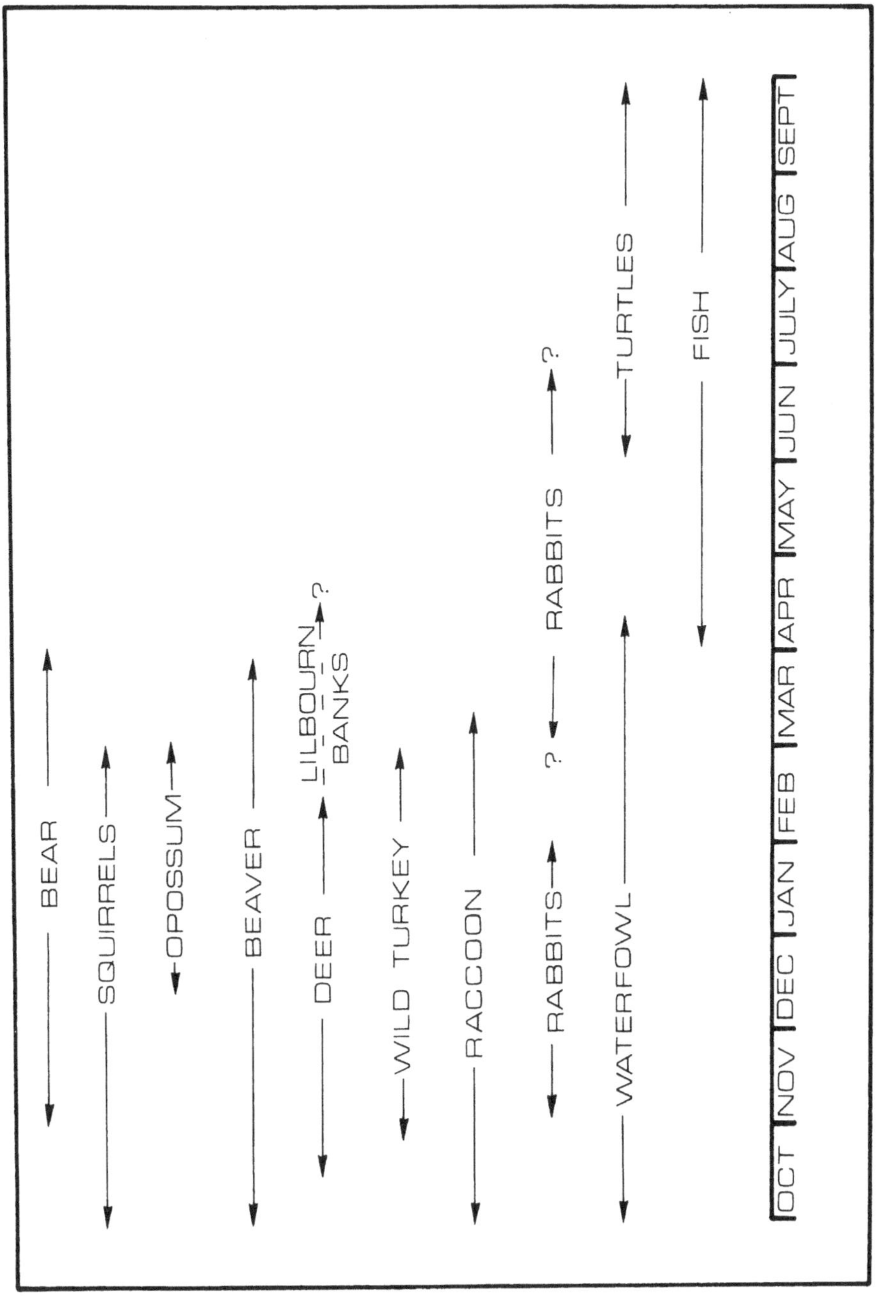

Fig. 10. Projected primary seasons of exploitation of 13 animal species/species groups.

Indian groups in the southeast United States by Swanton (1946:255-265). While giving little specific information concerning the seasonal exploitation of animal populations by early historic Indian groups in the southeast, Swanton considered the annual economic cycle to be generally similar throughout much of the southeast ("we are plainly dealing with one economic province" p. 296) and provides a general outline of this cycle in the following passage:

> Throughout the rest of the Southeast ... corn, beans, pumpkins, and a few other vegetables were raised, and the fields where these grew usually determined the sites of the towns. This was because they required labor and protection and because most of the crop was stored for later consumption. Dried meat was also stored there, but it was never possible to tell where game animals were to be found while the location of the field was definite. This of course meant that the people were generally in or near their villages in summer. They had to return to them in spring to plant, and a certain amount of cultivation was also necessary during the growing season, though the Indians did not worry themselves on this point as much as our farmers. However, it was also necessary to have someone watch the fields during the sprouting season to keep the ubiquitous crow and other birds in check. Between planting and harvest they did, however, often get time for a shorter hunt. After harvest they would remain in town until well toward winter to enjoy the produce of their fields and thus place it beyond the reach of human or animal depredation ... As the harvest was seldom sufficient to last–nor was it expected to last–until another crop came in, the Indians were obligated to seek natural food supplies elsewhere and, since such supplies were not usually concentrated, this meant that the people themselves scattered about in camps where they remained until planting time ... Nevertheless, even the inland tribes were not without opportunities to enjoy a fish diet in summer, for they had fish traps led to by converging lines of rocks, and it was then that they resorted to the poisoning of fish in pools in the shrunken streams, or drugged them for the same purpose. (Ibid.:256-257).

This general description of the annual economic cycle of Indian groups in the southeast includes a number of points that are pertinent to our present discussion:

1) Fish were harvested during the summer months;
2) Most of the hunting occurred during the winter months;
3) A shorter summer hunt often took place.

The first two points correspond to the pattern observed for the Middle Mississippi groups. A short summer hunt (point three) may correspond to the projected summer season of exploitation of rabbits, as well as the small number of summer-killed individuals of other species, including deer and raccoons.

These apparent general similarities in the annual economic cycle of early historic Indian groups in the southeast and the Middle Mississippi groups being studied are not surprising, since the subsistence base of both is generally similar, and the time span separating the two is not great. No attempt will be made, however, to draw any more specific comparisons between the seasonal pattern of animal exploitation of these late prehistoric and early historic Indian groups. This is not possible because of the questionable value of much of the ethnohistorical data relating to specific exploitation patterns during the contact period, and the lack of more detailed information about historic Indian tribes in our area of interest.

VARIATION BETWEEN ZONES IN EXPLOITATION OF ANIMAL POPULATIONS

An east-west transect of the northern division of the lower alluvial valley of the Mississippi River intersects a number of quite different environmental zones, four of which are of interest in the present study. Each of the four environmental zones delineated herein contains a biotic community that differs in important ways from those of the other three zones. This difference between zones in terms of the composition and relative abundance of plant and animal populations has been discussed in some detail in section I, and will be discussed further in site appendixes.

The extent to which this variation in the composition and relative abundance of the biotic communities is paralleled by a variation in the pattern of exploitation of animal populations at the Middle Mississippi sites located in each of the four zones will be considered in the present chapter.

The seasonal nature of exploitation of each of the thirteen species/species groups was projected in the preceding section, and it was found that the annual economic cycle could be separated into a winter and summer period of exploitation of faunal resources.

Those species that were probably exploited primarily during the winter months (deer, raccoon, turkey, beaver, opossum, bear, elk, gray and fox squirrels, and swamp and cottontail rabbits) will be considered first in the present discussion; migratory waterfowl, also primarily winter-killed, will be considered separately.

Let us now take a closer look at the relative representation of each of these eleven winter-killed species at each of the sites, keeping in mind the location of each site within the Mississippi valley. Working from data presented in the site appendixes and in Tables 2, 3, and 4, each species was ranked numerically according to its relative importance at each site, with "importance" measured in terms of both projected meat yield for each species and the minimum number of individuals of each species. The results of this ranking procedure are shown in Figure 11. It should be remembered that the eleven species shown in Figure 11 were ranked in relation to each other, rather than in relation to all the animal species represented at each site. The mean rank value of species based on the criteria of projected meat yield is measured along the horizontal axis, while mean rank values based on the criteria of minimum number of individuals represented at each site is measured along the vertical axis. The box drawn around each mean rank value is two standard deviations in size, and gives an indication of the variance of the mean rank values. The eleven species ranked in Figure 11 can be seen to separate out into three groups.

The three species in the first group (beaver, black bear, and wapiti) all fall above the diagonal (the distance from the two dimensional rank value of each species to the diagonal gives an indication of the disparity between the mean rank value of the animal in terms of projected meat yield, and its representation in terms of minimum number of individuals). Each of these three species has a large yield of edible meat per individual, yet each was exploited in low numbers, possibly because of their low annual productivity. The low representation of the wapiti, or eastern elk in these Middle Mississippi sites is almost certainly a result of its extremely low prehistoric density within the central section of the Mississippi valley. The sites in question fall right on

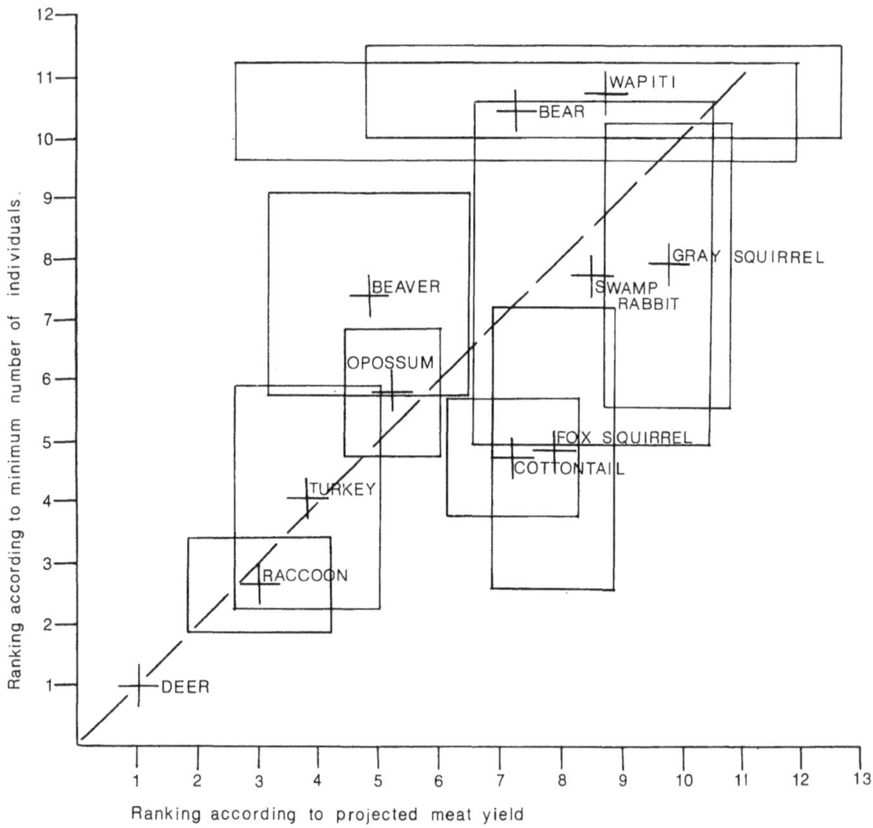

Fig. 11. The rank value and variance of 11 winter-killed animal species.

the edge of the estimated southern boundary of its original range (Murie, 1951: Figure 6).

The four species in the second group (cottontail and swamp rabbit, and gray and fox squirrel) all fall below the diagonal, indicating that although they rank relatively high in terms of minimum number of individuals, they were not of primary importance in the diet of these Middle Mississippi groups, in part because they were small (low meat yield per individual), and because they did not concentrate in high densities within small geographical areas (see below).

The four species that make up the third group (deer, raccoon, turkey, and opossum) all fall close to the diagonal, and all have relatively high mean rank values according to both criteria of importance. The deer, raccoon, and turkey, in that order, have the highest mean rank values along both axes, and would seem to have been the terrestrial animal species of primary importance in the exploitation strategy of these Middle Mississippi groups. The white-tailed deer ranked first at every site according to both criteria of importance, while the raccoon ranked lower than third only three times, and the turkey ranked lower than fifth only once. Thus, even though the Middle Mississippi sites being considered are situated in quite different environmental zones, the animal species that were of primary importance during the winter season of exploitation were the same from zone to zone (excluding migratory waterfowl for the moment). The white-tailed deer was by far the most important winter-killed species, and accounted for a high percentage of the total winter protein yield at every site. While the raccoon and the turkey were much less important than deer in terms of total winter protein yield, they were consistently represented in significant quantities.

These three species, along with the opossum, formed the basic framework of the winter period of exploitation of animal populations by the Middle Mississippi groups being studied. This basic reliance upon deer, raccoon, turkey, and opossum was augmented by occasional killing of large species such as the beaver and black bear, and killing of smaller species such as squirrels and rabbits. The beaver and black bear were not depended upon for a consistent annual harvest, however, for reasons that will be discussed in the next section (p. 137).

The single variation in the relative importance of these eleven terrestrial species from zone to zone was within the second group of species (squirrels and rabbits). While rabbits and squirrels are represented at consistently low levels throughout the valley, there is an interzone variation in the utilization of swamp vs. cottontail rabbits, and gray vs. fox squirrels. At those sites located within the meander belt zone the swamp rabbit outnumbers the cottontail rabbit, and the gray squirrel is as common as the fox squirrel. Outside of the meander belt, the swamp rabbit/cottontail rabbit and gray squirrel/fox squirrel ratios strongly favor the latter species. This inter-zone variation is largely a function of the greater abundance of the swamp rabbit and gray squirrel within the river bottom hardwood forest of the meander belt zone.

Unlike most of the winter-killed species just discussed, migratory waterfowl were clearly not used uniformly throughout the Mississippi valley area. The Banks site and the Lilbourn site have much higher species counts, minimum numbers of individuals represented, and poundage estimates than the sites situated outside the meander belt zone. Migratory waterfowl represents 14.6 to 29.9 percent of the non-deer meat at the two meander belt sites, while accounting for only 0.6 percent (Snodgrass) to 2.4 percent (Chucalissa) of the non-deer meat at the other sites.

This inter-site variation in exploitation of waterfowl is partly because of poor preservation at the Powers Phase sites, but certainly also reflects the excellent accessibility of the Banks and Lilbourn sites to the migrating duck populations. As the migrating waterfowl populations move south into the central section of the flyway in the fall, they land on the numerous oxbow lakes and backwater areas of the meander belt to feed, rest, or stay the winter. Both the Banks site, which was situated directly adjacent to a large, permanently flooded, oxbow lake, and the Lilbourn site, which was quite close to a number of oxbow lakes, were within this zone of unparalleled waterfowl habitat. It is not surprising, then, that more types of waterfowl, in greater numbers, occur at these two sites, since waterfowl populations would have occurred in great densities within the meander belt zone during the winter months, and could have been exploited on a consistent basis.

The Chucalissa site, on the other hand, had fewer species represented, and only three strongly migratory species occurred in the sample. This suggests that the location of the Chucalissa site on the eastern bluffs of the Mississippi River did not allow easy access to oxbow lakes in the Mississippi valley. Thus, there is a relatively high representation of species that would be expected to occur along the upland streams (wood duck and hooded merganser). It is also interesting to note that all of the three migratory species represented at the Chucalissa site will use available land food sources as well as the aquatic vegetation of shallow water areas, and are more apt to occur in areas away from oxbow lakes.

The samples of waterfowl skeletal elements recovered from the sites of the Powers Phase are small partly because of poor preservation, but since the Powers Phase area is located at the extreme western edge of the Mississippi flyway, and waterfowl habitat would have been less impressive, ducks and geese were certainly used to a significantly lesser extent than at the Banks and Lilbourn sites. The high proportion of wood duck, a year-round resident at the Powers Phase sites, supports this hypothesis of low utilization of migratory species in the Powers Phase area.

Thus, while Middle Mississippi groups situated in such optimum locations as the Banks and Lilbourn sites could have intensively and continually exploited waterfowl populations in rather small geographical areas throughout the winter, those groups situated outside the meander belt zone would have been severely restricted in their access to this potential winter food source.

It is evident that this inter-zone variation in exploitation of migratory waterfowl is primarily a reflection of the relative abundance of these species in the meander belt zone.

When we add migratory waterfowl to the list of winter-killed species already discussed, we find that within the meander belt zone migratory waterfowl contributed significantly to the winter diet, ranking second in importance at the Lilbourn site and third at the Banks site, while in the other zones they were comparable to the fox squirrel in importance.

This importance of waterfowl within the meander belt zone affected the basic, valley-wide winter pattern of exploitation of animal populations in the following way: because of the presence of an additional reliable food source, the relative importance of the other species of animals was lower in the meander belt zone. The rankings of other species is consistent from zone to zone, however, when waterfowl are deleted from the model.

The relative utilization of numerous species of fish during the summer period of exploitation apparently differs from zone to zone in a pattern similar to the one just described for migratory waterfowl. Fish account for 20.3 to 66.4 percent of the non-deer meat at the Lilbourn site. While only 9.2 percent of the non-deer meat at the Banks site is made up by fish, its relative dietary importance was judged to be higher by the excavator (see appendix B), but lack of adequate recovery techniques clearly biased the fish bone sample that was recovered. Percentage estimates of the importance of fish at sites outside the meander belt are significantly lower. While it is probable that fish were exploited more intensively at the two meander belt sites, it is not possible to quantitatively measure the variation in exploitation from zone to zone, because of the lack of uniform preservation and recovery of fish bone.

Although it is not possible to accurately determine the difference in importance of fish between zones, I think that it is safe to say that the Middle Mississippi populations located within the meander belt zone were exploiting fish more intensively, since they had greater access to oxbow lake and backwater pond areas.

A basic pattern of exploitation of animal populations has been described for the Middle Mississippi groups being studied. This pattern is fairly uniform throughout the four environmental zones being considered, with two exceptions: (1) the relative exploitation of gray and fox squirrels and swamp and cottontail rabbits varied from zone to zone with the relative abundance of each species, and (2) migratory waterfowl and fish were exploited much more intensively within the meander belt of the Mississippi River.

The second of these variations from the basic pattern is of some importance. Migratory waterfowl and fish represented a significant additional winter and summer source of animal protein respectively, one that was available to a much greater extent within the meander belt of the Mississippi River. The availability of these two resources is an effect of location on the Mississippi River floodplain. The abundant shallow water aquatic vegetation of the oxbow lakes and seasonally flooded areas of this large river attracted and supported large populations of fish during the spring and summer, and wintering flocks of ducks and geese during the colder months. A similar situation would be expected to exist in other major river valleys in the eastern United States, with the abundance of these two food sources being directly related to the size and accessibility of oxbow lakes and seasonally flooded backwater areas.

It has been stated by some archaeologists that most of the larger Middle Mississippi sites were located on former natural levees of major rivers primarily because of the agricultural potential of the soils in such areas, and this is certainly true. The availability of large populations of migratory waterfowl through the winter months, as well as large numbers of fish during the summer, however, was certainly an important factor in supporting such large, permanently occupied villages throughout the year: "No wonder the former levees of the lower Mississippi Valley south of St. Louis, along cutoff lakes, with their fish and bird life, were a favorite place for Mississippian people" (Griffin, 1967:15).

The importance of this greater availability of migratory waterfowl and fish in supporting large, year-round prehistoric settlements should, of course, be seen as a single, but very important, facet of the higher carrying capacity of such meander belt zones.

In the detailed discussion of the environmental setting of the Banks and Lilbourn sites, contained in the site appendixes, it will be pointed out that the location of these sites was significant in that the areas immediately around the sites contained a great diversity of micro-ecological zones within relatively small geographical areas, with a resultant maximization of edge or interface areas between micro-ecological zones. This, and the water resources described above, combined to produce a habitat area that supported a rich variety of animal species in relatively high densities within a small geographical area.

Thus, the higher human population levels in meander belt zones during the Mississippi period are a function of both the abundance of animal populations and the higher quality of agricultural land.

As this Middle Mississippi cultural adaptation, which first developed in the meander belt of the Mississippi River, spread outward, the most significant inroads appeared first, and were most firmly established, in areas that were most similar to the meander belt of the Mississippi River in their ecological diversity and composition, and geographically closest along river routes. Middle Mississippi expansion along the routes of major rivers should not be considered simply a result of ease of transportation but expansion within linear zones most preferred for settlement and exploitation. As the Middle Mississippi cultural adaptation became established in more "marginal" areas such as the Powers Phase area, shifts in the pattern of exploitation of animal populations occurred. I think that such shifts should not be considered significant changes in the pattern of exploitation, but rather shifts in emphasis in the relative exploitation of various animal species to offset the lesser abundance of migratory waterfowl and fish in such areas. This shift in the pattern of exploitation in such marginal areas would quite probably result in more intensive exploitation of winter-killed species other than waterfowl during the colder months, and perhaps a greater utilization of species other than fish during the summer, although there is no archaeological evidence from the Powers Phase area for the latter.

SELECTIVITY OF EXPLOITATION OF THE BIOTIC COMMUNITY BY MIDDLE MISSISSIPPIAN POPULATIONS

The biotic community that existed in the Mississippi valley area during the Mississippi period included a great variety of animal species. Only a relatively small percentage of these potentially available species of animals were selected by the Middle Mississippi groups being considered, and of the species selected, only a few contributed in any significant way to the Middle Mississippi diet. We have studied in some detail niche reconstruction, seasonality of exploitation, possible procurement techniques, relative importance, and variation in utilization from zone to zone for those species/species groups which did.

The basic Middle Mississippi pattern of exploitation, and the observed inter-zone variation, have been adequately defined and discussed, but we have yet to consider why the pattern of exploitation took the form it did. Why were these species/species groups exploited to the relative exclusion of other species? Why were some of the most important species represented in fairly consistent percentages throughout the Mississippi valley?

Let us now consider the first of the three hypotheses that were proposed on page 17 as offering possible explanations of the Middle Mississippi pattern of exploitation of animal species:

H_0: Middle Mississippi populations exploited all animal populations in direct proportion to the potential annual yield of each species (the null hypothesis).

The almost complete absence of certain species with high potential productivity (e.g., mice) in the faunal samples strongly suggests that this hypothesis should be rejected. It will be tested as far as is possible, however, since the results may suggest alternative hypotheses.

A number of problems are involved in testing this null hypothesis. Potential annual yield values are easily determined for many species of land animals, and can be applied with a high degree of confidence. It is quite difficult, however, to produce such potential yield values, density or biomass values for groups such as fish and migratory waterfowl.

If the annual productivity values could be determined for fish and migratory waterfowl, the null hypothesis could be tested in its entirety, with the annual productivity of each species/species group compared with its representation at the sites being considered. Even if a high correlation were found to exist between the productivity values of the thirteen species/species groups and their representation in the faunal samples, however, the null hypothesis could not yet be accepted. The relative productivity of animal species other than those discussed in the present study would still have to be considered before the hypothesis could be provisionally confirmed. It would, of course, not be necessary to move into this second stage of testing if the hypothesis was rejected during the first stage.

While it is impossible to test the null hypothesis in its entirety because of the lack of data for migratory waterfowl and fish, it can be tested for those species for which such productivity estimates are available. Before the null hypothesis is tested in this restricted manner, we shall consider the relative exploitation of species within the fish and migratory waterfowl species groups.

Since it is not possible to project density or productivity values for these two species groups, they cannot be compared to other species/species groups in terms of such criteria of abundance. But the importance of the various species within each of these species groups can be determined. Buffalo fish, for example, composed 40 to 54 percent of the Lilbourn fish sample, while the Canada goose accounted for 23 percent of the waterfowl meat yield at the same site. By comparing such percentage values for the species within these two groups with similar present day percentage estimates, some idea of the extent to which exploitation of species of fish and waterfowl was a function of relative abundance of the species in the biotic community can be obtained.

The Lilbourn site contained the only fish bone sample large enough to allow such a comparison, while the Chucalissa, Banks and Lilbourn sites had sufficiently large migratory waterfowl samples.

The percentage values for the different types of fish represented at the Lilbourn site correspond closely to the percentage values for different fish types represented in the commercial catch on the Mississippi River in 1895 (Carlander, 1954: Figure 16). Buffalo fish made up 40 to 54 percent of the Lilbourn sample, and approximately 45 percent of the 1895 catch, while catfish (21 percent of the Lilbourn sample), were approximately 24 percent of the 1895 catch. Freshwater drum, which made up approximately 11 percent of the 1895 sample, accounted for 17 percent of the Lilbourn sample. On the basis of this interesting correlation between representation of various types of fish in the Lilbourn sample and in the Mississippi River (assuming the 1895 catch is a random sample), we can say that the Lilbourn fish harvest probably represents a non-selective sample of the fish population. Because of small sample size, the correlation between representation of fish types at other sites and their relative abundance in the biotic community cannot be determined.

The situation for the migratory waterfowl group is more difficult to assess. The Canada goose and mallard/black duck, which are 69, 68, and 56 percent of the waterfowl meat yield at the Chucalissa, Banks, and Lilbourn sites respectively, account for a comparable percentage of the waterfowl populations that winter in the central section of the flyway today, suggesting that there is a correlation between the degree of exploitation and relative abundance of various species of ducks and geese. The very low occurrence of species of diving ducks (lesser scaup, bufflehead, etc.), however, may indicate selective exploitation of shallow water and land feeders. Because of the low percentage of diving ducks within waterfowl populations, it is difficult to determine if selective exploitation of dabbling ducks did in fact exist. Such selective exploitation would be very difficult to demonstrate without a large sample, even in a present day situation, and would therefore represent a very small variation from a non-selective pattern of exploitation.

Thus while the limited data available suggests that fish and migratory waterfowl were exploited in a non-selective manner, the quality of the data does not permit more detailed analysis.

Let us now turn to a restricted test of the null hypothesis, based upon the nine terrestrial species listed in Table 30. The first column of Table 30 lists both the projected potential annual yield of each species for a ten square mile area, expressed in pounds of edible meat, and the percentage of the total potential annual yield represented by each species. The corresponding actual values for each species for each site are listed for comparison.

It can be seen in Table 30 that while the white-tailed deer represents only 15.1 percent of the potential annual productivity of edible meat for this group of species, it represents from 84 to 94 percent of the edible meat yield for the listed species at the seven sites. The raccoon and turkey were represented in the faunal samples in percentages approaching their estimated annual productivity, while rabbits, squirrels, and the opossum were not taken in percentages anywhere close to their productivity levels.

The null hypothesis (H_0) can therefore be rejected. There is no overall correlation between the potential annual yield of species and the extent to which they were exploited by Middle Mississippi populations. This is not to say, however, that potential productivity is never relevant to relative exploitation of certain species. Larger species such as the black bear and the beaver, for instance, were exploited infrequently, and the low reproduction rates of these species are certainly an important factor in their low representation in prehistoric samples.

Season of exploitation of these species helps explain the lack of correlation between the potential annual productivity estimates and relative representation of these nine species at the Middle Mississippi sites. Even if a species

TABLE 30

PROJECTED ANNUAL MEAT YIELD, AND PERCENTAGE OF TOTAL ANNUAL MEAT YIELD, OF NINE ANIMAL SPECIES COMPARED WITH THEIR REPRESENTATION AT EACH OF SEVEN MIDDLE MISSISSIPPI SITES[1]

ANIMAL SPECIES	PROJECTED ANNUAL PRODUCTIVITY	CHUCALISSA	BANKS SITE	LILBOURN SITE	TURNER SITE	SNODGRASS SITE	POWERS FORT	GOOSENECK SITE
Deer	14,500	10,192	7,250	2,797	2,948	12,031	515	1,092
	15.1	90	88	88	86	94	84	94
Racoon	3600	296	368	144	184	624	24	8
	3.8	2	4	4	5	4	3	.6
Turkey	4080	178	145	69	26	43	36	36
	4.2	1	2	2	.7	.3	5	3
Opossum	21,420	86	133	35	26	45	17	9
	22.4	.7	2	1	.7	.3	2	.7
Rabbits	44,375	74	78	78	9	25	9	2
	46.3	.6	1	2	.2	.1	1	.1
Squirrels	7200	78	13	45	6	7	5	3
	7.5	.6	.2	1	.1	.05	.8	.2
Black Bear	630	420	210		210			
	0.7	3	3		6			

1. The projected annual yield values given here are slightly different than those given in an earlier publication (Smith, 1974*b*)

has a high birth rate, with resultant high population density levels during the spring and early summer, this is of little significance if a subsequent high juvenile mortality rate substantially reduces the population density prior to a fall-winter hunting season.

If the Middle Mississippi exploitation of fall-winter killed species was non-selective, one would expect those species with the highest fall-winter biomass levels (rather than the highest potential productivity levels) to have the highest projected meat yield values.

Thus a logical alternative hypothesis concerning selectivity of exploitation is the following:

H_1: Animal species primarily exploited during the fall-winter period of the annual cycle were taken in direct proportion to their fall-winter biomass levels.

This hypothesis is similar to the one formulated and tested by Munson et al. (1971:425) for a terminal Middle Woodland village located in west-central Illinois (the Scovill site). The fall-winter biomass values projected in the present study differ from those given by Munson et al. Their biomass values for squirrels and raccoon are two and three times as high as those given herein. These higher density and biomass values are clearly a result of selecting data from a single secondary source. In using general approximations of density values given in Shelford (1963:25, 47), which were in part derived from a study done in a highly modified environmental situation (a park in Cleveland, Ohio) during the 1930s (Williams, 1936), Munson et al. did not take advantage of the wealth of excellent population studies that have been produced in the intervening years.

Although the population density estimates utilized by Munson et al. differed from the ones employed here, and the composition of their species groups was slightly different, their results are fairly similar to ours (Table 31).

Column one in Table 31 lists the estimated winter biomass values for seven winter-killed species, and the percentage of the total estimated biomass values represented by each species. The meat yield values for each species for each site are listed for comparison. The white-tailed deer is 63.8 percent of the estimated fall-winter biomass for this group of species, and consistently accounts for higher percentages of the faunal samples (from 86 to 95 percent). The representation of the raccoon and turkey at the seven sites approaches their biomass values, while the opossum, rabbits and squirrels are significantly underrepresented in the faunal samples. While the black bear occurs infrequently, average percentage values (1.8 percent) correspond to its projected biomass level.

This comparison between the biomass values and relative representation of these seven species at the sites being considered forces us to reject H_1 (since the opossum and squirrels were not exploited up to their estimated biomass percentage levels). There is little overall correlation between estimated biomass levels and the extent to which animal species were exploited by the Middle Mississippi groups being studied.

It is clear from Table 31 that the Middle Mississippi groups being studied were highly selective in their winter exploitation of animal species. A number of important points concerning this pattern of selectivity can be made from Table 31.

TABLE 31

ESTIMATED WINTER BIOMASS LEVELS OF NINE ANIMAL SPECIES (EXPRESSED IN TERMS OF POUNDS OF EDIBLE MEAT AND PERCENTAGE OF TOTAL) COMPARED WITH THEIR REPRESENTATION AT EACH OF SEVEN MIDDLE MISSISSIPPI SITES[1]

ANIMAL SPECIES	ESTIMATED BIOMASS LEVELS 10 SQUARE MILES	CHUCALISSA SITE	BANKS SITE	LILBOURN SITE	TURNER SITE	SNODGRASS SITE	POWERS FORT	GOOSENECK SITE
Deer	36250	10192	7622	2797	2948	12031	515	1092
	63.8	90	88	90	86	94	86	95
Raccoon	3200	296	368	144	184	624	24	8
	5.6	2	4	4	5	4	4	.6
Turkey	1700	178	145	69	26	43	36	36
	3.0	1	2	2	.7	.3	.6	3
Opossum	5270	86	133	35	26	45	17	9
	9.3	.7	2	1	.7	.3	2	.7
Rabbits	4500	74	78	78	9	25	9	2
	7.9	.6	.9	2	.2	.1	1	.1
Squirrels	4800	78	13	45	6	7	5	3
	8.5	.6	.2	1	.1	.04	.8	.2
Black Bear	1050	420	210		210			
	1.8	3	3		6			

1. The fall winter biomass estimates given here differ slightly from those of an earlier publication (Smith, 1974*b*)

Using biomass levels as a reference base, Table 31 shows that:

1) Deer, raccoon, and turkey were selectively exploited to the relative exclusion of other winter-killed species (data for the beaver are not available). Thus their consistent high ranking in the Middle Mississippi faunal samples is not simply a function of either productivity or higher biomass levels, but is a result of more intensive exploitation,

2) The white-tailed deer was exploited much more intensively than the other species being considered. It is the only species that was consistently taken in amounts higher than its projected biomass levels.

3) The raccoon and turkey were exploited at levels approaching their projected biomass levels, and much more intensively than rabbits, squirrels, and the opossum.

4) Although the opossum, rabbits and squirrel were represented at all the sites being considered, and are species that clearly played some role in the winter subsistence pattern of these groups, they were exploited at a very low level relative to their available biomass levels.

A variety of causative factors probably combined to make deer, raccoon and turkey both more susceptible to winter exploitation by Middle Mississippi groups, and more attractive to hunters than other species.

Only four primary causative factors allow us to construct a hypothesis that will adequately explain this selective pattern of winter exploitation. The four inter-related primary factors which influenced the selectivity of exploitation were the following:

1) Biological potential of the species–biological potential should be viewed as a restricting factor that ruled out certain species with low reproductive rates, such as the beaver and black bear. These species were not important in the diet of the groups being studied because they could not sustain even moderate exploitation levels on a consistent basis. Once biological potential reached a certain minimum level, however, it ceased to be an important factor.

2) Amount of edible meat per individual–the size of the prey species was of importance only in relation to factors one and four. Large species were not of potential value if they could not support annual harvesting because of low reproductive rates, while smaller species were potentially important if they occurred in large numbers in small geographical areas during some season of the year (i.e. migratory waterfowl, fish). But if each of two species were distributed fairly equally over the landscape, had sufficiently high biotic potential to support human exploitation on a continual basis, and were equally susceptible to exploitation, the larger of the two species would be more apt to be exploited.

3) Ease of capture–the relative ease with which various species could have been killed by Middle Mississippi hunters is obviously difficult to determine accurately, yet in the detailed discussions of the various species in

Section II, it was evident that the deer, raccoon, and turkey are highly susceptible to certain available techniques of procurement. These techniques will be briefly restated in a moment.

4) Seasonal peaks in density levels–probably the most important factor in determining selectivity of exploitation was seasonal peaks in density levels–high density levels of prey populations in relatively small geographical areas during a specific season of the year. It has already been noted that both fish and migratory waterfowl, which were important food sources, especially within the meander belt zone, occurred in high population densities within relatively small geographical areas. I think that deer, turkeys, and raccoons were selectively exploited during the fall-winter primarily because they, too, could be found in high population densities in small geographical areas.

In the detailed discussion of the white-tailed deer contained in Section II, it was pointed out that deer occur in high densities during the fall-early winter mast season in relatively restricted geographical areas (upland hardwoods and lowland ridge tops), and that because of rut-induced behavioral changes they are more susceptible to the stalking-attraction hunting techniques that were widely employed by early historical Indian groups in the southeast United States. Deer occurred in higher densities and were easier to exploit during this period of the year.

Turkeys, like deer, subsist almost entirely on acorns throughout the fall and part of the winter. This shift to a more localized food resource causes the formation of larger flocks in the late fall, which last until the end of March. These large winter flocks are concentrated in the upland hardwood areas, and represent a high population density level of a potential food source in relatively small geographical areas. Accounts of early historical Indian groups hunting such flocks by flushing them into trees and then killing large numbers of them were given in Section II.

The raccoon, like the deer and turkey, depends upon acorns as a primary fall-winter food source, feeding mainly in upland hardwood areas. Their denning trees, however, are located in relatively small linear bands within 500 feet of streams or lakes, and are quite easy to locate. Significant numbers of raccoons can be harvested in fairly small geographical areas by the simple process of locating dens and extracting raccoons.

Many other species which have high biomass levels, such as rabbits and squirrels, are distributed more evenly over the landscape during the fall and winter, partly because of their small home ranges. This lack of high, localized density levels, and their small size, make these species less desirable food sources.

This exploitation strategy of selectively harvesting animal species that occur in high densities in small geographical areas supports the second hypothesis on page 17.

H_2: Middle Mississippi populations selectively exploited animal populations according to the concept of maximization–they attempted to gain a maximum meat yield with a minimum of effort.

While it is not possible to quantitatively test this hypothesis, I think that it can be provisionally accepted on the basis of the data presented herein concerning the selective nature of Middle Mississippi exploitation of animal populations.

The Middle Mississippi groups being studied selectively exploited a restricted segment of the biotic community. By concentrating on those species that occurred in high densities in small geographical areas (resulting in localized high biomass values), Middle Mississippi groups maximized their annual meat yield in relation to the energy necessary to exploit them.

This exploitation strategy of maximization of return for energy expended, through seasonal exploitation of localized, abundant food resources is not only a fairly common pattern among hunting and gathering people, but is also characteristic of many species of animals.

The Middle Mississippi groups being considered clearly employed a seasonal round in terms of exploitation of animal populations, but because of the occurrence of many micro-environmental zones within small geographical areas, the distance they were required to move to exploit seasonally abundant animal populations was very small. This abundance of micro-environmental zones, along with the presence of agricultural crops such as maize and beans, allowed permanent year-round villages to be established.

It is quite possible that such an exploitation strategy is not unique to the Mississippi period, but was present over a long period of prehistory in major river valleys in the eastern United States. The relative representation of fish, migratory waterfowl, deer, raccoon, and turkey at a Middle Woodland site in the Illinois valley recently analyzed by Parmalee et al. (1972) suggests such an exploitation strategy existed prior to the Mississippi period.

MAN'S ROLE IN THE ECOSYSTEM DURING THE MISSISSIPPI PERIOD

The Middle Mississippi groups under study influenced the surrounding biotic community in innumerable ways. Some of the effects of human interaction with the ecosystem are obvious, and are easily observed in the archaeological record, while other, more subtle, effects have left no trace. The most obvious point of interaction between Middle Mississippi groups and the faunal section of the biotic community is the human exploitation of animal populations. This human predation has already been analyzed in some detail in defining the pattern of exploitation and exploitation strategy and will therefore be only briefly discussed in this section. Little has been said, however, concerning the other, less obvious ways in which these pre-historic Indian groups influenced the faunal section of the biotic community. These topics will be considered in the present chapter within the framework of coaction pairs.

Coaction can be defined as "reciprocal behavior of two individuals of the same or different species; complex coactions involve the interaction of one group or community with another" (Lawrence, 1971:397). Relations between different species can be classified according to the outcome of such reciprocal behavior: coaction can affect an individual's activity in one of three ways—decelerate the given activity (-), leave it unchanged (o), or accelerate it (+).

The Middle Mississippi groups in question formed a coaction pair with each of the other animal species in the biotic community, and each of these coaction pairs can theoretically be placed into one of the following five categories (Lawrence, 1971:598; Clarke, 1954:364):

1) Toleration (oo),
2) Mutualism (++), } Symbiosis
3) Commensalism (+o), } Symbiosis
4) Competition (--), } Antagonism
5) Exploitation (-+). } Antagonism

Toleration—Toleration, or neutrality, encompasses coaction pairs in which neither species gains or loses; neither species is influenced by the other. Such coaction pairs can therefore be considered as not really being relationships at all. The great majority of the coaction pairs formed between Middle Mississippi populations and animal populations within the biotic community certainly fell into this category. By their nature, such non-relationships are difficult, if not impossible, to infer from the archaeological record. In the present discussion, only those coaction pairs that can be classed with some confidence as being either symbiotic or antagonistic will be considered. This is not meant to indicate that other animal species are assumed to have had a neutral relationship with the human population, but rather that there is not enough information available to assess the status of the interrelationship.

Symbiosis—The provision of food is the most frequently received benefit when members of two species form a symbiotic relationship. The association may be transitory or continual, and in some cases the two species influence each other without actual contact. The term "mutualism" (++) has been applied to those coaction pairs in which both species benefit, while "commensalism" (o+) refers to associations in which only one species benefits and neither is harmed.

The aboriginal dog (*Canis familiaris*) is one animal species that may have formed a mutualistic coaction pair with the Middle Mississippi groups being studied. The aboriginal dog populations that existed on the margin of each village benefited from the village refuse, which almost certainly represented the bulk of their diet. The value of such dog populations to the Middle Mississippi villages is, however, impossible to assess. Dogs were rarely eaten, judging from their scarcity in the faunal samples, and were probably rarely utilized for hunting. They could, however, have helped the villages by reducing the occurrence of disease vectors through scavenging village refuse, and by serving as a peripheral warning mechanism. It is impossible to determine if such activities by the dog population actually benefited the villages. Therefore the human-dog interaction pair can be termed symbiotic, but cannot be classed as either mutualistic or commensalistic.

In addition to providing nourishment for aboriginal dogs, village refuse undoubtedly served as a food source for many other scavenging organisms, including numerous rodents and mammals (the raccoon, opossum, eastern wood rat, marsh rice rat, etc.) as well as numerous species of insects and bacteria. Such coaction pairs can be classed as being commensalistic.

In clearing forest areas for their villages and fields, the Middle Mississippi groups significantly altered the environment, setting up commensalistic coaction pairs with many animal species. Removal of the forest canopy encouraged the growth of a whole new group of plant species. The most obvious were the cultigens deliberately planted by the Indian groups (maize, beans, etc.). But in addition to these domesticated species, a variety of wild species of plants would have competed for the newly opened areas. The edges of the forest clearing would have supported low level herbaceous bush and shrub species. Thus these clearings would have supported domesticated cultigens, "weeds," and forest edge species of plants.

This vegetational situation would in turn have created a higher "carrying capacity" than that of the surrounding forest for a number of animal species.

These non-forested areas would have supported higher populations of species of small animals, including the plains pocket gopher (*Geomys bursarius*), the eastern mole (*Scalopus aquaticus*), the marsh rice rat (*Oryzomys palustris*), the hispid cotton rat (*Sigmodon hispidus*), the eastern wood rat (*Neotoma floridana*), and various species of deer mice (*Peromyscus spp.*).

The low level herbaceous plant species along the forest-clearing edges would have provided cover and food for numerous "edge" species of animals, including the white-tailed deer, cottontail rabbit, raccoon, and turkey. These and other herbivorous species would have been supported in higher densities in the vicinity of these clearings than in the surrounding forest because of the increase in plant food resources, and would in turn have attracted predator species such as the gray fox, coyote, wolf, striped skunk, mink, weasel, hawk and owl. The coaction pairs that existed between the prehistoric human populations in question and these animal species contained aspects of commensalism insofar as these species benefited from the alteration of the environment caused by human activity.

It is possible, in fact, that the coaction pairs formed by these prehistoric human populations and the nonhuman predator populations just mentioned included aspects of mutualism. Human alteration of the forest cover increased the abundance of prey populations exploited by these species of nonhuman predators, while the predator populations, in controlling these prey populations, reduced their use of agricultural crops, benefiting the human population. That the coaction pairs formed by some of these animal species and the Indian groups were not restricted to a commensalistic or mutualistic level, but contained strong aspects of antagonism as well, will be seen more clearly in the next few pages.

There is no evidence for the existence of any coaction pairs in which the human population was on the receiving end of a commensalistic relationship.

Antagonism—The general heading of antagonism covers relationships between different species in which one or both are harmed. These antagonistic relations "are not necessarily harmful for the population or for the species as a whole. From the broader viewpoint interspecific antagonism may have beneficial effects through controlling abundance. . ." (Clarke, 1954:381). Antagonism can be separated into two categories: competition (−−), in which both species of a coaction pair are harmed out of a common need for some feature of the environment that exists in short supply, and exploitation (+−), in which one species benefits at the expense of the other.

The Middle Mississippi groups being studied used a variety of plant species, both wild and domesticated. This use of plants meant competition with a wide variety of animal species. Acorns, for instance, were an important food source for over one hundred species in the eastern United States, as well as for humans. The coaction pairs that existed between the human populations and animal species that used the same wild plant species would contain aspects of competition. The level of competition in each coaction pair would vary with the availability of the specific plant species and its importance in the diet of each member of the coaction pair. The domesticated cultigens planted by Middle Mississippi groups most certainly were a food source for a number of species of animals. The coaction pairs existing between the Middle Mississippi villages and the animal species attracted to these domesticated crops would similarly contain aspects of competition.

Thus, by clearing forest areas, these villages benefited a number of animal species, establishing coaction pairs with aspects of commensalism. A number of species, however, also ate the domesticated crops occurring in such clearings. In doing so, these species added aspects of competition to their relationship with the Middle Mississippi villages.

The coaction pairs that existed between the human populations and animal species were therefore complex in nature, containing aspects of both symbiosis and competition. As will be seen shortly, many of these complex coaction pairs also contained aspects of exploitation, as indicated by the occurrence of these species in the faunal samples recovered from these sites.

In addition to the competition for plant food sources that existed between the human populations and numerous animal populations, there was a similar competition for animal food sources between the Indian groups and numerous nonhuman predator populations. The predator species that competed most strongly with the human populations, judging from the primary prey species for each predator, were the wolf (*Canis lupus*), mountain lion (*Felis concolor*), coyote (*Canis latrans*), gray fox (*Urocyon cineroargenteus*), black bear (*Ursus americanus*), and raccoon (*Procyon lotor*). The last two species competed with human populations rarely, except for common utilization of acorns, and fish in backwater pools. The low representation of these or any other predator species (except the raccoon) in the faunal samples recovered indicates that competition between Middle Mississippi groups and these species rarely involved direct aggression.

The level of competition between human and nonhuman predators was probably fairly low. The white-tailed deer was the primary animal food source for Middle Mississippi groups, and for the wolf. Smith (1974*a*) has shown through the study of the age composition of the deer kill for each species that these two predator species were not as competitive in their exploitation of deer populations as one might think.

The age composition of the Middle Mississippi harvests of a number of other prey species, including raccoon, opossum, squirrels, and rabbits, suggests a somewhat similar situation, with nonhuman predator species taking primarily young of the year and older individuals, while human predation concentrated on the middle portion of the age range.

This difference in the age composition of human and nonhuman predation of a number of species is of course largely a result of the seasonal nature of human exploitation, and the great difference between human and nonhuman procurement techniques. Because the Middle Mississippi groups exploited many species primarily during the fall and winter, they competed with nonhuman predators for only half of the year. During the spring and summer period of high juvenile mortality for prey species, mortality due to predation was quite likely almost entirely a result of nonhuman predation (except for fish, turtles, and perhaps rabbits). During the winter period of exploitation, however, competition for prey species would have existed between human and nonhuman predator populations. While it is difficult to accurately assess the level of competition during the fall-winter hunting season, the procurement techniques probably used by the human populations were relatively nonselective, while nonhuman predation concentrated on the weaker and older individuals.

Exploitation—Exploitation occurs when the members of one species benefit by using another species. The most common manifestation of interspecific exploitation is the use of another species as a source of food.

Indians at the seven Middle Mississippi sites being considered exploited a wide variety of animal species, mainly for food. Certain species such as passerine and predatory birds, and box turtles, were obtained, however, for non-dietary reasons (feathers and claws for personal decoration, shells for bowls, etc.), and species such as the white-tailed deer yielded more than just meat (hides, bone tools and gaming devices, etc.). The coaction pairs formed between these Middle Mississippi groups and most of the animal species represented in the faunal samples recovered from each site contained aspects of exploitation (the occurrence of remains of species of small rodents, such as *Geomys bursarius* or *Sigmodon hispidus*, represents natural death assemblages, however, rather than human exploitation).

Many of the coaction pairs formed between the human populations and the species represented in the faunal samples cannot be classed simply as predatory relationships, however, since aspects of competition and commensalism were oftentimes also included. The interrelationships that existed between Middle Mississippi populations and other animal populations should therefore not be viewed as being either simply neutral or predator-prey relationships, but rather should be recognized as being complex coaction pairs often containing aspects of both symbiosis and antagonism. The complex coaction pair formed between the human groups and the white-tailed deer, for example, contained aspects of: commensalism—deer benefited from the forest clearing efforts of the Middle Mississippi groups; competition—both deer and human populations would use common plant food sources, both wild species like acorns and domesticated species like maize or beans; and exploitation—the deer was the primary source of animal protein for these human groups. Even if we restrict our discussion to the aspect of predation that existed in these man—animal coaction pairs, it is still not possible to describe the predation as being clearly exploitative in nature, at least at the species level. Certainly Middle Mississippi predation on animal species was simple exploitation on the individual level, with the hunter gaining from each successful encounter, and the individual prey animal losing, but the effect of human predation at the species level is more difficult to assess.

Human predation of animal populations in the southeast United States had existed for at least eight to nine thousand years prior to the Mississippi period. Man's role in the ecosystem of the eastern Deciduous Woodlands had been evolving slowly over a long period of time. Certainly the pattern and intensity of human predation had changed during this eight thousand year span, but many of the man-animal predator-prey relationships that existed during the Mississippi period were of long standing. In any ecosystem, member components of the biotic community do not evolve in isolation, but rather within a web of complex interrelationships, including predation, with other species within the ecosystem. It is important, therefore, to remember that prehistoric human populations, including Middle Mississippi groups, were integral, functioning components within the ecosystem, and that human predation during the Mississippi period was but one aspect of a very complex web of interaction and interdependence that had developed between prehistoric human populations and other species within the ecosystem over a long period of time.

Human predation was also only one of many mortality factors that many of the animal species within the ecosystem had adjusted to through time.

It is probably better, therefore, not to think of predation by Middle Mississippi groups as being strongly exploitative at the species level. Since the annual mortality due to human hunting was, in a sense, anticipated by the animal populations in question, and was a single aspect of a mortality pattern that the prey populations had adjusted to over a long period of time, it was not really damaging to the prey population as long as it continued within anticipated limits. This concept of annual mortality due to human predation being maintained within an anticipated range is an interesting and important point. It is clear that over a long period of prehistory, human predation on animal populations in the eastern Deciduous Woodlands was, in most cases, not intensive enough to seriously deplete prey populations. Such an intensive pattern of predation would, of course, be unsuccessful in the long run. Prehistoric human populations may have occasionally harvested prey populations in local areas to low enough densities that it was more advantageous for them to shift their hunting to another area for a year or two. The prey population density levels at which such shifts would have taken place, however, would have been high enough to allow the local prey population to increase back within needed density levels within a year or two.

What would happen, on the other hand, if the level of Middle Mississippi predation on prey populations was decreased? Such a question is impossible to answer in any conclusive way, since the level of Middle Mississippi predation on different animal populations is difficult to assess. If Middle Mississippi predation was a major mortality factor, and was withdrawn, the resultant increase in the density of the prey population might have serious consequences. If Middle Mississippi predation was a relatively minor source of mortality, a decrease may have had little effect on the prey population.

The degree to which compensatory mortality may have offset any such decrease in Middle Mississippi predation is also difficult to assess. Certainly as Middle Mississippi predation was relaxed, prey population mortality due to nonhuman predation would have increased, but the degree to which this increased nonhuman predation would have compensated for reduced human predation would depend both upon the degree of compensation required, and the ability of the nonhuman predator populations to respond to the situation.

Thus it is obvious, I think, that the relationships that existed between these Middle Mississippi groups and the animal species present in the Mississippi valley area should not be considered primarily exploitative in nature.

Because of the nature of the available data, the predation on animal populations by prehistoric Indian groups is usually emphasized at the expense of other aspects of interaction within the ecosystem, as it has been in this study. But just because evidence concerning mutualistic, commensalistic, or competitive aspects of human-animal coaction pairs is lacking in the archaeological record does not mean that the role of prehistoric human populations in the ecosystem was primarily predatory. The Middle Mississippi populations that have been considered in this study filled a complex niche in the ecosystem, influencing other components, and in turn being influenced in many subtle yet important ways. Predation of animal populations was only a single aspect of this interaction with the biotic community, and in many cases it was a relatively unimportant aspect of their overall role in the ecosystem.

Appendix A

THE CHUCALISSA SITE

THE Chucalissa site (40 Sy 1) is located nine miles south of Memphis, Shelby County, Tennessee, on the grounds of the T. O. Fuller State Park. In publications prior to 1960, the site is referred to as either the T. O. Fuller site (Beaudoin, 1953) or the Shelby site (Phillips, Ford, Griffin, 1951:48). Situated just south of the confluence of Nonconnah Creek with the Tennessee Chute, Chucalissa sits atop a natural bluff formation which delineates the eastern edge of the Mississippi Valley.

The central plaza of the site measures 175 feet on each side, and is bounded on the west, south, and east by a horseshoe-shaped high status residential ridge. A large, flat-topped pyramidal mound faces the north side of the plaza. A small pyramidal mound is located on the western edge of the plaza.

In addition to the main village midden area, which extends north and northeast from the central ceremonial area, there are two village midden areas on nearby ridges to the south and east, both of which are separated from the plaza by narrow ravines.

Based on $Carbon^{14}$ samples (Crane and Griffin, 1959), Chucalissa was quite likely occupied prior to A.D. 1000 (M-583 - 930 ± 200 years B.P.), while a sample taken near the surface indicates a terminal dating of A.D. 1590 (M-788 - 360 ± 150 years B.P.).

Gerald P. Smith, who has been directing recent excavations at Chucalissa, believes that

> there are at least three Mississippian components on the site, with discontinuities in the occupation between each. The Walls Phase component is basically Stratum I and should date to the first half of the 1500s. The Boxtown component appears to date about A.D. 1400 (personal communication, 1973).

The third component (Mitchell) dates to around A.D. 1185 (I-5781 - 765 ± 95 B.P.). The large platform mound dates to the Walls Phase, with a possible

Boxtown core. The smaller mound on the west side of the plaza is an Ensley and Mitchell platform mound on an Ensley Phase village area (with the transition to shell tempering coming at the end of the Ensley Phase component). The residential ridge around the plaza consists of Walls Phase house mounds over Boxtown, Mitchell, and Ensley Phase middens (personal communication, 1973).

Because of its location atop the eastern bluffs of the Mississippi Valley, Chucalissa was not discovered during the early archaeological surveys of the Mississippi Valley, and its existence was not, in fact, brought to the attention of archaeologists until the 1930s, when a Civilian Conservation Corps crew encountered midden debris while digging foundations for their camp buildings.

Since the site was discovered, excavations have been carried out by a number of groups. The location of these excavation units is shown in Figure 12.

(1) During the summer of 1940, a University of Tennessee crew directed by T. M. N. Lewis excavated a number of trenches northeast of the central plaza. Unfortunately, all records of the 1940 excavations were later lost.

(2) The Memphis Archaeological and Geological Society excavated a one thousand square foot area approximately 250 feet north of the temple mound during the summers of 1952-53. Working in arbitrary 5 inch levels, and excavating to various depths (mostly within Stratum I), the Memphis Archaeological and Geological Society did not screen any fill. They nevertheless recovered a sizable sample of animal skeletal elements.

On the 10,040 bone fragments recovered during the 1952-53 excavations, the following numerical analysis was done (Beaudoin, 1953):

Species	Number of Bones	Percentage
White-tailed deer (*Odocoileus virginianus*)	6148	61.0
Eastern box turtle (*Terrapene carolina*)	831	8.3
Wild turkey (*Meleagris gallopavo*)	417	4.0
Fish (*Pisces*)	756	7.5
Black bear (*Ursus americanus*)	383	3.8
Other mammals and birds	924	9.2
Unidentified bone	521	5.2

In addition to this analysis, lists of species represented at the site were prepared by William R. Adams (n.d.) (mammals), Herbert Friedman (1953) (amphibians, reptiles, and birds), and W. T. Leapley (1953) (fish). Those species identified from the 1952-53 sample are indicated in column 2 of Table 32.

(3) After a lapse of a year, excavations were resumed at Chucalissa under the direction of Charles H. Nash. The Memphis Archaeological and Geological Society and Tennessee State Parks both excavated at the site

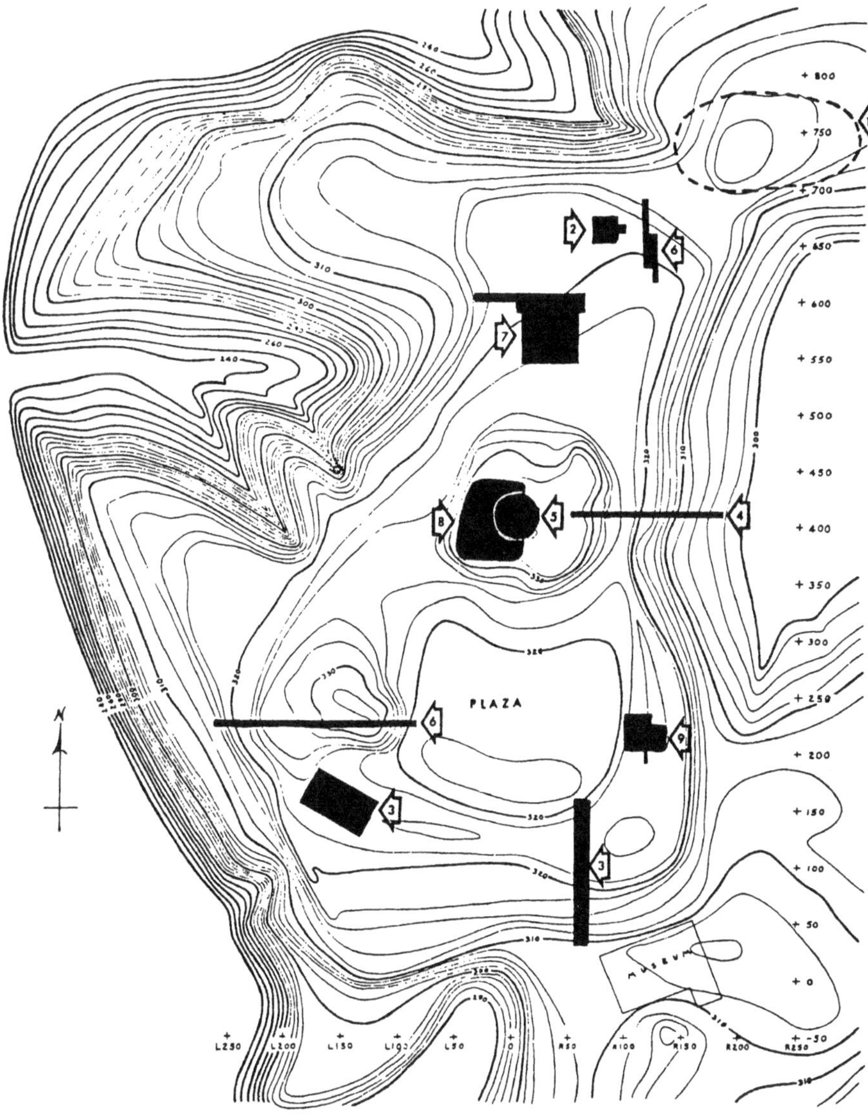

Fig. 12. The location of excavation units at the Chucalissa site.

during 1955. Two excavation units were opened on the high status residential ridge south of the plaza area. The west unit was carried to subsoil, while the east unit was carried to upper Stratum IV. All excavations from 1955 to 1967 were done with mattocks in arbitrary 6 inch levels, without screening fill dirt.

(4) A narrow east-west trench was excavated just east of the temple mound by the Tennessee State Parks during the summer of 1957.

The animal bone recovered during the 1955 and 1957 seasons was sent to Paul W. Parmalee for identification and analysis (Parmalee, 1960), Parmalee's report, like the reports from the 1952-53 seasons, treated the animal bone recovered from all levels of all areas as a single sample. The species identified by Parmalee, and the number of skeletal elements assigned to each is listed in column 3-4 of Table 32.

(5) During the summer of 1959, the Tennessee State Parks excavated a roughly circular area on the top of the temple mound.

(6) During the 1961 and 1962 seasons, Memphis State University excavated trenches west of the Plaza and north of the temple mound. Both trenches were taken to subsoil.

(7) Memphis State University spent five field seasons (1963-67) excavating a large block unit north of the temple mound, taking it to the top of Stratum IV. The animal bone recovered from this excavation was identified and analyzed by B. D. Smith. Skeletal element counts, minimum number of individuals counts, and projected meat yields are listed in the last three columns of Table 32. This faunal sample has been treated as a single unit in this study because exact cultural affiliation of specific provenience units has not yet been determined. Provenience information has been retained for each skeletal element, however, and more detailed analysis of the faunal sample in terms of Walls, Boxtown, and Mitchell components will be done as cultural affiliation for provenience units becomes available.

(8) Memphis State University opened a large block excavation in the temple mound during the 1969-71 seasons, taking it to the top of the last intact construction stage. All occupation debris from this excavation were water-screened using window screen. This faunal material was identified and analyzed by me, and skeletal element counts, minimum number of individual counts, and projected meat yields are listed in Table 33.

(9) Memphis State University opened a block excavation unit on the residential ridge to the east of the plaza. Work is continuing at this time.

The faunal sample recovered from the Chucalissa village midden area is clearly biased, with strong selection against very small skeletal elements (i.e., fish, mice, etc.) There does not, however, seem to be too great a bias against somewhat larger species such as squirrels and migratory waterfowl in the village midden sample (based on the relative occurrence of these species in the village midden and in the water screened material recovered from the temple mound). Preservation was quite good at the site, as indicated by the numerous small fish elements recovered from the water screened pyramidal mound samples.

It has long been assumed that the substructural pyramidal mounds that occur on Middle Mississippi sites had a primarily ceremonial function, and may also have served as a residence for high status individuals. If access to these pyramidal mounds were in fact restricted, and the activities that took place there largely ceremonial in nature, one would expect a faunal sample recovered from the substructural pyramidal mound at Chucalissa to differ from the village midden sample taken from the same site. One might expect fewer skeletal elements, or a smaller species range concentrating on "favored" species, or skeletal elements representing choice meat cuts to occur in the pyramidal mound sample. On the contrary, the only difference in relative importance of species between Mound C and the village midden can be attributed to differences in recovery technique. The relative occurrence of skeletal elements in the pyramidal mound sample does not indicate the presence of choice cuts of meat, but rather represents a uniform distribution of body parts.

This similarity of the faunal samples recovered from the village midden and the pyramidal mound may, of course, simply be the result of construction of the mound with midden soil. Thus, the similarity of the two samples does not at this stage of analysis shed any new light on the function of such mounds.

DESCRIPTION OF THE CHUCALISSA SITE LOCATION

The Chucalissa site is situated on a ridge top at the very edge of the eastern bluff slope. The bluff face just west of the site is rather steep, with a one hundred foot change in elevation occurring within a horizontal distance of four hundred yards. The rugged topography that exists in the uplands to the east and south of the Chucalissa site is due to the erosive action of a number of creeks, all of which empty into a triangular floodplain area just northeast of the site. The largest of these is Nonconnan Creek, which enters the Tennessee Chute about two miles northeast of the site. Cypress Creek joins Nonconnan Creek after crossing the small triangular floodplain area formed at the confluence of Nonconnan Creek and the Tennessee Chute. In addition to the many branches of Cypress Creek, which drain most of the area east of the site, two small unnamed creeks flow north out of the uplands just east of the site. Except for Nonconnan Creek, these watercourses are largely seasonal in nature, with their upper reaches containing runoff only after sizable showers. Although the numerous branches of Cypress Creek have formed narrow, steep-sided ravines, a few relatively flat areas still remain east of the site, and some relatively flat land can be found in the creek valley. The general topography of the upland area to the east and south of the site has probably changed very little since the site was occupied.

Assuming that a climax forest situation existed when the Chucalissa site was occupied, the ridge top areas, including the ridge the site is located upon, would have supported a forest composed largely of beech, a number of oak species, and hickory. The ravine slopes would have supported a typical mixed mesophytic forest, with beech being the most commonly occurring species in both the canopy and the second story. The lower slopes of the stream valleys, as well as the flat areas in the Cypress Creek valley would have supported a forest composed mostly of mixed mesophytic species, with a few floodplain species present. Although these different forest types would have been distinguishable to the trained eye, there would have been no distinct boundaries between forest areas, no definable edge areas. The forest canopy would have been closed throughout the uplands, with forest sub-type areas defined by gradual changes in representation of different species, rather than distinct boundaries. This upland area would have been a fairly uniform environmental setting. Except for the stream margin areas, it would have supported lower population densities of most animal species than the floodplain of the Mississippi River a few miles to the west.

The relative extent to which the Middle Mississippi groups that occupied the Chucalissa site used the Mississippi floodplain to the north and west, or the upland loess area to the south and east is a complex and interesting problem.

The meander belt soils of the Mississippi floodplain would have been superior to the loess soils of the uplands for agriculture. Agriculture could, however, have been carried out to a limited extent on the relatively flat areas and more gradual slopes of the uplands, as well as on the alluvial fans of loess formed where the small creeks entered the floodplain. It would be difficult, of course, to determine if crops were grown to any extent in the uplands. Nash's reference to possible terracing on the bluff slope just west of the site (1955) is, however, interesting in this regard.

The floodplain to the west obviously was a much more advantageous area to plant crops than the uplands, but the floodplain was not an unlimited resource area. Because of the shifting course of the Mississippi River, the amount and character of floodplain land that was open for use and readily accessible to the Chucalissa site did not remain constant, but changed during the six hundred year period of occupation. The different channel stages of the Mississippi River are shown in Figure 13.

In 1944, Harold N. Fisk defined the approximate sequence of channel location of the Mississippi River. He worked back from the known location of the river in 1765 (channel stage 17), with each channel stage identified representing a one hundred year interval. Fisk's channel stage 13, for example, theoretically approximates the specific location of the Mississippi River within its meander belt for the period A.D. 1265-1365. The channel stages we are interested in (11–15) are indicated by arrows. According to Fisk's chronology, channel stage 10 represents the course of the Mississippi River during the hundred year span from A.D. 965 to A.D. 1065, stage 11 the period A.D. 1065 to 1165, and so on. The Chucalissa site was occupied intermittently from approximately A.D. 1000 to A.D. 1590. By spending a little time looking at the location of channel stage remnants 11 through 15 in Figure 13, a number of interesting points can be made.

If east-west and north-south axes are drawn through the Chucalissa site, the southeast quadrant is upland loess hills, the southwest and northwest quadrants are floodplain, and the northeast quadrant is composed of some floodplain and some upland areas. Of the three floodplain quadrants, let us consider the southwest and northwest first. The stage 11 and 12 meanders (A.D. 1065–1265) flowed quite close to the eastern bluff line. During these channel stages relatively little accessible floodplain existed in the southwest and northwest quadrants, since the extreme eastern course of the river formed a formidable barrier against movement into these quadrants. There was, however, some natural levee land available at the base of the bluff during channel stages 11 and 12. In subsequent channel stages (13, 14, 15) the river gradually moved west as the meander moved downstream. Through each of these succeeding channel stages, more land became available for use in the southwest quadrant, while the river moved only slightly further west in the northwest quadrant. The northwest quadrant, therefore, can be considered as remaining essentially inaccessible during the period of occupation of the Chucalissa site. As the meander moved downstream in the southwest quadrant, the land areas opening up would have included significant former natural levee areas, as well as cutoff oxbow lakes similar to the stage 15 cutoff lake shown in the lower center of Figure 13 (Horn Lake).

Prior to 1265 there would have been a certain amount of natural levee area available in the southwest quadrant, but no easily reached oxbow lake areas would have existed. With the gradual western shift of the meander, more and more natural levee area would have opened up and oxbow lake areas would have become more accessible to the Chucalissa site. The floodplain area in the northeast quadrant most likely had some land area open for exploitation during channel stages 11 and 12, but the recent channel shifts (16, 17, 18, 19) have largely obscured the exact course of channel stages 11 and 12 in this quadrant. They probably were quite close to the bluff line, however, judging from channel remnants farther north. With the westward shift of the river during channel stages 13, 14, and 15, more natural levee and oxbow lake areas would have opened up for exploitation in the northeast quadrant. The small triangular floodplain area where Nonconnan and Cypress creeks join the Mississippi River was open for exploitation throughout the period of occupation of the Chucalissa site, and offered good agri-

Fig. 13. The location of the Chucalissa site on the eastern bluffs of the Mississippi valley.

cultural land, as well as numerous seasonally inundated, shallow water areas.

This brief description of the shifting course of the Mississippi River in the vicinity of the Chucalissa site during the period A.D. 1065 to A.D. 1565 allows us to draw a few preliminary conclusions. The small triangular floodplain area just northeast of the site was accessible throughout the period of occupation, affording excellent farmland for agricultural pursuits, as well as a variety of habitat areas that would have supported a number of potentially important animal species not found in the uplands. Much of the main floodplain area was inaccessible before 1265 without moving five to ten miles north or south along the bluff line. After 1265, the western movement of the river improved access to some extent.

These conclusions are important and interesting when considering potential vs. actual exploitation of floodplain species of mammals, fish, and birds by Chucalissa inhabitants. Thus, the relative exploitation of floodplain animal populations was probably not a matter of selective exploitation, but was influenced by changes in the amount of floodplain area that was accessible to the Chucalissa inhabitants. The faunal sample from the Chucalissa site has unfortunately not yet been placed into a chronological sequence according to provenience unit, and as a result we cannot consider the relative representation of floodplain species through time to see if there is, in fact, an increase in exploitation of floodplain species after 1265. We are forced to consider the faunal sample in a single temporal block (A.D. 1000–1590).

We can, however, consider the extent to which Chucalissa groups exploited floodplain species of animals as opposed to upland species. Many broad niche species exploited by the Chucalissa population, such as the white-tailed deer (*Odocoileus virginianus*) and the raccoon (*Procyon lotor*), occur in abundance in both the upland and floodplain habitats, and are therefore not good indicators of floodplain exploitation. Since they would have been restricted almost exclusively to the floodplain zone, backwater species of fish, migratory waterfowl, and swamp rabbits (*Sylvilagus aquaticus*) are, on the other hand, fairly good indicators of the extent to which the animal species of the floodplain habitat zone were used by the inhabitants of the Chucalissa site. More specifically, a high representation of both backwater species of fish and migratory waterfowl indicates access to, and exploitation of, floodplain oxbow lakes. These two species groups, which were intensively exploited by the meander belt Lilbourn and Banks populations, represented a very small percentage of the diet at the Chucalissa site. This low representation of floodplain–oxbow lake species at the Chucalissa site is all the more interesting considering its location on the edge of the floodplain.

If a circle of ten square miles is drawn using the Chucalissa site as a center point, it will circumscribe significant portions of both the Mississippi River floodplain and the eastern bluff loess hills zone. Within these two major

ecological zones, a number of habitats can be identified. Those micro-ecological zones occurring in the floodplain will be described in some detail in Appendix B. The eastern bluff zone contained three micro-ecological zones:
1) oak-beech ridge top forest,
2) mixed mesophytic slope forest, and
(3) mixed mesophytic–floodplain species–stream margin communities.
The forest canopy in the upland loess hills zone would be continuous. The different micro-ecological zones would be identifiable through the relative representation of different species of trees, rather than by any distinct edge or interface areas. This relatively uniform upland habitat zone is quite different from the very complex and varied environmental situation that existed in the Mississippi River meander belt, and it is surprising that the abundant and varied fauna of the floodplain was not more intensively exploited by the Chucalissa population. The answer to this contrast between the low representation of floodplain species at Chucalissa, and the seeming abundance of accessible floodplain areas within a ten square mile area around the site may well be that floodplain areas were for the most part not very accessible to exploitation, judging from channel stage remnants, and the seeming abundance of floodplain area did not in fact exist.

TABLE 32

ANIMAL SPECIES REPRESENTED AT THE CHUCALISSA VILLAGE MIDDEN 40 Sy 1.

	2	3-4	SKELETAL ELEMENTS	MINIMUM NO. OF INDIVIDUALS	PROJECTED MEAT YIELD (IN POUNDS)
Pisces		65	36		
Amia calva					
Bowfin	*	17			
Lepisosteus sp.					
Gar	*	25			
Ictiobus cyprinellus					
Bigmouth buffalofish		2			
Ictiobus niger/bubalus					
Black/smallmouth buffalofish		1			
Family Catostomidae					
Suckers		1			
Ictalurus punctatus/furcatus					
Channel/blue catfish		6			
Ictalurus sp.					
Catfish/bullhead	*	4			
Micropterus sp.					
Bass		2			
Aplodinotus grunniens					
Freshwater Drum	*	7			
Unidentified			36		
Amphibians and Reptiles		1048	1803	154	82.3
Rana catesbeiana					
Bullfrog	*		5	3	–
Rana sp.					
Frog		1	1	1	–
Chelydra serpentina					
Snapping turtle	*	14	35	3	22.5
Kinosternon subrubrum					
Mud turtle			7	1	.3

Table 32 cont'd

	2	3-4	SKELETAL ELEMENTS	7 MINIMUM NO. OF INDIVIDUALS	PROJECTED MEAT YIELD (IN POUNDS)
Terrapene carolina Box turtle	*	631	804	109	32.7
Chrysemys picta Painted turtle			92	17	4.3
Pseudemys scripta/floridana Pond slider/cooter	*	63	25	4	6.0
Pseudemys/Graptemys/Chrysemys Slider/Map/Painted turtles		331	75	9	13.5
Trionyx sp. Softshell turtle		4	18	2	3.0
Colubridae Non-poisonous snakes			3	1	–
Crotalus horridus Canebreak rattlesnake		4	3	2	–
Crotalidae Poisonous snakes			17	2	–
Unidentified turtle			618		
Aves		187	614	48	246.8
Branta canadensis Canada goose	*	2	23	4	22.0
Chen caerulescens/hyperborea Blue/snow goose		17	7	2	8.0
Anas platyrhynchos/rubripes Mallard/black duck	*	3	26	4	8.0
Anas discors Blue winged teal		1			
Mareca americana Baldpate	*				
Spatula clypeata Shoveller			3	1	1.0

Table 32 cont'd

	2	3-4	SKELETAL ELEMENTS	7 MINIMUM NO. OF INDIVIDUALS	PROJECTED MEAT YIELD (IN POUNDS)
Aix sponsa Wood duck	*	2	13	4	4.0
Lophodytes cucullatus Hooded merganser			13	5	5.0
Buteo jamaicensis Red-tailed hawk	*	1	1	1	2.0
Aquila chrysaetos Golden eagle			1	1	5.0
Haliaeetus leucocephalus Bald eagle	*		1	1	5.0
Meleagris gallopavo Wild turkey	*	154	313	21	178.5
Grus canadensis Sandhill crane		7	3	1	6.0
Strix varia Barred owl	*		1	1	2.0
Corvus brachyrhynchos Common crow			2	1	0.3
Passerine Perching birds			1	1	–
Unidentified			206		
Mammalia		2339	9551	326	11,891.4
Didelphis marsupialis Opossum	*	25	56	10	85.0
Scalopus aquaticus Eastern mole			1	1	.2
Sylvilagus floridanus Eastern cottontail	*	87	220	22	44.0
Sylvilagus aquaticus Swamp rabbit	*	19	81	10	30.0

Table 32 cont'd

	2	3-4	SKELETAL ELEMENTS	7 MINIMUM NO. OF INDIVIDUALS	PROJECTED MEAT YIELD (IN POUNDS)
Sylvilagus sp.					
Cottontail/swamp rabbit		4	22	9	22.5
Marmota monax					
Woodchuck			3	1	4.0
Sciurus carolinensis					
Gray squirrel	*	8	51	6	6.0
Sciurus niger					
Fox squirrel	*	105	507	48	72.0
Castor canadensis					
Beaver	*	11	18	4	80.0
Oryzomys palustris					
Marsh rice rat	*	6	126	14	1.4
Sigmodon hispidus					
Hispid cotton rat			20	7	1.8
Neotoma floridana					
Eastern wood rat		2	2	1	.5
Ondatra zibethicus					
Muskrat	*	1	13	3	6.0
Canis lupus					
Gray wolf		2	4	2	60.0
Canis familiaris					
Domestic dog	*	27	211	8	64.0
Urocyon cinereoargenteus					
Gray fox	*	3	21	4	20.0
Ursus americanus					
Black bear	*	36	13	2	420.0
Procyon lotor					
Raccoon	*	50	183	37	296.0
Mustela vison					
Mink		2	7	4	8.0

Table 32 cont'd

	2	3-4	SKELETAL ELEMENTS	7 MINIMUM NO. OF INDIVIDUALS	PROJECTED MEAT YIELD (IN POUNDS)
Mephitis mephitis Striped skunk	*	4	18	3	28.0
Lutra canadensis River otter		1	2	1	10.0
Felis concolor Mountain lion		6	3	1	60.0
Lynx rufus Bobcat	*	6	10	2	30.0
Cervus canadensis Wapiti	*		1	1	350.0
Odocoileus virginianus White-tailed deer	*	1803	3230	125	10192.0
Unidentified small mammal			213		
Unidentified large mammal			4515		

TABLE 33

ANIMAL SPECIES REPRESENTED AT THE CHUCALISSA TEMPLE MOUND.

	SKELETAL ELEMENTS	MINIMUM NUMBER OF INDIVIDUALS	PROJECTED MEAT YIELD (IN POUNDS)
Pisces	79	12	20.5
Amia calva Bowfin	6	1	1.0
Lepisosteus platostomus Shortnose gar	1	1	2.0
Lepisosteus sp. Gar	8	3	3.0

Table 33 cont'd

	SKELETAL ELEMENTS	MINIMUM NUMBER OF INDIVIDUALS	PROJECTED MEAT YIELD (IN POUNDS)
Moxostoma sp. Redhorse	1	1	3.0
Ictalurus punctatus Channel catfish	5	3	4.5
Ictalurus sp. Catfish/bullheads	10	2	3.0
Aplodinotus grunniens Freshwater drum	3	1	4.0
Unidentified	45		
Amphibians and Reptiles	106	15	12.5
Rana sp. Frog	7	2	–
Chelydra serpentina Snapping turtle	3	1	7.5
Terrapene carolina Box turtle	55	8	2.0
Trionyx sp. Softshell turtle	1	1	3.0
Colubridae Non-poisonous snakes	1	1	–
Crotalus horridus Canebreak rattlesnake	3	1	–
Crotalidae Poisonous snakes	1	1	–
Unidentified turtle	35		
Aves	56	7	33.0
Branta canadensis Canada goose	3	2	11.0

Table 33 cont'd

	SKELETAL ELEMENTS	MINIMUM NUMBER OF INDIVIDUALS	PROJECTED MEAT YIELD (IN POUNDS)
Anas platyrhynchos/rubripes Mallard/black duck	3	1	2.0
Anas sp. Mallard/Black/Pintail group	1	1	2.0
Aix sponsa Wood duck	1	1	1.0
Meleagris gallopavo Wild turkey	9	2	17.0
Unidentified	39		
Mammalia	381	21	299.7
Scalopus aquaticus Eastern mole	1	1	.2
Sylvilagus floridanus Eastern cottontail	5	1	2.0
Sylvilagus aquaticus Swamp rabbit	2	1	3.0
Sciurus carolinensis Gray squirrel	2	2	2.0
Sciurus niger Fox squirrel	23	7	10.5
Castor canadensis Beaver	1	1	20.0
Oryzomys palustris Marsh rice rat	5	2	.2
Sigmodon hispidus Hispid cotton rat	1	1	.2
Canis familiaris Domestic dog	4	1	8.0
Procyon lotor Raccoon	1	1	8.5

Table 33 cont'd

	SKELETAL ELEMENTS	MINIMUM NUMBER OF INDIVIDUALS	PROJECTED MEAT YIELD (IN POUNDS)
Odocoileus virginianus White-tailed deer	90	3	245.1
Unidentified small mammal	153		
Unidentified large mammal	93		

Appendix B

THE BANKS SITE

The Banks village site is located one and one half miles north of Clarkdale, Crittenden County, Arkansas, on land owned by Mrs. Henry Banks. Situated on the south edge of what was at the time of occupation a large oxbow lake (Lake Wapanocca), the Banks village site is roughly rectangular in shape. Extending along the lake for 1470 feet, and averaging 300 feet in width, it covers a little more than ten acres. A plaza area measuring 175 feet on each side has been located adjacent to the lake in the northwest area of the site. A radiocarbon date of A.D. 1535 (M - 916 425 ± 150 B.P.) has been obtained from this site. Unlike earlier Mississippian sites, the Banks site contains no identified refuse pits. There are, however, extensive refuse deposits at the edge of the village away from the lake.

Under the direction of Gregory Perino of the Thomas Gilcrease Foundation, portions of the Banks site were extensively tested during the late 1950s (Perino, 1966). Perino's extensive excavations included: (a) the excavation of 56 ten by ten foot squares in the area north of the plaza area, (b) the excavation of large refuse areas, (c) the excavation of seven structures, and (d) the uncovering of more than 550 human skeletons in both single and group burial situations, including four group burial pits.

The excavation units in the refuse areas on the edge of the village away from the lake produced almost all the animal skeletal elements, with small amounts being obtained from house floor areas and from burial fill.

All bones found during the Banks site excavations were retained, with the exception of exceedingly numerous small fish elements such as ribs, vertebrae, and scales (Perino, personal communication). The numerous fish bones, as well as the generally excellent condition of the recovered skeletal elements, indicate that soil conditions at the Banks site were conducive to bone preservation. An objective measure of the preservation qualities of the soil through a soil analysis, however, is not available. Dirt removed during the excavations was not screened. An obviously biased faunal sample is produced by not screening the fill dirt (a fairly common practice prior to the 1960s). There is almost certainly an under-representation of remains of fish and of small species of mammals, birds, reptiles, and amphibians in the faunal list (Table 34).

The faunal remains from the Banks site were identified by Dr. Paul W. Parmalee of the Illinois State Museum (Parmalee, 1959*a*, 1966). The sample of 5,397 identifiable animal bone fragments analyzed by Parmalee included at least nine fish species, four turtle species, twenty-six avian species, and eighteen mammal species. The ratio of identifiable to unidentifiable bone fragments is not known, since only identifiable fragments were retained. The species identification and skeletal element counts shown in Table 34 are essentially those originally done by Parmalee. Re-analysis of the Banks faunal collection at the Illinois State Museum during the summer of 1972 resulted in the additional data presented in this study.

DESCRIPTION OF THE BANKS SITE LOCATION

As can be seen in Figure 14, the Banks site is situated on the downstream, outside edge of a meander of channel stage 13 (Fisk, 1944, plate

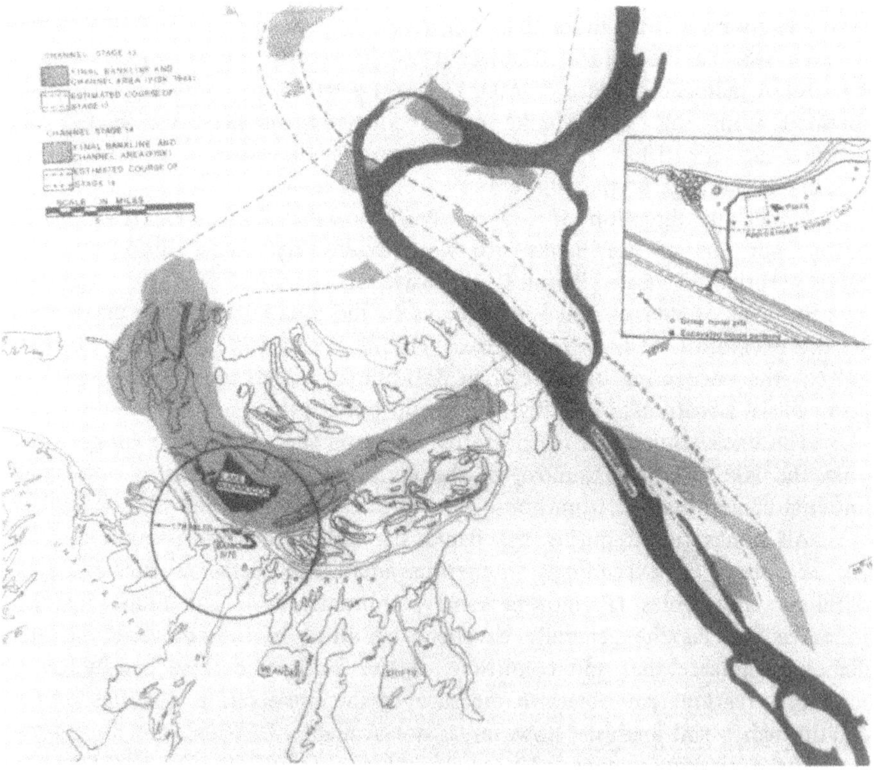

Fig. 14. The location of the Banks site on a levee remnant of the Mississippi River.

22, sheet 5). Channel stage 12 followed the same general course as the stage 13 meander, with the resulting natural levee of both channel stages being locally referred to as Bradley Ridge. Phillips, Ford, and Griffin note that natural levee areas are almost always highest in such downstream outside corner areas. This channel stage 13 meander was cut off by a meander shift at approximately A.D. 1365, according to Fisk's chronology, with the subsequent stage 14 course of the river moving about six miles east of the Banks site (Fig. 14). The resultant oxbow lake slowly filled in through the annual deposition of soil from spring floods, and Lake Wapanocca, which is located just east of the Banks site, represents the only portion of the cutoff oxbow lake that still contains water throughout the year.

The single radiocarbon date obtained for the Banks site was A.D. 1535 ± 140 (Perino, 1966:140). Since the standard deviation of the date obtained comes close to overlapping the cutoff date for the stage 13 meander (A.D. 1365), it is not possible to determine if the Banks site was occupied while channel stage 13 was still the main channel of the river. It was certainly occupied after the channel 13 meander became an oxbow lake, however.

I think, for a number of reasons, that the Banks site was not established until after the eastward meander shift. It is difficult to believe that the Banks site could have existed for very long in the outside downstream area of a meander of the main channel, since it would have been subjected to the full force and velocity of spring flood waters. Once the meander was cut off and became an oxbow lake, however, the area became quite different, in both the vegetation and the variety and number of animal species that were present. Middle Mississippi groups located within the meander belt zone attached great importance to the fauna that occurred in these oxbow lake areas. I think that the Banks site, and perhaps many other meander belt Middle Mississippi sites, were established in oxbow lake areas quite soon after they were formed by shifts in the meander pattern of the river, and that the establishment of these sites represented expansion into newly formed, unexploited niche areas (see Phillips, Ford, and Griffin, 1951:300). These oxbow lake areas, such as the Banks site stage 13 meander, represented newly available, prime environmental locations for Middle Mississippi groups to settle.

The natural levees, which were excellent farm land, would perhaps now be easier to use. We are assuming that main channel levee areas were not as suitable for habitation as former levee areas because of the force of flood waters, and that farming areas had to be close to village sites, in order to control and protect field areas, and minimize walking time to and from field areas.

Since the deepest portion of the stage 13 oxbow lake was directly adjacent to the Banks site, the Banks site was situated on the edge of a large lake, extending out from the present site of Lake Wapanocca. This location on the edge of a large oxbow lake had great importance in terms of availability of a number of animal species that also would have moved into the newly formed oxbow lake area, particularly backwater species of fish and migratory waterfowl.

Once the cutoff occurred, the vegetational sequence toward a cypress swamp would begin around the edges of the permanent water areas of the former channel bed. But because of the long period of time needed for mature cypress swamps to develop (i.e., 100-150 years for favorable conditions for cypress seeding around lake margins) the former channel bed would still have been in an early successional stage during the Banks site occupation, with swamp cottonwood, black willow, water tupelo, pumpkin and green ash, silver and red maple, and box elder predominating in the channel bed. Extensive stands of black willow would be expected in the early stages of succession, with bald cypress seedlings not occurring until approximately one hundred years after cutoff. The entire channel bed would be inundated during spring flood stages, and numerous shallow water areas would persist well into the summer dry period. The deeper portions of the channel bed would, of course, contain water on a permanent basis.

Except during a few very old channel stages (prior to 0 A.D.) the area to the south and west of the Banks site has been unaltered by meander shifts. The modern topography of the area is therefore similar to that which existed at approximately A.D. 1535. Because the area south and west of the Banks site was undisturbed by the shifting river, it is quite possible that mature floodplain plant communities had developed prior to, and existed during, the period of time the site was occupied. Since the distribution and composition of plant communities within the meander belt is dictated by elevation above mean low water levels, and since the topography of the area south and west of the Banks site has probably changed little during the last five hundred years, it is possible to reconstruct in general outline the probable distribution of vegetation in the Bradley Ridge area circa A.D. 1535.

The ridge area itself probably supported a ridge bottom plant community, with the higher elevation allowing more advanced species such as white and cherrybark oak and shagbark hickory to join the other numerous bottomland oak species. The understory probably included dense stands of cane. It is possible that the tulip-oak community described by Shelford (1954) existed on Bradley Ridge. Certainly this climax community had time to fully develop, but since Shelford states that it occurs only in areas forty to forty-five feet above low water levels, Bradley Ridge may not have been high enough for climax development.

The lower slopes of the ridge, and the relatively drier areas of the bottomlands to the south and west would have supported a hardwood bottom (oak-hickory) community that was similar to the ridge top vegetation except that it would lack the more advanced species of oaks. Sweetgum, red maple, elm, and numerous species of oaks would predominate. Those bottom areas that remained flooded through a longer period of the growing season would support an earlier successional stage community similar to that existing in the stage 13 channel bed.

Probably the two most important points to remember concerning the location of the Banks site in terms of micro-ecological zones are these:

1) A variety of different micro-ecological zones occurred within easy reach of the site—a circle of ten square miles with the Banks site at the center included significant areas of
    a) open water and lake margin zones,
    b) seasonally flooded ponds, sloughs, and swamp areas,
    c) ridge slope and hardwood bottom forest areas, and
    d) ridge top cane break and oak-hickory forest.
2) The complex curvilinear nature of the topography produced maximum interface or edge area between the different micro-ecological zones.

These two factors, a variety of micro-ecological zones within a small area, and maximum linear interface between zones, create an environmental setting that will support a variety of both broad and narrow niche animal species at relatively high population densities. A similar situation existed in the Lilbourn site area.

TABLE 34

ANIMAL SPECIES REPRESENTED AT THE BANKS VILLAGE SITE

	SKELETAL ELEMENTS	MINIMUM NUMBER OF INDIVIDUALS	PROJECTED MEAT YIELD (IN POUNDS)
Pisces	415	64	160.0
Amia calva Bowfin	18	5	5.0
Lepisosteus spatula Alligator gar	16	4	4.0
Lepisosteus platostomus Shortnose gar	1	1	2.0
Lepisosteus osseus Longnose gar	22	4	4.0
Lepisosteus spp. Gar	129	16	16.0
Ictiobus cyprinellus Bigmouth buffalofish	3	1	8.0
Ictiobus niger/bubalus Black/smallmouth buffalofish	3	1	8.0
Ictiobus spp. Buffalofish	31	3	24.0
Family Catostomidae Suckers	12	6	48.0
Ictalurus spp. Catfish/bullheads	126	17	20.0
Micropterus spp. Bass	4	2	1.0
Aplodinotus grunniens Freshwater drum	50	4	20.0
Amphibians and Reptiles	114	18	71.4
Chelydra serpentina Snapping turtle	24	8	60.0

Table 34 cont'd

	SKELETAL ELEMENTS	MINIMUM NUMBER OF INDIVIDUALS	PROJECTED MEAT YIELD (IN POUNDS)
Terrapene carolina Box turtle	4	3	0.9
Pseudemys scripta/floridana Pond slider/cooter	66	5	7.5
Pseudemys/Graptemys/Chrysemys Slider/Map/Painted turtle group	4	–	–
Trionyx sp. Softshell turtle	16	2	3.0
Aves	771	149	467.3
Phalacrocorax auritus Double-crested cormorant	14	4	12.0
Ardea herodias Great blue heron	5	2	8.0
Casmerodius albus Common egret	1	1	4.0
Cygnus columbianus (?) Whistling swan	6	1	10.0
Cygnus buccinator Trumpeter swan	7	1	17.0
Branta canadensis Canada goose	95	11	60.5
Chen caerulescens/hyperborea Blue/snow goose	19	4	16.0
Anas platyrhynchos/rubripes Mallard/Black duck	273	55	110.0
Anas acuta Pintail	31	8	12.0
Anas spp. Mallard/Black/Pintail group	37	9	18.0
Anas discors Blue-winged teal	1	1	0.5

Table 34 cont'd

	SKELETAL ELEMENTS	MINIMUM NUMBER OF INDIVIDUALS	PROJECTED MEAT YIELD (IN POUNDS)
Anas carolinensis Green-winged teal	5	2	1.0
Anas streperus Gadwall	1	1	1.0
Mareca americana Baldpate	6	3	1.0
Aix sponsa Wood duck	10	3	3.0
Aythya collaris/affinis Ring-necked/Lesser scaup duck	12	2	2.0
Bucephala albeola Bufflehead	2	1	1.0
Lophodytes cucullatus Hooded merganser	26	6	6.0
Mergus spp. American/Red-breasted merganser	12	3	6.0
Anatidae Duck	42	5	5.0
Cathartes aura Turkey vulture	1	1	2.0
Buteo jamaicensis Red-tailed hawk	2	1	2.0
Haliaeetus leucocephalus Bald eagle	1	1	5.0
Circus cyaneus Marsh hawk	1	1	0.5
Meleagris gallopavo Wild turkey	138	17	144.5
Grus canadensis Sandhill crane	20	3	18.0

Table 34 cont'd

	SKELETAL ELEMENTS	MINIMUM NUMBER OF INDIVIDUALS	PROJECTED MEAT YIELD (IN POUNDS)
Fulica americana			
American coot	1	1	1.0
Corvus brachyrhynchos			
Common crow	2	1	0.3
Mammalia	3574	248	8394.2
Didelphis marsupialis			
Opossum	58	15	132.5
Scalopus aquaticus			
Eastern mole	25	4	0.8
Sylvilagus floridanus			
Eastern cottontail rabbit	75	13	26.0
Sylvilagus aquaticus			
Swamp rabbit	114	17	51.0
Sylvilagus spp.			
Cottontail/swamp rabbit	14	4	10.0
Sciurus carolinensis			
Gray squirrel	20	7	7.0
Sciurus niger			
Fox squirrel	18	4	6.0
Castor canadensis			
Beaver	28	3	60.0
Oryzomys palustris			
Marsh rice rat	25	4	0.4
Ondatra zibethicus			
Muskrat	9	2	4.0
Canis lupus			
Gray wolf	1	1	30.0
Canis familiaris			
Aboriginal dog	95	18	144.0
Ursus americanus			
Black bear	3	1	210.0

Table 34 cont'd

	SKELETAL ELEMENTS	MINIMUM NUMBER OF INDIVIDUALS	PROJECTED MEAT YIELD (IN POUNDS)
Procyon lotor Raccoon	228	46	368.0
Mustela vison Mink	19	5	10.0
Mephitis mephitis Striped skunk	4	1	4.0
Lutra canadensis River otter	5	2	20.0
Felis concolor Mountain lion	1	1	60.0
Odocoileus virginianus White-tailed deer	2832	100	7250.5

Appendix C

THE LILBOURN SITE (23 Nm 38)

The Lilbourn site is situated on the edge of a former tributary stream channel at the southwestern tip of Sikeston Ridge, about three miles southwest of New Madrid, Missouri.

Although it is the largest site in the Cairo Lowlands, encompassing forty-eight acres within its fortifications, almost no controlled excavations had been done at the site prior to 1970.

Potter's 1880 map of the site shows eight mounds, numerous house depressions, and a large plaza area. The largest of the three pyramidal mounds, which measured 280 feet by 140-210 feet, and was 21 feet high in 1951 (Williams, 1954) was tested by George C. Swallow in 1856 (Swallow, 1875). Swallow also excavated a burial mound in the southeast corner of the site in 1856. No faunal remains were saved from these excavations.

Although surface collections were obtained from the Lilbourn site in 1941 (Adams and Walker, 1942), and 1951 (Williams, 1954), no further controlled excavations were undertaken until the summer of 1970.

University of Missouri archaeological survey crews, under the direction of Dr. Carl H. Chapman, conducted excavations at the Lilbourn site during the summers of 1970, 1971, 1972, and 1973. Three of the features excavated during the summer of 1971 yielded the faunal materials that were identified and analyzed for this study. The location of these features is shown in Fig. 15 (Features 71-9, 71-12, and 71-25 are referred to here as structures 9, 12, and 25 respectively).

Structure 9 (feature 71-9) consisted of two superimposed wall trench structures. Although the faunal sample analyzed was recovered from structure fill, it was not possible to determine to which construction phase the materials belonged. Dense fish bone deposits encountered at or near the house floor were water screened using window screen. The structure was not totally excavated.

Structure 12 (feature 71-12) was a burned structure area immediately north of feature 71-9. Approximately three-fourths of the burned area was excavated, with no well-defined floor area or structure outline being identified.

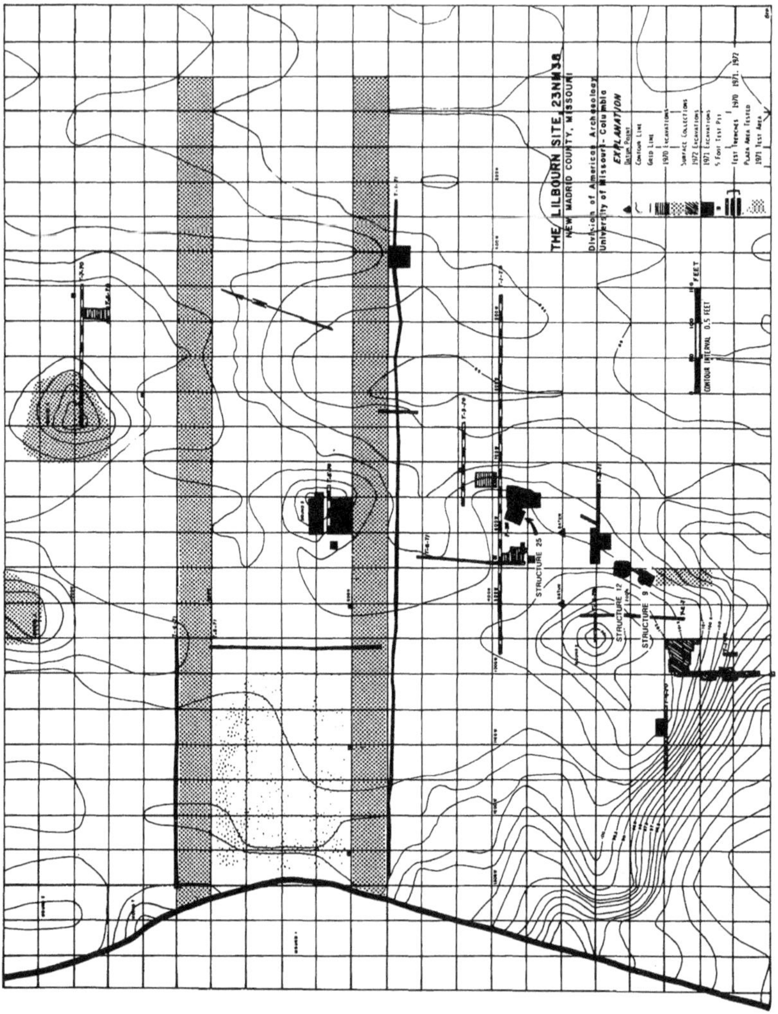

Fig. 15. The location of structures 9, 12, and 25 at the Lilbourn site.

Structure 25 (feature 71-25) was a single post wall structure located northeast of structures 9 and 12. Structure 25 contained three distinct strata, with the lowest strata occurring just below a floor level deposit, which in turn was overlain by a general trash midden deposit that postdated the structure. The faunal sample analyzed here was taken from all three strata, and analyzed as a single unit.

The faunal samples drawn from each of the structures should best be considered as samples of general midden accumulation rather than as total samples of the animal bone recovered from structure floor context. They do not represent total faunal samples from the structures in question, nor are they from well-controlled house floor deposits.

The faunal remains recovered from structure 25 have since been analyzed in terms of the three strata present by Gregory Waselkov (see Cottier and Waselkov, 1974). All three structures probably date to the earlier of two Middle Mississippi occupations at the Lilbourn site (circa A.D. 1000-1200.)

DESCRIPTION OF THE LILBOURN SITE LOCATION

The Lilbourn site is situated on the edge of a former tributary stream channel at the southwestern tip of Sikeston Ridge, about three miles southwest of New Madrid, Missouri. Sikeston Ridge is a low sand ridge extending thirty-five miles from the Commerce Hills south to New Madrid, Missouri, where it expands to a width of five miles and descends to almost floodplain level. Separating the Morehouse and Cairo lowlands, Sikeston Ridge was bordered on both sides by low swampy areas during the early historic period, and supported prairie vegetation with occasional oak groves (Williams, 1954:150). The low swampy areas to the east and west of Sikeston Ridge were termed East Lake and West Lake respectively by early settlers. Potter's 1880 map of Sikeston Ridge (Fig. 16) shows clearly both the location of the Lilbourn site in relation to Sikeston Ridge, and the low backswamp areas to either side. A number of former tributary stream channels are shown in Potter's map, and since they are identified as "cypries" or cypress bayous, a fairly long period of time must have elapsed since they were continuously active stream channels. One of these cypries passes just south of the Lilbourn site, and its former channel bed has been traced for some distance up the west side of Sikeston Ridge (Fisk, 1944:Plate 15, Sheet 1). It is difficult to determine the exact status of this stream channel during the period of time the Lilbourn site was occupied, but it was most likely a seasonally flooded but otherwise rather swampy area containing isolated stagnant pools during the dry season.

The Lilbourn site, as is shown in Figure 17, is not actually located within the active meander belt of the Mississippi River (the western edge of

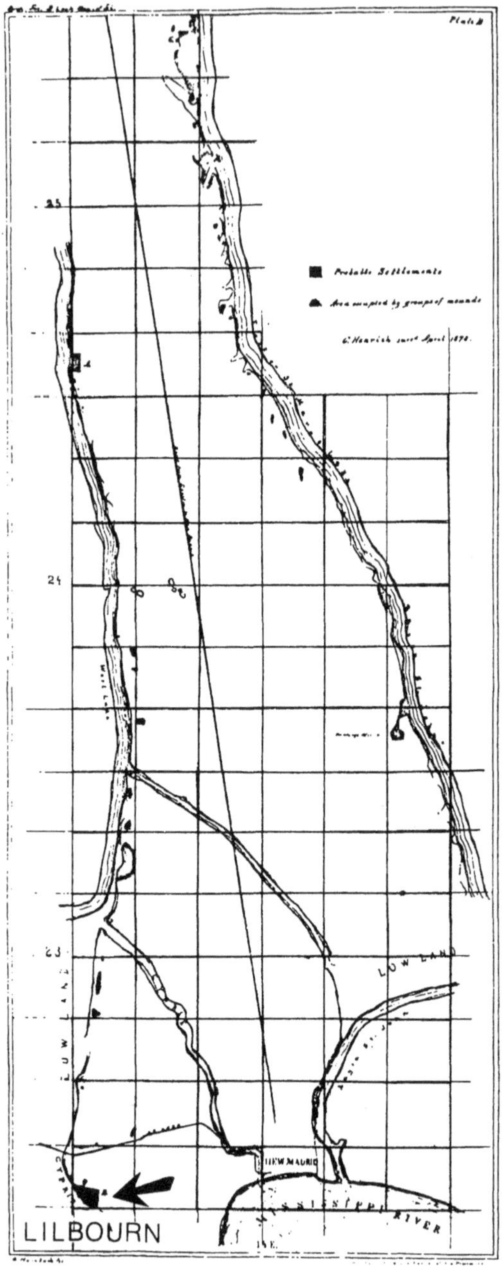

Fig. 16. The location of the Lilbourn site on Potter's 1880 map of Sikeston Ridge.

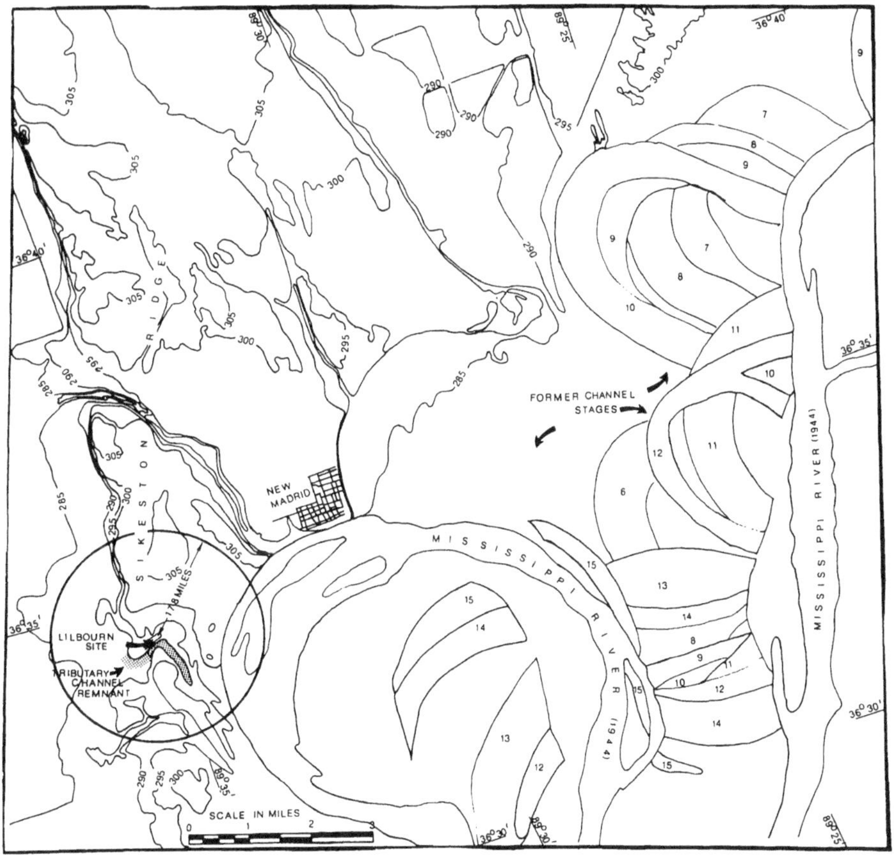

Fig. 17. The location of the Lilbourn site at the south end of Sikeston Ridge.

which is defined by the present day channel) but rather is situated a few miles west of it. Although the Lilbourn site is not situated on a former natural levee of the Mississippi River, as is the Banks site, the high elevation and good drainage afforded by its Sikeston Ridge location serves the same purpose as a levee in providing easily accessible areas of excellent farmland and protection from all but severe flooding.

The vegetation reconstruction of the New Madrid area done by Shelford (1954, 1963) clearly shows the location of the Lilbourn site at the interface of the tulip-oak zone on Sikeston Ridge and the hardwood bottom oak-hickory zone, but does not fully indicate the diversity of micro-ecological zones that probably existed during the occupation of the Lilbourn site. A climax tulip-oak forest probably existed on the southern end of Sikeston Ridge, including the area around the Lilbourn site. This climax forest community would be similar to the western mesic forest, with tulip, white basswood, chinkapin oak, shumard oak, silver maple, winged elm, sugarberry, and elm making up the overstory and first understory, described by Braun (1950). This tulip-oak community eventually gave way to a long grass prairie environment on the higher portions of the ridge further north, but the exact location of the interface between forest and prairie, and the composition of the prairie vegetation are not very well known, because of the large scale destruction of the prairie environment during early farming efforts by settlers. The former stream bed that passes just south of the Lilbourn site probably flowed actively only during the spring flood stage and after heavy rains. During the rest of the year numerous shallow pools and low swampy areas would occur in the channel bed. This stream bed could have supported a variety of successional stages of vegetation, including pioneer vegetation such as willow and cottonwood encroaching upon the shallow pool areas, and perhaps the development of early stages of cypress swamps.

In the lowland areas to the south and west of the Lilbourn site, which are now drained by ditches, there would have been numerous sloughs, cypress-tupelo swamp areas, and seasonally flooded ponds interspersed with hardwood-bottom climax communities made up of oak-hickory and sweetgum. Undergrowth would have been dense in the hardwood bottom forest community areas on the slightly higher sites, and a high overstory composed of large sweetgum and a variety of oak species would have existed.

The area to the southeast of the Lilbourn site would have contained former natural levees of the Mississippi River, supporting ridge bottom oak-hickory, as well as lower elevation plant communities. A number of oxbow lakes also probably occurred in this area, but because of the channel shifts of the river, it is difficult to be sure.

The variety of micro-ecological zones existing in the Lilbourn site area, as well as the amount of edge area between zones, is comparable to that found in the Banks site area. A circle of ten square miles drawn around the Lilbourn site will circumscribe significant areas of

(1) tulip-oak climax forest,
(2) open water and pool margin areas,
(3) backswamp cypress-tupelo areas,
(4) hardwood ridge bottom oak-hickory areas,
(5) hardwood bottom sweetgum-oak areas,

and may include open prairie and prairie-tulip-oak forest edge zones, depending on the southern extent of the prairie zone on Sikeston Ridge.

All species of animals have a variety of habitat requirements, including adequate sources of food and water and cover from predator populations. The probability that a specific area will satisfy all the habitat requirements of a certain species correlates closely with the variety of micro-ecological zones that exist within the designated area. The greater the diversity of a specific area in terms of vegetation, cover, etc., the greater the probability that it will contain all the habitat requirements of a given animal species. Diversity of micro-ecological zones in relatively small areas is especially critical for animals with small home ranges and diverse diet requirements. Many animal species eat a wide variety of different species of plants and animals throughout the year, with the food species quite often located in different micro-ecological zones. Thus localities such as the Banks and Lilbourn sites can support a greater variety of animal species, and at higher population densities, than habitat areas that are uniform in composition. The abundance of animal species obviously has relevance for the distribution of Middle Mississippi sites. Climax forest situations, for example, have much lower population densities of many animal species in the uniform habitat areas of the deep forest than in forest edge or interface areas. Edge areas support more animal species because of the relative abundance and variety of low vegetation types. Along forest edge or interface areas where the forest overstory canopy is broken, low vegetation can survive, and provide cover and food for numerous edge or sub-climax animal species. With the increase in herbivorous species, there is a corresponding increase in predatory species. Edge areas are thus capable of supporting a much richer and more varied faunal community than uniform habitat areas.

These observations are not original; wildlife ecologists have been saying the same things for some time, but they are basic, important points to remember when looking at the different species of animals that were exploited by Banks and Lilbourn groups. The environmental setting of the Banks and Lilbourn sites contained both a variety of micro-ecological zones, and a correspondingly large linear distance of interface areas. These two factors combined to produce a habitat area that supported a rich variety of animal species in relatively high densities in relatively small geographical areas. The opportunities for exploitation of faunal resources in such locales are obvious.

TABLE 35

ANIMAL SPECIES REPRESENTED AT THE LILBOURN SITE–STRUCTURE 9

	SKELETAL ELEMENTS	MINIMUM NUMBER OF INDIVIDUALS	PROJECTED MEAT YIELD (IN POUNDS)
Pisces	7885	294	893.1
Amia calva			
Bowfin	1084	23	15.0
Lepisosteus platostomus			
Shortnose gar	25	5	2.5

Table 35 cont'd

	SKELETAL ELEMENTS	MINIMUM NUMBER OF INDIVIDUALS	PROJECTED MEAT YIELD (IN POUNDS)
Lepisosteus osseus Longnose gar	10	2	5.0
Lepisosteus sp. Gar	189	6	6.6
Ictiobus cyprinellus Bigmouth buffalofish	25	8	69.0
Ictiobus niger Black buffalofish	9	5	45.0
Ictiobus niger/bubalus Black/smallmouth buffalofish	11	6	53.0
Ictiobus bubalus Smallmouth buffalofish	19	9	95.0
Ictiobus sp. Buffalofish	257	17	160.0
Moxostoma macrolepidotum Northern redhorse	3	3	1.0
Moxostoma sp. Redhorse	12	9	3.0
Family Catostomidae Suckers	68	12	88.8
Ictalurus punctatus Channel catfish	143	31	42.5
Ictalurus furcatus Blue catfish	42	9	14.0
Ictalurus natalis Yellow bullhead	8	5	2.0
Ictalurus melas Black bullhead	58	12	3.7
Ictalurus nebulosus Brown bullhead	10	5	1.0

Table 35 cont'd

	SKELETAL ELEMENTS	MINIMUM NUMBER OF INDIVIDUALS	PROJECTED MEAT YIELD (IN POUNDS)
Ictalurus sp. Catfish/bullhead	653	85	116.5
Pylodictis olivaris Flathead catfish	14	7	31.5
Micropterus salomidaes Largemouth bass	4	2	1.0
Micropterus sp. Bass	29	4	2.0
Aplodinotus grunniens Freshwater drum	129	29	135.0
Unidentified	5083		
Amphibians and Reptiles	198	23	29.2
Bufo sp. Toad	10	1	–
Rana catesbeiana Bullfrog	2	1	–
Rana sp. Frog	1	1	–
Chelydra serpentina Snapping turtle	34	2	15.0
Kinosternon subrubrum Mud turtle	7	1	.3
Terrapene carolina Box turtle	41	4	1.2
Chrysemys picta Painted turtle	31	3	.7
Graptemys sp. Map turtle	5	1	1.5
Pseudemys scripta/floridana Pond slider/cooter	24	3	4.5

Table 35 cont'd

	SKELETAL ELEMENTS	MINIMUM NUMBER OF INDIVIDUALS	PROJECTED MEAT YIELD (IN POUNDS)
Pseudemys/Graptemys/Chrysemys Slider/Map/Painted turtle	14	–	–
Trionyx sp. Softshell turtle	14	4	6.0
Colubridae Non-poisonous snakes	6	1	–
Crotalidae Poisonous snakes	9	1	–
Aves	1207	110	229.7
Podilymbus podiceps Pied-billed grebe	2	1	.5
Phalacrocorax auritus Double-crested cormorant	4	1	3.0
Botaurus lentiginosus American bittern	3	1	2.0
Olor buccinator Trumpeter swan	2	1	17.0
Branta canadensis Canada goose	23	8	44.0
Anas platyrhynchos/rubripes Mallard/black duck	110	13	26.0
Anas acuta Pintail	4	2	3.0
Anas spp. Mallard/Black/Pintail group	59	19	38.0
Anas discors Blue-winged teal	13	5	2.5
Anas carolinensis Green-winged teal	14	4	2.0
Spatula clypeata Shoveller	20	4	4.0

Table 35 cont'd

	SKELETAL ELEMENTS	MINIMUM NUMBER OF INDIVIDUALS	PROJECTED MEAT YIELD (IN POUNDS)
Aix sponsa			
Wood duck	38	6	6.0
Bucephala albeola			
Bufflehead	3	1	1.0
Lophodytes cucullatus			
Hooded merganser	20	4	4.0
Mergus spp.			
American/Red-breasted merganser	1	1	2.0
Anatidae			
Duck	105	22	22.0
Haliaeetus leucocephalus			
Bald eagle	6	1	5.0
Tympanuchus cupido			
Greater prairie chicken	15	3	4.5
Meleagris gallopavo			
Wild turkey	16	3	25.5
Grus canadensis			
Sandhill crane	6	2	12.0
Fulica americana			
American coot	2	1	1.0
Strix varia			
Barred owl	2	1	2.0
Corvus brachyrhynchos			
Common crow	5	2	.6
Passerine			
Perching birds	4	2	.1
Bucephala clangula			
Common goldeneye	7	2	2.0
Unidentified	723		
Mammalia	2090	100	1525.1

Table 35 cont'd

	SKELETAL ELEMENTS	MINIMUM NUMBER OF INDIVIDUALS	PROJECTED MEAT YIELD (IN POUNDS)
Didelphis marsupialis Opossum	2	2	17.0
Scalopus aquaticus Eastern mole	1	1	.2
Sylvilagus floridanus Eastern cottontail	63	7	14.0
Sylvilagus aquaticus Swamp rabbit	46	5	15.0
Sylvilagus sp. Cottontail/swamp rabbit	22	7	17.5
Spermophilus tridecemlineatus Thirteen-lined ground squirrel	1	1	.4
Sciurus carolinensis Gray squirrel	23	5	5.0
Sciurus niger Fox squirrel	86	10	15.0
Geomys bursarius Plains pocket gopher	1	1	.7
Castor canadensis Beaver	2	1	20.0
Oryzomys palustris Marsh rice rat	75	17	1.7
Peromyscus spp. Deer mice	2	1	–
Sigmodon hispidus Hispid cotton rat	19	5	1.3
Neotoma floridana Eastern wood rat	1	1	.5
Ondatra zibethicus Muskrat	35	5	10.0

Table 35 cont'd

	SKELETAL ELEMENTS	MINIMUM NUMBER OF INDIVIDUALS	PROJECTED MEAT YIELD (IN POUNDS)
Canis familiaris			
Domestic dog	1	1	8.0
Canis spp.			
Coyote/Wolf/Dog	10	1	10.0
Urocyon cinereoargenteus			
Gray fox	3	1	5.0
Procyon lotor			
Raccoon	57	6	48.0
Mustela vison			
Mink	9	4	8.0
Mephitis mephitis			
Striped skunk	2	1	4.0
Odocoileus virginianus			
White-tailed deer	504	17	1323.8
Unidentified small mammal	431		
Unidentified large mammal	694		

TABLE 36

ANIMAL SPECIES REPRESENTED AT THE LILBOURN SITE–STRUCTURE 12

	SKELETAL ELEMENTS	MINIMUM NUMBER OF INDIVIDUALS	PROJECTED MEAT YIELD (IN POUNDS)
Pisces	736	26	64.6
Amia calva			
Bowfin	74	4	3.0
Lepisosteus spatula			
Alligator gar	1	1	1.0
Lepisosteus platostomus			
Shortnose gar	2	1	1.0

Table 36 cont'd

	SKELETAL ELEMENTS	MINIMUM NUMBER OF INDIVIDUALS	PROJECTED MEAT YIELD (IN POUNDS)
Lepisosteus sp.			
Gar	14	2	2.0
Ictiobus sp.			
Buffalofish	10	2	19.0
Moxostoma macrolepidotum			
Northern redhorse	1	1	.7
Moxostoma sp.			
Redhorse	14	3	2.1
Family Catostomidae			
Suckers	6	3	22.2
Ictalurus melas			
Black bullhead	1	1	.3
Ictalurus sp.			
Catfish/bullheads	26	4	4.8
Pylodictis olivaris			
Flathead catfish	4	1	.5
Aplodinotus grunniens			
Freshwater drum	5	3	8.0
Unidentified	578		
Amphibians and Reptiles	115	10	16.2
Chelydra serpentina			
Snapping turtle	7	1	7.5
Terrapene carolina			
Box turtle	8	3	.9
Chrysemys picta			
Painted turtle	6	1	.3
Pseudemys scripta/floridana			
Pond slider/cooter	8	2	3.0
Pseudemys/Graptemys/Chrysemys			
Slider/map/painted turtle group	6	2	3.0

Table 36 cont'd

	SKELETAL ELEMENTS	MINIMUM NUMBER OF INDIVIDUALS	PROJECTED MEAT YIELD (IN POUNDS)
Trionyx sp. Softshell turtle	7	1	1.5
Unidentified	73		
Aves	475	62	97.4
Botaurus lentiginosus American bittern	1	1	2.0
Branta canadensis Canada goose	3	1	5.5
Chen caerulescens/hyperborea Blue/snow goose	2	1	4.0
Anas platyrhynchos/rubripes Mallard/black duck	21	5	10.0
Anas acuta Pintail	2	2	3.0
Anas spp. Mallard/black/pintail group	22	10	20.0
Anas discors Blue-winged teal	6	6	3.0
Anas carolinensis Green-winged teal	1	1	.5
Spatula clypeata Shoveller	7	2	2.0
Aix sponsa Wood duck	3	2	2.0
Bucephala clangula Common goldeneye	4	2	.1
Bucephala albeola Bufflehead	2	1	1.0
Lophodytes cucullatus Hooded merganser	6	2	2.0

Table 36 cont'd

	SKELETAL ELEMENTS	MINIMUM NUMBER OF INDIVIDUALS	PROJECTED MEAT YIELD (IN POUNDS)
Anatidae			
Duck	82	17	17.0
Haliaeetus leucocephalus			
Bald eagle	1	1	5.0
Tympanuchus cupido			
Greater prairie chicken	3	1	1.5
Meleagris gallopavo			
Wild turkey	7	2	17.0
Fulica americana			
American coot	1	1	1.0
Bartramia longicauda			
Upland plover	1	1	.2
Otus asio			
Common screech owl	1	1	.2
Corvus brachyrhynchos			
Common crow	1	1	.3
Passerine			
Perching birds	1	1	.1
Unidentified	297		
Mammalia	699	41	673.8
Didelphis marsupialis			
Opossum	1	1	8.5
Sylvilagus floridanus			
Eastern cottontail	15	3	6.0
Sylvilagus aquaticus			
Swamp rabbit	12	3	9.0
Sylvilagus sp.			
Cottontail/swamp rabbit	4	2	5.0
Sciurus carolensis			
Gray squirrel	13	3	3.0

Table 36 cont'd

	SKELETAL ELEMENTS	MINIMUM NUMBER OF INDIVIDUALS	PROJECTED MEAT YIELD (IN POUNDS)
Sciurus niger Fox squirrel	8	3	4.5
Castor canadensis Beaver	4	1	20.0
Oryzomys palustris Marsh rice rat	61	6	.6
Ondatra zibethicus Muskrat	9	4	8.0
Canis familiaris Domestic dog	2	1	8.0
Canis sp. Coyote/wolf/dog	2	2	20.0
Urocyon cinereoargenteus Gray fox	1	1	5.0
Procyon lotor Raccoon	19	4	32.0
Odocoileus virginianus White-tailed deer	152	7	544.2
Unidentified small mammal	29		
Unidentified large mammal	367		

TABLE 37

ANIMAL SPECIES REPRESENTED AT LILBOURN SITE–STRUCTURE 25

	SKELETAL ELEMENTS	MINIMUM NUMBER OF INDIVIDUALS	PROJECTED MEAT YIELD (IN POUNDS)
Pisces	6543	83	148.0
Amia calva Bowfin	170	8	6.0

Table 37 cont'd

	SKELETAL ELEMENTS	MINIMUM NUMBER OF INDIVIDUALS	PROJECTED MEAT YIELD (IN POUNDS)
Lepisosteus sp. Gar	2014	38	34.0
Family Catostomidae Suckers	237	6	44.5
Ictalurus sp. Catfish/bullhead	92	13	18.0
Pylodictis olivaris Flathead catfish	4	1	.5
Aplodinotus grunniens Freshwater drum	314	17	45.0
Unidentified	3712		
Amphibians and Reptiles	560	31	62.0
Bufo sp. Toad	11	2	
Rana pipiens Leopard frog	2	1	
Chelydra serpentina Snapping turtle	112	6	45.0
Chrysemys picta Painted turtle	224	8	2.0
Pseudemys scripta/floridana Pond slider/cooter	150	10	15.0
Colubridae Non-poisonous snakes	54	3	–
Crotalus horridus Canebreak rattlesnake	7	1	–
Aves	505	105	179.8
Phalacrocorax auritus Double-crested cormorant	4	2	6.0
Ardea herodias Great blue heron	3	1	4.0

Table 37 cont'd

	SKELETAL ELEMENTS	MINIMUM NUMBER OF INDIVIDUALS	PROJECTED MEAT YIELD (IN POUNDS)
Branta canadensis			
Canada goose	18	3	16.5
Chen caerulescens/hyperborea			
Blue/snow goose	12	3	12.0
Anas platyrhynchos/rubripes			
Mallard/black duck	275	28	56.0
Anas acuta			
Pintail	8	4	6.0
Anas discors			
Blue-winged teal	25	8	4.0
Anas carolinensis			
Green-winged teal	30	9	4.5
Spatula clypeata			
Shoveller	34	11	11.0
Aix sponsa			
Wood duck	29	7	7.0
Bucephala clangula			
Common goldeneye	10	3	3.0
Bucephala albeola			
Bufflehead	3	2	2.0
Lophodytes cucullatus			
Hooded merganser	19	5	5.0
Haliaeetus leucocephalus			
Bald eagle	3	1	5.0
Tympanuchus cupido			
Greater prairie chicken	8	3	4.5
Colinus virginanus			
Bob-white	1	1	–
Meleagris gallopavo			
Wild turkey	5	3	25.5

Table 37 cont'd

	SKELETAL ELEMENTS	MINIMUM NUMBER OF INDIVIDUALS	PROJECTED MEAT YIELD (IN POUNDS)
Fulica americana American coot	7	2	2.0
Bartramia longicauda Upland plover	2	1	.2
Ectopistes migratorius Passenger pigeon	1	1	.3
Strix varia Barred owl	3	2	4.0
Chordeiles minor Booming nighthawk	1	1	.1
Melanerpes sp. Woodpecker	1	1	.3
Corvus brachyrhynchos Common crow	3	3	.9
Mammalia	813	92	1120.6
Didelphis marsupialis Opossum	1	1	8.5
Sylvilagus floridanus Eastern cottontail	9	2	4.0
Sylvilagus aquaticus Swamp rabbit	78	10	30.0
Sciurus carolinensis Gray squirrel	72	9	9.0
Sciurus niger Fox squirrel	29	5	7.5
Castor canadensis Beaver	3	2	40.0
Oryzomys palustris Marsh rice rat	122	19	1.9
Peromyscus spp. Deer mice	16	5	–

Table 37 cont'd

	SKELETAL ELEMENTS	MINIMUM NUMBER OF INDIVIDUALS	PROJECTED MEAT YIELD (IN POUNDS)
Sigmodon hispidus			
Hispid cotton rat	37	5	1.3
Synaptomys cooperi			
Southern bog lemming	9	4	–
Microtus ochrogaster			
Prairie vole	3	1	–
Ondatra zibethicus			
Muskrat	7	3	6.0
Urocyon cinereoargenteus			
Gray fox	5	2	10.0
Procyon lotor			
Raccoon	83	8	64.0
Mustela frenata			
Long-tailed weasel	1	1	2.0
Mustela vison			
Mink	3	3	6.0
Odocoileus virginianus			
White-tailed deer	335	12	930.4

Appendix D

POWERS PHASE SITES

THE TURNER SITE (23 Bu 21 A)

The Turner site is approximately one mile west of Neelyville, Butler County, Missouri, and is within 300 yards of the Snodgrass site (23 Bu 21 B). It was not until 1965 that the Turner and Snodgrass sites were brought to the attention of professional archaeologists.

Containing 41 rectangular structures arranged in rows and columns around a central courtyard, the Turner site was quite possibly fortified, although no evidence of a fortification ditch has been uncovered as yet for this two acre site (Fig. 18).

The Turner site is one of a series of at least six fortified villages arranged in a semicircular pattern around Powers Fort, and was apparently occupied for a very short period of time, circa A.D. 1300.

One indication of the short period of occupation at the Turner site is the small amount of animal bone that has been recovered. Table 38 lists the animal species represented in the faunal sample obtained from almost all 41 structures and numerous extra-edificial pits at the Turner site.

Preservation of animal bone at both the Turner and Snodgrass sites is poor, and this is in part responsible for the low occurrence of smaller species of animals, but it does not explain the low representation of larger species such as the white-tailed deer.

The 41 structures of the Turner site have all been excavated by University of Michigan crews over the last seven years (1966-1973), under the field direction of Dr. James E. Price. All fill dirt from the structures was sifted through quarter-inch mesh screen. Faunal materials from the Turner site were processed, identified, and analyzed by the author.

A more detailed distributional analysis of the Turner site faunal sample will appear in future reports on the Powers Phase.

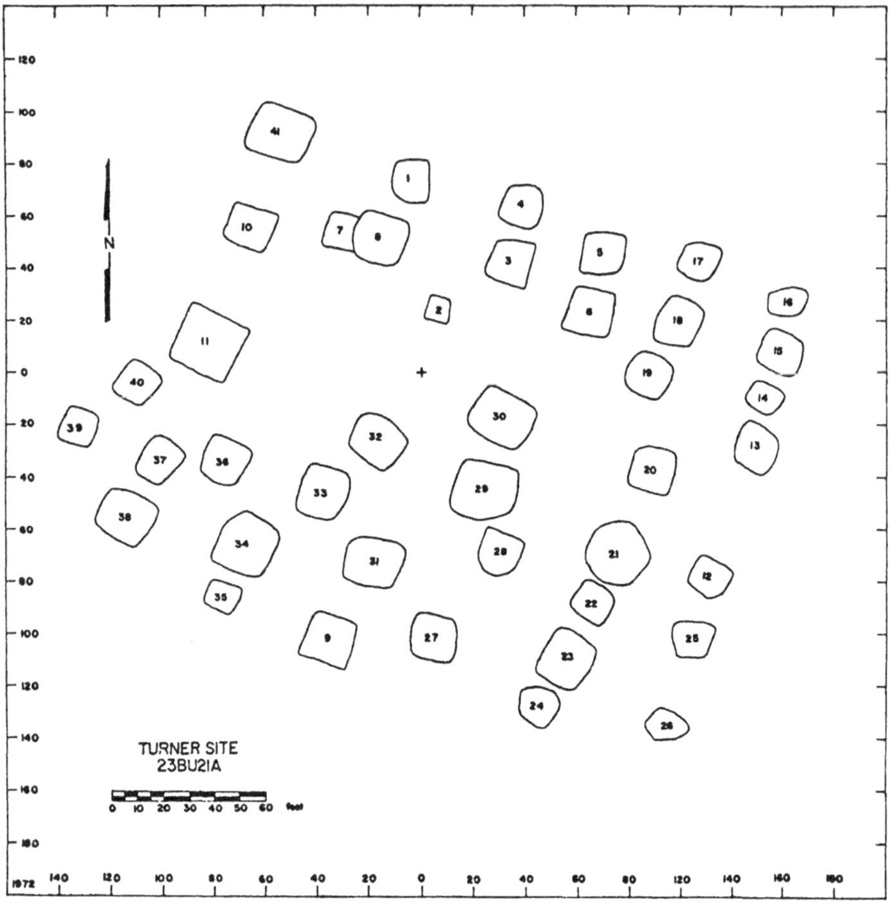

Fig. 18. Site plan of the Turner site.

THE SNODGRASS SITE (23 Bu 21 B)

The Snodgrass site is located just east of the Turner site, in Butler County, Missouri. It is approximately two and a half acres in size, and was surrounded by a palisade and fortification ditch (Fig. 19). The Snodgrass site contains ninety rectangular structures, an internal white wall, and three courtyard areas.

The Snodgrass site, like the Turner site, is believed to have been occupied for only a short period of time, circa A.D. 1300, with this short occupation reflected in the relatively small amount of recovered bone refuse.

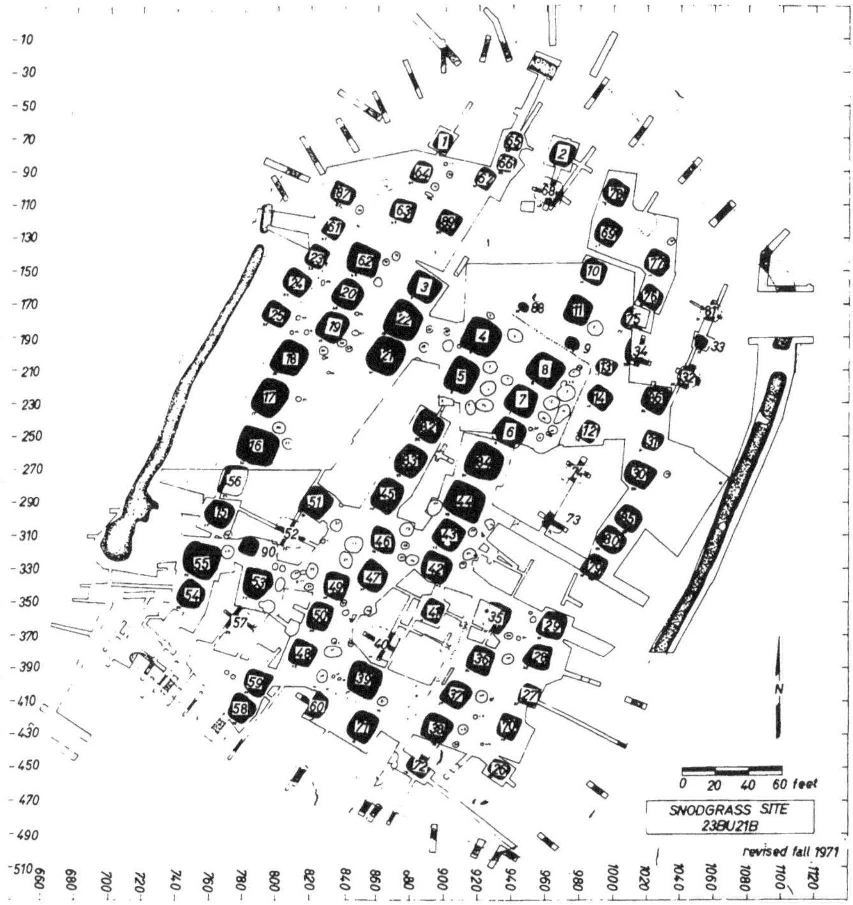

Fig. 19. Site plan of the Snodgrass site.

Sixty-seven of the ninety structures have been fully excavated by University of Michigan crews over the last seven years. Eight more structures, as well as numerous extra-edificial pits, have been partially excavated. Table 39 lists the animal species represented in the faunal sample obtained from all excavated structures and pits.

All fill dirt from the structures was screened through half-inch screen, and recovery was excellent.

Preservation of faunal materials at the Snodgrass site was poor, clearly creating a bias against many smaller species of animals. B. D. Smith processed, identified, and analyzed all faunal materials from the Snodgrass site.

A more detailed analysis of the distribution of faunal materials within the Snodgrass site will appear in later Powers Phase reports.

POWERS FORT

Located approximately one half mile northeast of Naylor, Butler County, Missouri, Powers Fort is the civic-ceremonial center of Powers Phase. A fortification wall and ditch enclose three sides of the twelve acre site, while the east side of the site fronts on a cypress swamp area. Within the fortified area there are four mounds: a large flat-topped temple mound and associated plaza area, and three subsidiary mounds. It is estimated that Powers Fort was occupied for approximately fifty years, circa A.D. 1300.

Powers Fort was first described by Cyrus Thomas in 1894. A map made of the site at that time is reproduced in Figure 20. No controlled excavation was carried out at the site before the summer of 1966. James E. Price, field director of the Powers Phase Project, excavated a single burial at the site during the summer of 1966. During the summer of 1969, a University

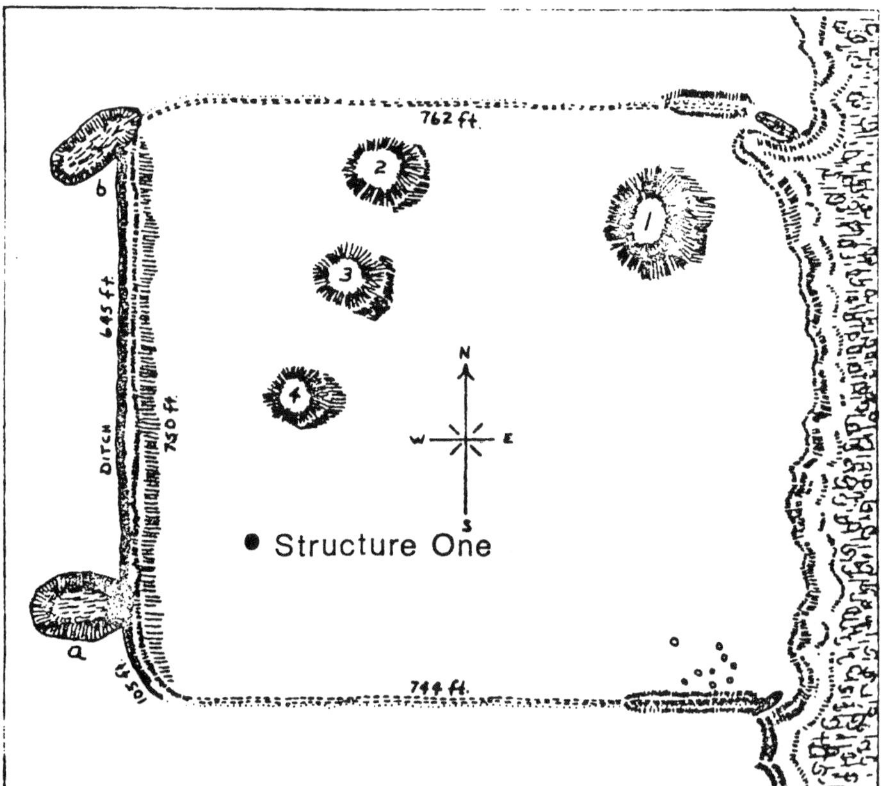

Fig. 20. The location of structure 1 at Powers Fort (map from C. Thomas, 1894).

of Michigan crew excavated a single structure at Powers Fort. Because access to the site is difficult, no further excavations have been undertaken to date.

The approximate location of the excavated structure is shown in Figure 20. Measuring approximately eighteen by eighteen feet, structure one showed evidence of having been rebuilt three times during its occupation.

The faunal sample recovered from structure one at Powers Fort is shown in Table 40. All dirt was sifted through quarter-inch screen, and recovery was excellent.

Preservation of bone at Powers Fort was better than at the Snodgrass and Turner sites, but the sample is still biased to some degree against species with delicate, small skeletons (i.e., fish and small rodents).

DESCRIPTION OF THE LOCATION OF THE LOWLAND SITES OF THE POWERS PHASE

The lowland sites of the Powers Phase are located at the extreme western edge of the Mississippi Valley, directly adjacent to the Ozark escarpment.

The low sand "ridges" upon which the lowland sites of the Powers Phase are located (stippled areas in Fig. 21), which rise five to ten feet above the surrounding area, are segmented remnants of former natural levees of the braided Mississippi River.

This topographic pattern is generally similar to the one described earlier for the meander belt Banks and Lilbourn sites. These former natural levee areas of the Mississippi River, which afforded protection from the spring flooding of the Little Black River, as well as providing fertile, well-drained, sandy soils for agricultural pursuits, were divided by braided Mississippi River channel remnants which were poorly drained prior to modern drainage efforts.

Similarly, the distribution of forest vegetation in the Powers Phase area when the sites were occupied was probably comparable to that already described for the meander belt zone sites. Vegetational succession in the Powers phase, however, could very well have reached a climax stage, and we shall assume that such was the case.

The subdivisions of bottomland forest defined by Braun (1950:291) are the most useful tool for projecting the distribution of vegetation in the Powers Phase area.

Braun's ridge bottom forest subtype would have covered the higher, and therefore better drained, sand ridge areas. In addition to those hardwood bottom species, advanced successional species, such as shagbark hickory, white oak, and cherrybark oak, would occur in the higher elevations of the sand ridge area overstory. It is possible that a tulip-oak climax forest could have existed on these ridge areas, in which case tulip, white basswood, chinkapin

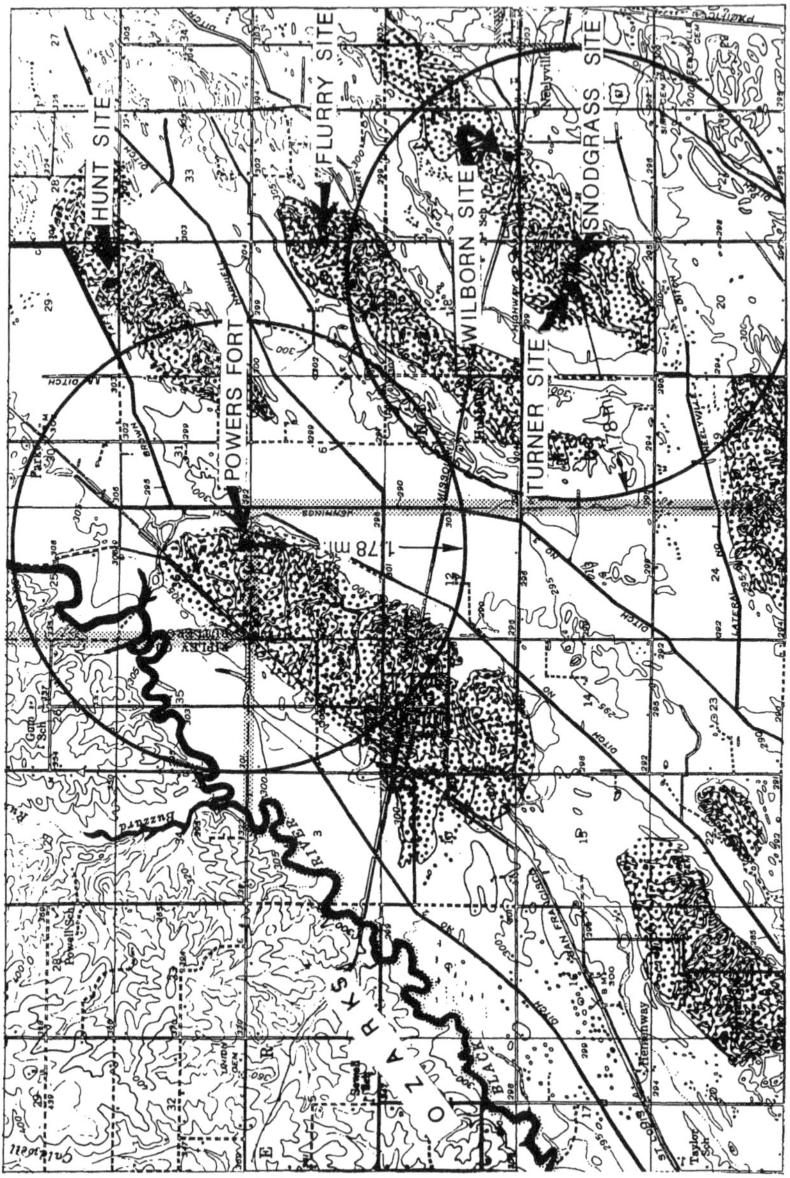

Fig. 21. The location of Powers Phase sites on segmented former natural levees of the Mississippi River.

oak, shumard oak, cherrybark oak, silver maple, winged elm, pin oak, sugarberry, and elm would have occurred in significant numbers.

The ridge bottom forest subtype would merge with the hardwood bottom forest subtype on the lower slopes of the sand ridges. The hardwood bottom forest subtype would also occur on the better drained portions of the lowland areas, with sweetgum, red maple, elm, sugarberry, and numerous species of oaks predominating in the overstory. Undergrowth would be quite dense, and overstory trees quite large.

In those poorly drained areas between the sand ridges that were inundated throughout the year (Shelford's [1963] aquatic habitat), mature cypress-tupelo swamps would have existed during the occupation of the Powers Phase sites. Bald cypress and water tupelo would have been the dominant overstory species, with silver maple, red maple, water and pumpkin ash, and box elder occurring in the understory.

Although it is difficult to accurately determine the extent to which cypress swamps filled these low former channel beds between the sand ridges, there are some indications that much of the lowland area may have consisted of mature cypress swamp. A few cypress still exist along drainage ditches south of Naylor, and there is a quite sizable cypress swamp area directly adjacent to Powers Fort. During the spring high water stage of the Little Black River, much of the low area between ridges is flooded, sometimes for weeks at a time. Prior to modern drainage efforts, it is quite possible that many areas were submerged well into the summer.

From this brief discussion of the topography and projected distribution of vegetation in the Powers Phase area, it is evident, I think, that the Powers Phase sites were comparable in many ways to the meander belt Banks and Lilbourn sites. All were situated on high former natural levee areas that provided good farmland, yet were close to a number of other micro-ecological zones.

Ten square mile circles drawn around Powers Fort and the Turner and Snodgrass sites, circumscribe significant areas of the three vegetational subtypes described above, with the following micro-ecological zones:

1) Ridge bottom forest areas,
2) Hardwood bottom sweetgum-oak areas,
3) Cypress-tupelo swamp areas,
4) Stream margin areas,
5) Seasonally flooded ponds and shallow water areas, and
6) Ozark upland areas.

There are a number of important differences, however, between the Powers Phase locale and the meander belt location of the Banks and the Lilbourn sites, in the variety and composition of accessible micro-ecological zones in each area. The Powers Phase area, because it is situated at the margin of the alluvial valley, does not contain the whole spectrum of micro-ecological zones that occur within the meander belt zone.

The Little Black River, which is the only major watercourse in the Powers Phase area, influences the character of the local environment far less than the Mississippi River influences the meander belt zone. Because of this lesser influence from the Little Black River, certain potentially important micro-ecological zones are missing in the Powers Phase area. The meander belt of the Little Black River is quite small, and the shifting of this rather slow moving river created very few new land areas. The forest cover would rarely have been broken by newly available areas such as cutoff meanders of the river. Oxbow lakes would have been infrequent and small in size, in contrast to the situation in the meander belt zone. This lack of newly available unforested areas, and oxbow lakes, would have had a number of consequences. The amount of forest edge area would have been less, which would in turn have reduced the density of a number of animal species.

The lack of sizable oxbow lake areas, combined with the location of the Powers Phase at the western edge of the Mississippi flyway, would have meant a significantly lower seasonal availability of migratory waterfowl.

Both the Powers Phase sites and the meander belt Banks and Lilbourn sites had access to a variety of micro-ecological zones, but the available micro-ecological zones were not identical in each area. This variation in the composition of accessible ecological zones in the two areas is reflected in the relative extent to which certain species or species groups were exploited at the different sites.

TABLE 38

ANIMAL SPECIES REPRESENTED AT THE TURNER SITE 23 Bu 21 A.

	SKELETAL ELEMENTS	MINIMUM NUMBER OF INDIVIDUALS	PROJECTED MEAT YIELD (IN POUNDS)
Amphibians and Reptiles	91	15	48.9
Chelydra serpentina Snapping turtle	3	3	22.5
Macroclemys temmincki Alligator snapping turtle	3	3	22.5
Terrapene carolina Box turtle	57	8	2.4
Pseudemys scripta/floridana Pond slider/Cooter	16	1	1.5
Unidentified	12		
Aves	75	11	41.0
Branta canadensis Canada goose	1	1	5.5
Anas platyrhynchos/rubripes Mallard/Black duck	3	2	4.0
Anas spp. Mallard/Black/Pintail group	2	1	2.0
Aix sponsa Wood duck	2	1	1.0
Anatidae Duck	5	1	1.0
Buteo jamaicensis Red-tailed hawk	1	1	2.0
Meleagris gallopavo Wild turkey	10	3	25.5
Passerine Perching birds	2	1	–
Unidentified	49		

Table 38 cont'd

	SKELETAL ELEMENTS	MINIMUM NUMBER OF INDIVIDUALS	PROJECTED MEAT YIELD (IN POUNDS)
Mammalia	1619	88	3491.6
Didelphis marsupialis Opossum	4	3	25.5
Scalopus aquaticus Eastern mole	1	1	.1
Sylvilagus floridanus Eastern cottontail	4	3	6.0
Sylvilagus aquaticus Swamp rabbit	1	1	3.0
Sylvilagus sp. Cottontail/swamp rabbit	1	1	2.5
Marmota monax Woodchuck	1	1	4.0
Sciurus carolinensis Gray squirrel	1	1	1.0
Sciurus niger Fox squirrel	3	3	4.5
Geomys bursarius Plains pocket gopher	3	3	2.1
Castor canadensis Beaver	10	3	60.0
Ondatra zibethicus Muskrat	2	2	4.0
Canis familiaris Domestic dog	5	3	24.0
Urocyon cinereoargenteus Gray fox	3	2	10.0
Ursus americanus Black bear	2	1	210.0

Table 38 cont'd

	SKELETAL ELEMENTS	MINIMUM NUMBER OF INDIVIDUALS	PROJECTED MEAT YIELD (IN POUNDS)
Procyon lotor			
Raccoon	36	23	184.0
Mustela vison			
Mink	1	1	2.0
Odocoileus virginianus			
White-tailed deer	544	36	2948.9
Unidentified small mammal	37		
Unidentified large mammal	960		

TABLE 39

ANIMAL SPECIES REPRESENTED AT THE SNODGRASS SITE 23 Bu 21 B.

	SKELETAL ELEMENTS	MINIMUM NUMBER OF INDIVIDUALS	PROJECTED MEAT YIELD (IN POUNDS)
Pisces	4	4	2.7
Amia calva			
Bowfin	1	1	1.0
Ictalurus melas			
Black bullhead	2	2	1.2
Pylodictis olivaris			
Flathead catfish	1	1	.5
Amphibians and Reptiles	508	50	103.9
Chelydra serpentina			
Snapping turtle	40	5	37.5
Macroclemys temmincki			
Alligator snapping turtle	42	5	37.5
Kinosternon subrubrum			
Mud turtle	3	3	1.0

Table 39 cont'd

	SKELETAL ELEMENTS	MINIMUM NUMBER OF INDIVIDUALS	PROJECTED MEAT YIELD (IN POUNDS)
Terrapene ornata Ornate box turtle	1	1	.3
Terrapene carolina Box turtle	235	22	6.6
Pseudemys scripta/floridana Pond slider/Cooter	57	7	10.5
Pseudemys/Graptemys/Chrysemys Slider/Map/Painted turtle group	37	4	6.0
Trionyx sp. Softshell turtle	7	3	4.5
Unidentified	86		
Aves	104	8	51.0
Branta canadensis Canada goose	1	1	5.5
Anas platyrhynchos/rubripes Mallard/Black duck	2	1	2.0
Aix sponsa Wood duck	2	1	1.0
Meleagris gallopavo Wild turkey	24	5	42.5
Unidentified	75		
Mammalia	5477	287	13206.4
Didelphis marsupialis Opossum	5	5	42.5
Scalopus aquaticus Eastern mole	2	2	.4
Sylvilagus floridanus Eastern cottontail	17	11	22.0
Sylvilagus aquaticus Swamp rabbit	1	1	3.0

Table 39 cont'd

	SKELETAL ELEMENTS	MINIMUM NUMBER OF INDIVIDUALS	PROJECTED MEAT YIELD (IN POUNDS)
Sylvilagus sp. Cottontail/Swamp rabbit	1	1	2.5
Sciurus niger Fox squirrel	5	4	6.0
Sciurus carolinensis Gray squirrel	1	1	1.0
Geomys bursarius Plains pocket gopher	19	7	4.9
Castor canadensis Beaver	4	3	60.0
Oryzomys palustris Marsh rice rat	1	1	.1
Ondatra zibethicus Muskrat	3	3	6.0
Canis familiaris Domestic dog	15	4	24.0
Urocyon cinereoargenteus Gray fox	5	3	15.0
Procyon lotor Raccoon	155	78	624.0
Mustela vison Mink	3	3	6.0
Mephitis mephitis Striped skunk	2	2	8.0
Cervus canadensis Wapiti	1	1	350.0
Odocoileus virginianus White-tailed deer	3023	157	12,031
Unidentified small mammal	167		
Unidentified large mammal	2047		

TABLE 40

ANIMAL SPECIES REPRESENTED AT POWERS FORT–STRUCTURE 1,23Bu 10.

	SKELETAL ELEMENTS	MINIMUM NUMBER OF INDIVIDUALS	PROJECTED MEAT YIELD (IN POUNDS)
Pisces	2	2	1.5
Micropterus punctulatus Spotted bass	1	1	1.0
Micropterus sp. Bass	1	1	0.5
Amphibians and Reptiles	22	6	10.2
Chelydra serpentina Snapping turtle	1	1	7.5
Terrapene carolina Box turtle	19	4	1.2
Pseudemys scripta/floridana Pond slider/cooter	2	1	1.5
Aves	39	7	44.0
Anas platyrhynchos/rubripes Mallard/Black duck	2	1	2.0
Aix sponsa Wood duck	1	1	1.0
Haliaeetus leucocephalus Bald eagle	4	1	5.0
Meleagris gallopavo Wild turkey	11	4	36.0
Unidentified	21		
Mammalia	734	26	615.9
Didelphis marsupialis Opossum	4	2	17.0
Sylvilagus floridanus Eastern cottontail	21	3	6.0

Table 40 cont'd

	SKELETAL ELEMENTS	MINIMUM NUMBER OF INDIVIDUALS	PROJECTED MEAT YIELD (IN POUNDS)
Sylvilagus aquaticus Swamp rabbit	1	1	3.0
Sciurus niger Fox squirrel	9	3	4.5
Geomys bursarius Plains pocket gopher	8	2	0.7
Castor canadensis Beaver	4	1	20.0
Canis familiaris Domestic dog	4	1	8.0
Urocyon cinereoargenteus Gray fox	3	1	5.0
Procyon lotor Raccoon	13	3	24.0
Mephitis mephitis Striped skunk	5	3	12.0
Odocoileus virginianus White-tailed deer	172	6	515.7
Unidentified small mammal	36		
Unidentified large mammal	454		

Appendix E

THE GOOSENECK SITE (23 Ct 54)

The Hawes Memorial Campground is located in Gooseneck Hollow, on the west bank of the Current River, in southeast Missouri. The name "Gooseneck" is derived from the distinctive "s" shaped bend in the river at this point. Surface collecting within the Hawes Campground in the winter of 1970 yielded small amounts of Middle Mississippi material, with most of the recovered artifacts coming from the area along the edge of the second terrace. The presence of three slight rises in the terrace slope suggested possible midden accumulation, and the southernmost of these was chosen for excavation.

A crew of twelve, under the direction of Bruce Smith, excavated at the Gooseneck site during the summer of 1971, under a permit issued by the United States Department of Agriculture-Forest Service. The excavations were funded entirely through National Science Foundation Grant GS 3215. The University of Michigan Museum of Anthropology provided all needed tools and camping materials.

A total of twenty-two five-foot squares were excavated to varying depths. In all cases, the squares were excavated to sterile soil, but with the squares actually on the terrace slope, this depth was little more than a foot. Arbitrary 0.2 foot levels were established at the start of excavations, and since only gross stratigraphy was discerned in the first trench, and there were no well-defined cultural layers, these arbitrary levels were continued throughout the excavation.

The fill dirt from each level of each square was screened through quarter-inch mesh. The dirt from all levels of one square and at least one level of each square, randomly selected, was then flotated.

Table 42 represents an almost complete analysis of the faunal materials recovered from the site. It includes all of the animal bone recovered through excavation and primary screening, as well as all the bone recovered from sorting of flotation samples from the single square that was completely flotated (approximately one-fourth of the total flotation sample volume).

Small fish bones, and some small elements of eastern mole (*Scalopus aquaticus*), were the only skeletal elements that were recovered from the flotation materials sorted. Bone preservation was excellent.

The artifacts recovered from the site indicate that it was a single component Middle Mississippi site. Over 500 pottery sherds, all of which were shell tempered plain Middle Mississippi ware (Neeley's Ferry Plain), were recovered from all levels of the midden. While the general shape of rim sherds from the site is similar to vessel forms recovered from Powers Fort, it is not possible to confidently assign the site to the Powers Phase. The lack of radiocarbon dates for the site also makes it difficult to determine the exact cultural affiliation of the site. It may well date somewhat later in the cultural sequence than the Powers Phase.

Faunal evidence indicates that the site was occupied during the late fall-early winter (October-November), and was occupied at some time during the period of January-May.

DESCRIPTION OF THE LOCATION OF THE GOOSENECK SITE

The topography of the eastern Ozarks has remained largely unaltered since the Mississippi period, and the distribution of the different vegetation has also remained unchanged (Steyermark, 1959). This continuity of the environmental setting of the Gooseneck site area during the last seven hundred years allows a more precise analysis (site catchment analysis) of the area in terms of the availability and accessibility of different micro-ecological zones than was possible for the other six sites that have been discussed.

Using the Gooseneck site as the center point, a circle encompassing ten square miles was drawn on the air photo shown in Figure 22. A transparent overlay was then placed over the photo and those areas which fell into each of the vegetation zones were delineated. These areas included:

1) Current River floodplain–using stereo viewing to determine the base of the valley bluffs, the maximum extent of the lowlands of the Current River was defined.

2) Upland pine hardwood–since the air photos were taken during the early spring, the deciduous species were still without foliage, and the areas of pine-hardwood interspersion could be easily defined. These areas were usually the southern and western aspect of the ridge slopes.

3) Stream bottom hardwoods–again using stereo coverage, the stream bottom areas of the seasonally active streams were defined, and the drainage pattern checked against contour maps for accuracy.

4) Upland hardwood–Areas of upland hardwood were defined as those areas not placed within one of the first three categories. Since this category has a quality of including "everything else," the estimated values will

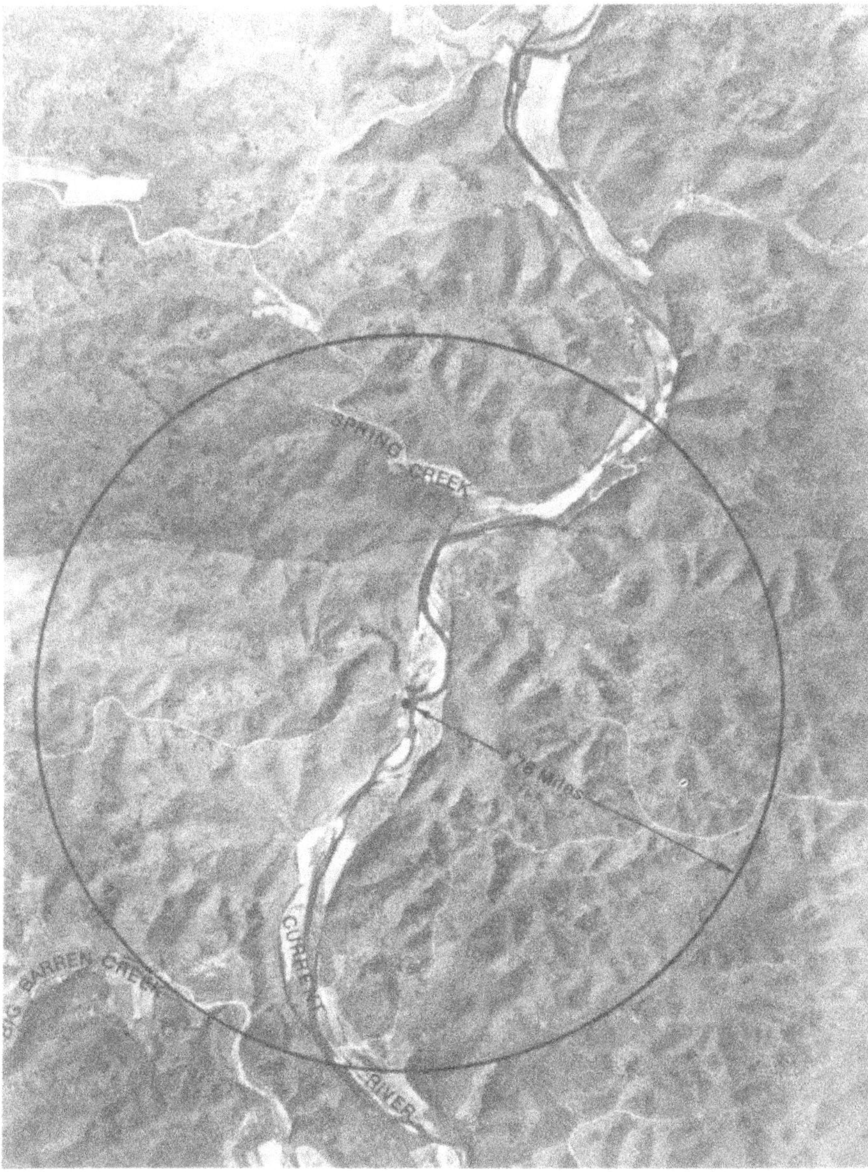

Fig. 22. The location of the Gooseneck site within the Current River valley.

obviously be higher than the actual value for upland hardwood areas, since it will include roads, houses, ditches, etc., but, since the area in question is largely undeveloped, this bias should not be of too much significance.

A dot grid (each dot equaling one acre) was placed over the transparency, and the number of acres within each of the four vegetation zones was determined. The relative representation of each of these vegetation zones within the circumscribed ten square mile area is shown in Table 41. The upland hardwood vegetation association is by far the most common in the ten square mile area, with the upland hardwood and upland pine–hardwood zones making up over eighty percent of the area. The circle that was drawn, however, represents a theoretical catchment area defined by strict geographical space, while catchment parameters should actually reflect ease of movement within each area. More realistic boundaries defined by movement would show expansion outward along the axis of the Current River valley, and contraction in areas of sheer cliffs and steep slopes. The catchment area boundaries would also vary seasonally, with changes in location of understory dense vegetation, and changes in the water table. Thus the upland vegetation zones are over-represented to a certain extent in this strictly geographical catchment analysis.

TABLE 41

NUMBER OF ACRES PLACED WITHIN EACH OF FOUR VEGETATION TYPES OCCURRING WITHIN A CIRCLE OF 10 SQUARE MILES, USING THE GOOSENECK SITE AS A CENTER POINT.

VEGETATION ASSOCIATION	NUMBER OF ACRES	RANK
Current River valley	441.6 (6.9%)	4
Stream bottom hardwood	729.6 (11.4%)	2
Upland hardwood	4595.2 (71.8%)	1
Upland pine-hardwood	633.6 (9.9%)	3

The vegetation zones that were present during the Mississippi period should correlate fairly closely with the modern distribution of vegetation, with the exception of the upland hardwood/upland pine-hardwood ratio, which could very well have been more balanced in A.D. 1300.

If traditional assumptions inherent in the site catchment studies done so far are to hold, the Gooseneck site would have depended largely upon the upland hardwood areas for its resource utilization, while the Current River bottom lands were of rather minor importance.

The location of the Gooseneck site within the Current River valley was not simply a function of easy access to river bottom species of animals and plants, but was, on the other hand, a function of two variables:

access to water, and to routes of movement. The Gooseneck site is well situated in terms of routes of movement, both north-south (the Current River valley), and east-west. It has an excellent location for easy access to both the immediate upland areas on both sides of the river, and the larger valleys which provide convenient routes of movement along an east-west axis.

This hypothesis–that the location of the Gooseneck site was dictated by ease of movement into upland areas, and that these upland areas were the primary areas exploited–is supported by the faunal samples from the site. River species such as fish, turtles, muskrat, and beaver were used to only a limited extent, while animal species that live in the upland areas during the fall and winter: white-tailed deer, raccoon, wild turkey, etc., are present in significant percentages.

TABLE 42

ANIMAL SPECIES REPRESENTED AT THE GOOSENECK SITE 23 Ct 54.

	SKELETAL ELEMENTS	MINIMUM NUMBER OF INDIVIDUALS	PROJECTED MEAT YIELD (IN POUNDS)
Pisces	21	8	7.5
Amia calva Bowfin	2	1	1.0
Hypentelium nigricans Hog sucker	2	2	2.0
Moxostoma duquesnei Black redhorse	2	2	2.0
Family Catostomidae Suckers	14	2	2.0
Micropterus amblоplites Rock Bass	1	1	0.5
Amphibians and Reptiles	91	10	11.4
Chelydra serpentina Snapping turtle	3	1	7.5
Terrapene carolina Box turtle	67	8	2.4
Pseudemys/Graptemys/Chrysemys Slider/Map/Painted turtle group	4	1	1.5

Table 42 cont'd

	SKELETAL ELEMENTS	MINIMUM NUMBER OF INDIVIDUALS	PROJECTED MEAT YIELD (IN POUNDS)
Unidentified	17		
Aves	43	6	38.0
Aix sponsa Wood duck	1	1	1.0
Lophodytes cucullatus Hooded merganser	1	1	1.0
Meleagris gallopavo Wild turkey	14	4	36.0
Unidentified	27		
Mammalia	994	22	1142.2
Didelphis marsupialis Opossum	1	1	8.5
Scalopus aquaticus Eastern mole	2	1	.2
Sylvilagus aquaticus Eastern cottontail	1	1	2.0
Sciurus carolinensis Gray squirrel	2	1	1.0
Sciurus niger Fox squirrel	2	1	1.5
Castor canadensis Beaver	2	1	20.0
Ondatra zibethicus Muskrat	1	1	2.0
Urocyon cinereoargenteus Gray fox	3	1	5.0
Procyon lotor Raccoon	1	1	8.0

Table 42 cont'd

	SKELETAL ELEMENTS	MINIMUM NUMBER OF INDIVIDUALS	PROJECTED MEAT YIELD (IN POUNDS)
Odocoileus virginianus White-tailed deer	224	13	1094.0
Unidentified small mammal	35		
Unidentified large mammal	720		

BIBLIOGRAPHY

Adams, Robert M. and Winslow M. Walker
1942 Archaeological Surface Survey of New Madrid County, Missouri. Missouri Archaeologist, Vol. 8, No. 2.

Adams, William
n.d. Laboratory of Comparative Osteology Reports Nos. 39*a*, 39*b*, 39*c*, 39*d*. Unpublished, Indiana University.

Allen, Glover M.
1920 Dogs of the American Aborigines. Bulletin of the Museum of Comparative Zoology, Vol. LXIII, No. 9. Cambridge, Mass.

Anderson, Paul
1965 The Reptiles of Missouri. The University of Missouri Press. Columbia, Mo.

Andrewartha, Herbert G. and L. C. Birch
1954 The Distribution and Abundance of Animals. University of Chicago Press. Chicago.

Appelget, John and Lloyd L. Smith, Jr.
1951 Determination of Age and Rate of Growth of Channel Catfish (*Ictalurus lacustris punctatus*) of the Upper Mississippi River from Vertebrae. Transaction of the American Fisheries Society, 80:119-139.

Bailey, W. R. and K. T. Rinell
1967 Events in the Turkey Year. *In* Hewitt, 1967.

Baker, R. H., C. C. Newman, and F. Wilke
1945 Food Habits of the Raccoon in Eastern Texas. Journal of Wildlife Management, 9:45-48.

Barkalow, E. J., W. J. Hamilton and B. Soots
1970 The Vital Statistics of an Unexploited Gray Squirrel Population. Journal of Wildlife Management, 34:489-500.

Bartlett, S. P.
1917 Fish Waste, Past and Present. Transactions of the American Fisheries Society, Vol. 47, No. 1.

Barton, B. S.
1805 On the Food of the Common Wild Turkey of the United States, *Meleagris palawa*. Barton's Medical and Physical Journal, 2:163-164.

Baumgartner, Luther L.
1943 Fox Squirrels in Ohio. Journal of Wildlife Management, 7:193-203.

Beaudoin, Kenneth L.
1953 A Report of Excavations Made at the T. O. Fuller Site, Shelby County, Tennessee. Printed privately, Memphis, Tennessee.

Bennitt, Rudolf and W. O. Nagel
1937 A Survey of the Resident Game and Fur Bearers of Missouri. University of Missouri Studies, 12:1-215.

Bradt, Glen W.
1938 A Study of Beaver Colonies in Michigan, Journal of Mammalogy, 19:139-162.

Braun, E. Lucy
1950 Deciduous Forests of Eastern North America. Hafner Publishers. New York.

Brohn, A. and D. Robb
1955 Age Composition, Weights and Physical Characteristics of Missouri Deer: 1944-1951. Missouri Conservation Commission, Pittman-Robertson Series: No. 3.

Burt, W. H.
1957 Mammals of the Great Lakes Region. University of Michigan Press. Ann Arbor.

Butterfield, Robert T.
1944 Populations, Hunting Pressure, and Movements of Ohio Raccoons. Transactions, North American Wildlife Conference, 9:337-344.

Carlander, H. B.
1954 History of Fish and Fishing in the Upper Mississippi River. The Upper Mississippi River Conservation Committee.

Carson, James D.
1961 Epiphyseal Cartilage as an Age Indicator in Fox and Gray Squirrels. Journal of Wildlife Management, 25:90-93.

Chaplin, Raymond E.
1965 Animals in Archaeology. Antiquity, 39:204-211.

Clarke, George L.
1954 Elements of Ecology. Wiley Publishers. New York.

Colton, Harold S.
1970 The Aboriginal Southwestern Indian Dog. American Antiquity, 35:153-159.

Conaway, C. H., H. M. Wight and K. C. Sadler
1963 Annual Production by a Cottontail Population. Journal of Wildlife Management, 27:171-175.

Cope, E. D.
1893 On a Jaw of an Indian Dog in C. B. Moore's Certain Shell Heaps of the St. John's River, Florida, Hitherto Unexplored. American Naturalist, 27:614.

Cottier, John W. and Gregory A. Waselkov
1974 The Environmental and Exploitative Reconstruction. *In* Investigation and Comparison of Two Nationally Registered Mississippi Archaeological Sites in Southeast Missouri. A Final Report to the National Endowment for the Humanities, Carl H. Chapman, Principal Investigator, pp. 48-75.

Crane, H. R., and James B. Griffin
1959 University of Michigan Radiocarbon Dates IV. American Journal of Science Supplement, 1:173-198.

Dalke, Paul D., William R. Clark, Jr. and Leroy J. Korschgen
1942 Food Habit Trends of the Wild Turkey in Missouri as Determined by Dropping Analysis. Journal of Wildlife Management, 6:237-243.

Dalke, Paul D., Aldo S. Leopold, and D. L. Spencer
1946 The Ecology and Management of the Wild Turkey in Missouri. Conservation Commission Federal Aid Wildlife Program, State of Missouri, Technical Bulletin 1.

Dasmann, Raymond F.
1964 Wildlife Biology. Wiley and Sons. New York.

Dice, Lee R. and Dora S. Dice
1941 Age Changes in the Teeth of the Cottontail Rabbit, *Sylvilagus floridanus*. Papers of the Michigan Academy of Science, Arts, and Letters, 26:219-228.

Dobie, James L.
1971 Reproduction and Growth in *Macroclemys temmincki*. Copeia, 4.

Dunkenson, Robert L.
1958 A Study of Deer Productivity and Breeding Season. State of Missouri–Surveys and Investigations, Project 13-R-12, Work Plan 1, Job 5. (mimeographed).

DuPratz, Lepage
1758 Histoire de la Louisiane, Vol. II. DeBure. Paris.

Edwards, William R.
1964 Evidence for a "Normal" Age Composition for Cottontails. Journal of Wildlife Management, 28:738-742.

Elder, William H.
1965 Primeval Deer Hunting Pressures Revealed by Remains from American Indian Middens. Journal of Wildlife Management, 29:366-370.

Ellis, James E. and John B. Lewis
1967 Mobility and Annual Range of Wild Turkeys in Missouri. Journal of Wildlife Management, 31:568-581.

Erickson, Albert W.
1959 The Age of Self-Sufficiency in the Black Bear. Journal of Wildlife Management, 23:401-405.

Featherstonhaugh, G. W.
1835 Geological Report of an Examination Made in 1834 of the Elevated Country Between the Missouri and Red Rivers. Washington, D.C.

Fisk, Harold N.
1944 Geological Investigation of the Alluvial Valley of the Lower Mississippi River. Mississippi River Commission. Vicksburg, Mississippi.

Fitch, H. S. and L. L. Sandidge
1953 Ecology of the Opossum on a Natural Area in Northeastern Kansas. University of Kansas Publication of the Museum of Natural History, 7:305-338.

Flannery, Kent V.
1966 The Postglacial "Readaptation" as Viewed from Mesoamerica. American Antiquity, 31:800-805.

Flyger, F. V.
1960 Movements and Home Range of the Gray Squirrel (*Sciurus carolinensis*) in Two Maryland Woodlots. Ecology, Vol. 41, no. 2.

Forbes, Stephen A. and Robert E. Richardson
1914 Studies on the Biology of the Upper Illinois River. Illinois State Laboratory of Natural History Bulletin, Vol. IX:481-571.
1920 The Fishes of Illinois (second edition). Illinois Natural History Survey. Springfield, Ill.

Friedman, Herbert
1953 Smithsonian Institution Report, January-May, 1953. Washington, D.C.

Friley, Charles E.
1949 Use of the Baculum in Age Determination of Michigan Beavers. Journal of Mammalogy, 30:261-267.

Gerstell, Robert
1939 The Growth and Size of Pennsylvania Black Bears. Pennsylvania Game News, 10:4-7.

Goodrum, Phil
1949 Wildlife and Longleaf Pine Forests. Mimeographed, 28 pages.

Grau, Gerald A., Glen C. Sanderson and John P. Rogers
1970 Age Determination of Raccoons. Journal of Wildlife Management, 34:364-371.

Griffin, James B.
1943 The Fort Ancient Aspect. University of Michigan Press. Ann Arbor.
1952*a* Archaeology of Eastern United States. University of Chicago Press. Chicago.
1952*b* Prehistoric Cultures of the Central Mississippi Valley. *In* Griffin 1952*a*.
1967 Eastern North American Archaeology: a Summary. Science, 156:175-191.

Guilday, John E.
1958 The Prehistoric Distribution of the Opossum. Journal of Mammalogy, 39: 39-43.
1971 Biological and Archaeological Analysis of Bones from a 17th Century Indian Village (46 Pu 31), Putnam County, West Virginia. West Virginia Geological and Economic Survey, Report of Archaeological Investigations, No. 4.

Gwynn, John V.
1964 Virginia Upland Game Investigations: Restoration of the Wild Turkey. Annual Report, Virginia Pittman-Robertson Project W-40-R-11. (mimeographed).

Haag, William
1948 An Osteometric Analysis of Some Aboriginal Dogs. University of Kentucky Reports in Anthropology, Vol. 8, No. 3.

Hale, James B.
1949 Aging Cottontail Rabbits by Bone Growth. Journal of Wildlife Management, 13:216-225.

Hall, E. Raymond and Keith R. Kelson
1959 The Mammals of North America. Ronald Publishers. New York.

Hallowell, A. Irving
1926 Bear Ceremonialism in the Northern Hemisphere. American Anthropologist, 28:1-175.

Halls, Lowell K. and John J. Stransky
1971 Atlas of Southern Forest Game. Southern Forest Experiment Station. Forest Service, U.S. Department of Agriculture.

Hamilton, William J., Jr.
1958 Life History and Economic Relations of the Opossum (*Didelphis marsupialis virginiana*) in New York State. Cornell Agricultural Experiment Station Memoirs, 354.

Harlow, Robert F.
1961 Characteristics and Status of Florida Black Bears. Transactions of the 26th North American Wildlife Conference, 481-495.

Haugen, A. O.
1941 Life History and Management Studies of the Cottontail Rabbit in Southwest Michigan. Unpublished Ph.D. thesis, University of Michigan. Ann Arbor.
1942*a* Home Range of the Cottontail Rabbit. Ecology, 23:354-367.
1942*b* Life History Studies of the Cottontail Rabbit in Southern Michigan. American Midland Naturalist, 28:204-244.

Hewitt, O. H., ed.
1967 The Wild Turkey and Its Management. Wildlife Society.

Hickerson, Harold
1965 The Virginia Deer and Intertribal Buffer Zones in the Upper Mississippi Valley. *In* Man, Culture, and Animals, A. Leeds and A. P. Vayda, eds. American Association for The Advancement of Science. Washington, D.C.

Holmes, Ann C. and Glen C. Sanderson
1965 Populations and Movements of Opossums in East-Central Illinois. Journal of Wildlife Management, 29:287-295.

Holmes, William H.
1903 Aboriginal Pottery of the Eastern United States. Twentieth Annual Report of the Bureau of American Ethnology, 1-201.

Hosley, Neil W.
1956 Management of the White-tailed Deer in its Environment. *In* Taylor 1956.

Kirkpatrick, Charles M. and Edward M. Barnett
1957 Age Criteria in Male Gray Squirrels. Journal of Wildlife Management, 21:341-347.

Korschgen, Leroy J.
1967 Feeding Habits and Foods. *In* Hewitt 1967

Lagler, K. P.
1943 Food Habits and Economic Relationships of the Turtles of Michigan, with Special Reference to Fish Management. American Midland Naturalist, 29:257-312.

Lambou, Victor W.
1959 Fish Populations of Backwater Lakes in Louisiana. Transactions of the American Fisheries Society, Vol. 88, No. 1.

Larson, Joseph S. and F. C. Van Nostrand
1968 An Evaluation of Beaver Aging Techniques. Journal of Wildlife Management, 32:99-103.

Larson, Lewis H.
1969 Aboriginal Subsistence Technology on the Southeastern Coastal Plain During the Late Prehistoric Period. Unpublished Ph.D. thesis, University of Michigan. Ann Arbor.
1972 Functional Considerations of Warfare in the Southeast During the Mississippi Period. American Antiquity, 37:383-392.

Latham, R. M.
1956 Complete Book of the Wild Turkey. Stackpole Co. Harrisburg, Pa.
1967 Turkey Hunting. *In* Hewitt 1967.

Lawrence, Barbara
1967 Early Domestic Dogs. Zeitschrift f. Saugetierkunde, 32:44-59.
1968 Antiquity of Large Dogs in North America. Tebiwa, 11:43-49.

Lawrence, David
1971 The Nature and Structure of Paleoecology. Journal of Paleoecology, 45:593-605.

Lay, Daniel W.
1942 Ecology of the Opossum in Eastern Texas. Journal of Mammalogy, 23:147-159.

Leapley, W. T.
1953 Smithsonian Institution Reports, May 12, 1953.

Lewis, James B.
1962 Statewide Wild Turkey Population Studies. Missouri Pittman-Robertson Project 13-R-16. (mimeographed).

Lincoln, Frederick C.
1935 The Waterfowl Flyways of North America. United States Department of Agriculture Circular 342.

Lord, Rexford D., Jr.
1961 Mortality Rates of Cottontail Rabbits, Journal of Wildlife Management, 25:33-40.

Lowe, Charles E.
1958 Ecology of the Swamp Rabbit in Georgia. Journal of Mammalogy, 39:116-127.

Madsen, Ruth M.
1967 Age Determination of Wildlife: A Bibliography. United States Department of the Interior, Department Library Bibliography, Mimeographed.

Marsden, H. M. and C. H. Conaway
1963 Behavior and the Reproductive Cycle in the Cottontail. Journal of Wildlife Management, 27:161-170.

Marsden, H. M. and N. R. Holler
1964 Social Behavior in Confined Populations of the Cottontail and the Swamp Rabbit. Wildlife Monograph, No. 13.

Martin, Alexander C., Herbert S. Zim and Arnold L. Nelson
1951 American Wildlife and Plants. Dover Publications. New York.

Martinson, R. K., J. W. Holten and G. K. Brakhage
1961 Age Criteria and Population Dynamics of the Swamp Rabbit in Missouri. Journal of Wildlife Management, 25:271-281.

Marzolf, Richard C.
1955 Use of Pectoral Spines and Vertebrae for Determining Age and Rate of Growth of the Channel Catfish. Journal of Wildlife Management, 19:243-249.

Mattox, N. T.
1935 Annular Rings in the Long Bones of Turtles and their Correlation with Size. Transactions of the Illinois State Academy of Science, Vol. 28, No. 1.

McMillian, Richard B.
1970 Early Canid Burial from the Western Ozark Highland. Science, 167: 1246-1247.

Meanley, Brooke
1956 Foods of the Wild Turkey in the White River Bottomlands of Southeastern Arkansas. Wilson Bulletin, 68:305-311.

Mech, L. David
1970 The Wolf: The Ecology and Behavior of an Endangered Species. American Museum of Natural History, Natural History Press. Garden City, New York.

Mech, L. David, Donald M. Barnes and John R. Tester
1968 Seasonal Weight Changes, Mortality and Population Structure of Raccoons in Minnesota. Journal of Mammalogy, Vol. 49, No. 1.

Membre, Z.
1852 Narrative of La Salles' Voyage Down the Mississippi (1682). *In* Historical Collections, Louisiana, B. F. French, ed., 4:165-184.

Mississippi Flyway Council
1958*a* A Guide to Mississippi Flyway Waterfowl Management. Mississippi Flyway Council (mimeographed).
1958*b* Waterfowl Distribution and Migration in the Mississippi Flyway. A Report by the Technical Section of the Mississippi Flyway Council, 1954-1957 (mimeographed).

Montgomery, G. G.
1964 Tooth Eruption in Preweaned Raccoons. Journal of Wildlife Management, 28:582-584.

Moore, W. H.
1967 Deer Browse Resources of the Atomic Energy Commission's Savannah River Project Area. United States Department of Agriculture, Forest Service Resources Bulletin, SE-6 (mimeographed).

Mosby, Henry S.
1969 The Influence of Hunting on the Population Dynamics of a Woodlot Gray Squirrel Population. Journal of Wildlife Management, 33:59-72.

Munson, Patrick J., Paul W. Parmalee and Richard A. Yarnell
1971 Subsistence Ecology of Scovill, a Terminal Middle Woodland Village. American Antiquity. 36:410-431.

Murie, Olaus J.
1951 The Elk of North America. Stackpole Co. Harrisburg, Pa.

Nash, Charles H.
1955 The Fuller Mounds. Tennessee Archaeologist, 11:49-53.

Newman, Charles
1948 A Survey of Florida Deer and Turkey Habitat and Populations. Paper presented at the Conference of the Southeastern Game Commission, Lexington, Ky. November 1-2 (mimeographed).

Old Timer
1898 On the Sunk Lands. Recreation, 8:209.

O'Roke, E. C. and F. N. Hamerstrom, Jr.
1948 Productivity and Yield of the George Reserve Deer Herd. Journal of Wildlife Management, 12:78-86.

Paloumpis, Andreas A.
1957 The Effects of Drought Conditions on the Fish and Bottom Organisms of Two Small Oxbow Ponds. Transactions of the Illinois State Academy of Science, Vol. 50.

Parmalee, Paul W.
1957 Vertebrate Remains from The Cahokia Site, Illinois. Transactions of the Illinois State Academy of Science, Vol. 50, No. 1.
1959*a* Animal Remains from the Banks Site, Crittenden County, Arkansas. Miscellaneous Paper No. 5. Tennessee Archaeological Society.
1959*b* Use of Mammalian Skulls and Mandibles by Prehistoric Indians of Illinois. Transactions of the Illinois State Academy of Science, 52:85-95.
1960*a* Vertebrae Remains from the Chucalissa Site. Tennessee Archaeologist, 16:84-90.
1960*b* Animal Remains from the Aztalan Site, Jefferson County, Wisconsin. Wisconsin Archaeologist, 41:1-11.
1962*a* Additional Faunal Remains from the Kingston Lake Site, Illinois. Transactions of the Illinois State Academy of Science, 55:6-12.
1962*b* Appendix A: Identification of the Faunal Remains from the Lawhorn Site. *In* The Lawhorn Site, by John Moselage, The Missouri Archaeologist, 24:95-96.
1966 Appendix A: Animal Remains from The Banks Site. *In* Perino 1966.

Parmalee, Paul W., Andreas A. Paloumpis and Nancy Wilson
1972 Animals Utilized by Woodland Peoples Occupying the Apple Creek Site, Illinois. Illinois State Museum Reports of Investigations: 23.

Parmalee, Paul W. and John E. Guilday
1973 Appendix I: Faunal Remains from the Zebree Site. *In* The Zebree Site, by D. F. Morse (unpublished manuscript).

Perino, Gregory
1966 The Banks Village Site. Memoir 4, Missouri Archaeological Society.

Petrides, George A.
1949 Sex and Age Determination in the Opossum. Journal of Mammalogy, 30:364-378.

Pflieger, William L.
1971 A Distributional Study of Missouri Fishes. University of Kansas Publications, Museum of Natural History, 20:225-570.

Phillips, Phillip, James A. Ford and James B. Griffin
1951 Archaeological Survey in the Lower Mississippi Alluvial Valley 1940-1947. Papers of the Peabody Museum of American Archaeology and Ethnology. Harvard University, Vol. XXV.

Pimlott, D. H.
1967 Wolf Predation and Ungulate Populations. American Zoologist, 7:267-278.
1970 Predation and Productivity of Game Populations in North America. Transactions of the 9th International Congress of Game Biology.

Pimlott, D. H., J. A. Shannon and G. B. Kolenosky
1969 The Ecology of the Timber Wolf in Algonquin Park, Ontario. Department of Lands and Forests.

Potter, Martha A. and Raymond S. Baby
1964 Hopewellian Dogs. The Ohio Journal of Science, 64:36-40.

Potter, W. B.
1880 Archaeological Remains in Southeastern Missouri. Contributions to the Archaeology of Missouri by the Archaeological Section of the St. Louis Academy of Science, 1:5-19.

Progulske, Donald R.
1956 Movements and Home Ranges of the White-tailed Deer (*Odocoileus virginianus*) in Central Missouri. Unpublished Ph.D. thesis, University of Missouri.

Progulske, Donald R. and Thomas S. Baskett
1958 Mobility of Missouri Deer and Their Harassment by Dogs. Journal of Wildlife Management, 22:184-292.

Ransom, S. B.
1966 Determining Age of White-tailed Deer From Layers in Cementum of Molars. Journal of Wildlife Management, 30:197-199.

Reynolds, Harold C.
1945 Some Aspects of the Life History and Ecology of the Opossum in Central Missouri. Journal of Mammalogy, 26:361-379.

Rhoads, Samuel N.
1897 A Contribution to the Zoology of Tennessee, Number 3–Mammals. Academy of Natural Science of Philadelphia. Proceedings, 1896:175-205.

Robertson, Ralph A. and Albert R. Shadle
1954 Osteologic Criteria of Age in Beavers. Journal of Mammalogy, 35:197-203.

Robertson, Walter V.
1969 Population Dynamics of White-tailed Deer. *In* White-tailed Deer in the Southern Forest Habitat. Southern Forest Experiment Station, Nacogooches, Texas. Forest Service, U.S. Department of Agriculture.

Rostlund, Erhard
1952 Freshwater Fish and Fishing in Native North America. University of California Publications in Geography, 9. University of California Press. Berkeley and Los Angeles.

Sanderson, Glen C.
1951 Breeding Habits and a History of the Missouri Raccoon Population From 1941-1948. Transactions of the North American Wildlife Conference, 16:445-461.
1961 Estimating Opossum Populations by Marking Young. Journal of Wildlife Management, 25:20-27.

Schorger, Arlie W.
1966 The Wild Turkey. University of Oklahoma Press. Norman, Okla.

Schwartz, Charles W.
1941 Home Range of the Cottontail in Central Missouri. Journal of Mammalogy, 22:386-392.

Schwartz, Charles W. and Elizabeth R. Schwartz
1959 The Wild Mammals of Missouri. University of Missouri Press. Columbia, Mo.

Segelquist, Charles A. and Walter E. Green
1968 Deer Food Yields in Four Ozark Forest Types. Journal of Wildlife Management, 32:330-337.

Segelquist, Charles A., Fred D. Ward and Robert G. Leonard
1969 Habitat–Deer Relations in Two Ozark Enclosures. Journal of Wildlife Management, 33:511-515.

Severinghaus, C. W.
1949 Tooth Development and Wear As A Criteria of Age in White-tailed Deer. Journal of Wildlife Management, 13:195-216.

Severinghaus, C. W. and E. L. Cheatum
1956 Life and Times of the White-tailed Deer. *In* Taylor 1956.

Shelford, Victor E.
1954 Some Lower Mississippi Valley Flood Plain Biotic Communities; Their Age and Elevation. Ecology, 35:126-142.
1963 The Ecology of North America. University of Illinois Press. Urbana, Ill.

Smith, Bruce D.
1974*a* Predator–Prey Relationships in the Eastern Ozarks: A.D. 1300. Human Ecology, Vol. 2:31-44.
1974*b* Middle Mississippi Exploitation of Animal Populations: A Predictive Model. American Antiquity, Vol. 39, No. 2.

Smith, Phillip W.
1961 The Amphibians and Reptiles of Illinois. Illinois Natural History Survey Bulletin, Vol. 28.

Sneed, Kermit E.
1951 A Method for Calculating the Growth of Channel Catfish (*Ictalurus lacustris punctatus*). American Fisheries Society Transactions, 90:174-183.

Sonenshine, Daniel E. and Elton L. Winslow
1972 Contrasts in Distribution of Raccoons in Two Virginia Localities. Journal of Wildlife Management, Vol. 36, No. 3.

Steyermark, Julian A.
1940 Studies of the Vegetation of Missouri. Field Museum of Natural History Botanical Series, 9:349-475.
1959 Vegetational History of the Ozark Forest. University of Missouri Studies, No. 31.

Stransky, John J.
1969 Deer Habitat Quality of Major Forest Types in the South. *In* White-tailed Deer in the Southern Forest Habitat. Southern Forest Experiment Station, Nacogooches, Texas. Forest Service, U.S. Department of Agriculture.

Stuewer, F. W.
1943 Raccoons: Their Habits and Management in Michigan. Ecological Monographs, 13:203-258.

Swallow, G. C.
1875 Inventory of Objects from Mounds in New Madrid County, and a Brief Description of Excavations. Eight Annual Report, Peabody Museum, Harvard University, 16-46.

Swank, William G.
1949 Beaver Ecology and Management in West Virginia. West Virginia Conservation Commission.

Swanton, John R.
1946 The Indians of the Southeastern United States. Bureau of American Ethnology, Bulletin 137. Washington, D.C.

Taber, Richard D.
1956 Characteristics of the Pelvic Girdle in Relation to Sex in Black tailed and White-tailed Deer. California Fish and Game, 42:15-21.

Taylor, Walter P., ed.
1956 The Deer of North America. The Stackpole Co. Harrisburg, Pa.

Thomas, Cyrus
1894 Report on the Mound Explorations of the Bureau of Ethnology. Bureau of American Ethnology, 12th Annual Report. Washington D.C.

Toll, J. E., T. S. Baskett, and C. H. Conaway
1960 Home Range, Reproduction, and Foods of the Swamp Rabbit in Missouri. American Midland Naturalist, 63:398-412.

Townsend, J. E.
1953 Beaver Ecology in Western Montana, with Special Reference to Movements. Journal of Mammalogy, Vol. 34, No. 4.

Twitchell, Allen R. and Herbert H. Dill
1949 One Hundred Raccoons from One Hundred and Two Acres. Journal of Mammalogy, 30:130-133.

Van Nostrand, F. C. and A. B. Stephenson
1964 Age Determination for Beavers by Tooth Development. Journal of Wildlife Management, 28:430-434.

Verts, B. J.
1963 Movements and Populations of Opossums in a Cultivated Area. Journal of Wildlife Management, 27:127-129.

Waselkov, Gregory
1972 A Faunal Assemblage from the Lilbourn Site (23Nm38) Missouri. Unpublished manuscript.

White, Theodore E.
1953 A Method of Calculating the Dietary Percentage of Various Food Animals Utilized by Aboriginal Peoples. American Antiquity, 18:396.

Williams, A. B.
1936 The Composition and Dynamics of a Beech-Maple Climax Community. Ecological Monographs, 6:317-405.

Williams, Stephen
1954 An Archaeological Study of the Mississippian Culture in Southeast Missouri. Unpublished Ph.D. thesis. Yale University. New Haven.

Yeager, Lee E. and R. G. Rennels
1943 Fur Yield and Autumn Foods of the Raccoon in Illinois River Bottomlands. Journal of Wildlife Management, 7:45-48.

www.ingramcontent.com/pod-product-compliance
Lightning Source LLC
LaVergne TN
LVHW050020250826
846302LV00008B/39
* 9 7 8 1 9 4 9 0 9 8 0 4 4 *